COLLINS
CHEERFUL
COOKING

PERFECT
CASSEROLES

© Wm. Collins Sons & Co. Ltd. 1973
First published 1973
New edition 1978
ISBN 0 00 435271 8

Devised, edited and designed by Youé & Spooner Ltd.

Printed in Great Britain by Collins Clear-Type Press

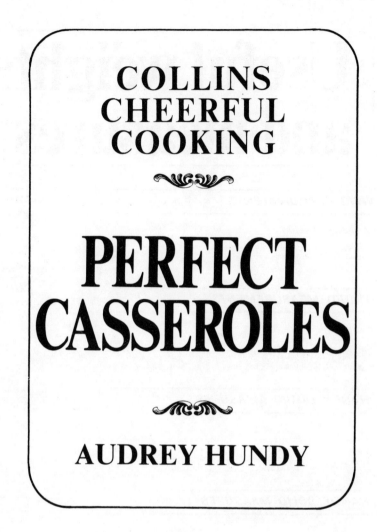

COLLINS
CHEERFUL
COOKING

PERFECT
CASSEROLES

AUDREY HUNDY

COLLINS
GLASGOW & LONDON

Useful weights and measures

WEIGHT EQUIVALENTS

Avoirdupois		Metric
1 ounce	=	28·35 grammes
1 pound	=	453·6 grammes
2·3 pounds	=	1 kilogram

LIQUID MEASUREMENTS

¼ pint	=	1½ decilitres
½ pint	=	¼ litre
scant 1 pint	=	½ litre
1¾ pints	=	1 litre
1 gallon	=	4·5 litres

HANDY LIQUID MEASURES

1 pint	=	20 fluid ounces	=	32 tablespoons
½ pint	=	10 fluid ounces	=	16 tablespoons
¼ pint	=	5 fluid ounces	=	8 tablespoons
⅛ pint	=	2½ fluid ounces	=	4 tablespoons
1/16 pint	=	1¼ fluid ounces	=	2 tablespoons

HANDY SOLID MEASURES

				Approximate
Almonds, ground	1 oz.	=		3¾ level tablespoons
Arrowroot	1 oz.	=		4 level tablespoons
Breadcrumbs fresh	1 oz.	=		7 level tablespoons
dried	1 oz.	=		3¼ level tablespoons
Butter and Lard	1 oz.	=		2 level tablespoons
Cheese, grated	1 oz.	=		3½ level tablespoons
Chocolate, grated	1 oz.	=		3 level tablespoons
Cocoa	1 oz.	=		2¾ level tablespoons
Desiccated Coconut	1 oz.	=		4½ tablespoons
Coffee—Instant	1 oz.	=		4 level tablespoons
Ground	1 oz.	=		4 tablespoons
Cornflour	1 oz.	=		2½ tablespoons
Custard powder	1 oz.	=		2½ tablespoons
Curry Powder and Spices	1 oz.	=		5 tablespoons
Flour	1 oz.	=		2 level tablespoons
Gelatine, powdered	1 oz.	=		2½ tablespoons
Rice, uncooked	1 oz.	=		1½ tablespoons
Sugar, caster and granulated	1 oz.	=		2 tablespoons
Icing sugar	1 oz.	=		2½ tablespoons
Syrup	1 oz.	=		1 tablespoon
Yeast, granulated	1 oz.	=		1 level tablespoon

AMERICAN MEASURES

16	fluid ounces	=	1 American pint
8	fluid ounces	=	1 American standard cup
0·50	fluid ounces	=	1 American tablespoon (slightly smaller than British Standards Institute tablespoon)
0·16	fluid ounces	=	1 American teaspoon

AUSTRALIAN MEASURES
(Cup, Spoon and Liquid Measures)

These are the measures in everyday use in the Australian family kitchen. The spoon measures listed below are from the ordinary household cutlery set.

CUP MEASURES

(Using the 8-liquid-ounce cup measure)

1 cup flour	4 oz.
1 cup sugar *(crystal or caster)*	8 oz.
1 cup icing sugar *(free from lumps)*	5 oz.
1 cup shortening *(butter, margarine, etc.)*	8 oz.
1 cup honey, golden syrup, treacle	10 oz.
1 cup brown sugar *(lightly packed)*	4 oz.
1 cup brown sugar *(tightly packed)*	5 oz.
1 cup soft breadcrumbs	2 oz.
1 cup dry breadcrumbs *(made from fresh breadcrumbs)*	3 oz.
1 cup packet dry breadcrumbs	4 oz.
1 cup rice *(uncooked)*	6 oz.
1 cup rice *(cooked)*	5 oz.
1 cup mixed fruit or individual fruit such as sultanas, etc.	4 oz.
1 cup grated cheese	4 oz.
1 cup nuts *(chopped)*	4 oz.
1 cup coconut	2½ oz.

SPOON MEASURES

	Level Tablespoon
1 oz. flour	2
1 oz. sugar *(crystal or caster)*	1½
1 oz. icing sugar *(free from lumps)*	2
1 oz. shortening	1
1 oz. honey	1
1 oz. gelatine	2
1 oz. cocoa	3
1 oz. cornflour	2½
1 oz. custard powder	2½

LIQUID MEASURES

(Using 8-liquid-ounce cup)

1 cup liquid	8 oz.
2½ cups liquid	20 oz. (1 pint)
2 tablespoons liquid	1 oz.
1 gill liquid	5 oz. (¼ pint)

Metric equivalents and oven temperatures are not listed here as they are included in all the recipes throughout the book.

When using the metric measures, in some cases it may be necessary to cut down the amount of liquid used. This is in order to achieve a balanced recipe and the correct consistency, as 1oz equals, in fact, 28·35gm.

Introduction

Whether you are a beginner or an expert in the kitchen, I am sure you will agree that casseroles are a cook's best friend. Casseroling is the most foolproof and yet the most exciting method of cooking and, with such an enormous variety of easily prepared dishes to choose from, there is always one suitable for the simplest or the grandest occasion.

The majority of casseroles are so good-tempered that they require very little attention during cooking and need not be eaten the minute they are cooked. If the family is late home or your guests are delayed, the oven temperature can be lowered and the casserole cooked a little longer.

Casseroling also means that the difficulties of getting everything ready to serve at the same time are avoided. You don't need to make the gravy at the last minute, carve at the table or be left with a kitchen full of washing up.

Apart from being so carefree, casseroling can be very economical, allowing you to make the fullest use of inexpensive meat, poultry and fish which become tender and succulent with slow, gentle cooking.

For easy preparation, and to save washing up, it is worth investing in a flameproof casserole, so that the same pot can be used for preliminary cooking on top of the stove as well as in the oven and serving at the table. There is an excellent choice in earthenware, flameproof glass and china, copper and enamel.

This collection of recipes, although concentrating on meat, poultry and fish, also covers vegetables and fruit to enable you to make the fullest use of the oven.

With the equipment now available, casserole cooking has become truly three-dimensional and it may be that you choose to use a pressure cooker or a slow crock cooker to prepare your recipe instead of the conventional casserole. These two methods fit in very well with our busy, modern way of life as they allow you to be away from home all day and still produce an excellent hot meal. With this in mind, I have added a footnote to several of the recipes in the first chapters of the book which can also be used as a guideline for adapting any of the other recipes.

Pressure Cooking

A pressure cooker is a great boon for the speedy cooking of casseroles: you are able to cut the cooking time to about one fifth of the original recipe if you are using a cooker at high pressure (15lb or H). Other pressure cookers which act on a lower pressure (7½lb or 8lb) will generally cut the cooking time to about one third of the original recipe but please consult your pressure cooker booklet and find a similar recipe to the one you want to use to check on the cooking time.

Remember that sufficient space must be left for the steam to circulate.

The complete cooker, including the base and cover, should never be more than half full.

Seasonings and herbs are accentuated in cooking so be sparing when adding these.

Add thickening agents at end of cooking.

Always refer to your own pressure cooker manual on how to use your particular model.

Slow Cooking Pots

With an electric slow cooker, the cooking is so gentle that the cooking time of casserole recipes can be extended to take several hours, allowing you to prepare the recipe and put it on in the morning and then leave it gently cooking whilst you are away.

There is never any need to stir and you must try to resist taking a peep as the cooker will lose heat and take longer.

Stews can safely be left without fear of burning or boiling over, even if you are delayed.

For taste and appearance, it is worth frying the meat and preparing the casserole in a saucepan before transferring it to the slow cooker.

If you need to speed up the meal, all the recipes can be cooked on High throughout in which case they will take half the time given in the footnotes in this book.

By using this book together with the manual of your slow cooker model, you will find it quite easy to adapt all the recipes.

Whichever method of preparation you use, I hope you enjoy both the cooking and the eating.

Audrey Hundy

Beef

Slow, gentle cooking makes the cheapest cuts of beef tender and full of flavour. On the following pages you will find plenty of dishes suitable for everyday, as well as those for special occasions.

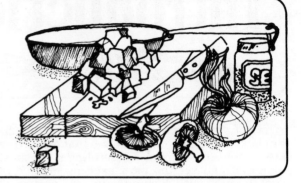

STEAK AND ONIONS
Serves 4–6

1lb (½ kilo) onions, peeled and sliced
salt and pepper
1½lb (¾ kilo) lean braising steak
1oz (25gm) butter or margarine
1oz (25gm) flour
4 tablespoons olive oil
5 dessertspoons cider vinegar
chopped parsley
4 anchovies, chopped
2–3 cocktail gherkins, chopped
¼ pint (125ml) hot water
watercress to garnish

1. Preheat oven to cool, 300 deg F or gas 2 (150 deg C).
2. Cover the bottom of a shallow casserole with half the onions and sprinkle with salt and pepper.
3. Cut meat into serving portions and place on top of onions.
4. Cover with remaining onions and season with salt and pepper.
5. Soften the butter or margarine and mix to a soft paste with the flour, then dot this over onions.
6. Cover closely with lid or foil and cook in centre of oven for 1 hour.
7. Sir together olive oil, vinegar, parsley, anchovies and gherkins and stir this mixture into casserole.
8. Cover and cook for a further hour, or until meat is tender.
9. Arrange meat on a serving dish leaving the liquid in the casserole. Stir hot water into casserole and pour sauce over meat.
10. Garnish with watercress and serve with baked tomatoes.

PEMBROKE BRAISE
Serves 4

1½lb (¾ kilo) braising steak, cut in four neat pieces
1oz (25gm) dripping or lard
1 large onion, peeled and chopped
4 carrots, peeled and sliced
2 sticks celery, trimmed, washed and cut into small pieces
1 dessertspoon soy sauce
1 tablespoon tomato ketchup
¼ pint (125ml) stock or water
2 teaspoons capers, drained and chopped
1 level teaspoon finely grated lemon rind (optional)

1. Preheat oven to moderate, 350 deg F or gas 4 (180 deg C).
2. Trim steak if necessary. Melt dripping or lard in a pan and fry meat until browned on both sides. Drain well over pan and keep on one side.
3. Add onion, carrots and celery to fat remaining in the pan and fry for 2–3 minutes, stirring with a metal spoon.
4. Transfer vegetables to a casserole using a draining spoon. Add soy sauce, tomato ketchup, stock or water and capers and stir well together.
5. Place meat on top of fried vegetables.
6. Cover closely with lid or foil and cook in centre of oven for about 2 hours, or until meat is tender.
7. Serve sprinkled with finely grated lemon rind if liked.

STEAK AND MUSHROOMS
Serves 4–6

1½lb (¾ kilo) stewing steak
1oz (25gm) butter
1 tablespoon oil
2 carrots, peeled and diced
1 large onion, peeled and chopped
1oz (25gm) plain flour
1 pint (approximately ½ litre) beef stock
1 dessertspoon soy sauce
½ level teaspoon dried mixed herbs
salt and pepper
1 tablespoon tomato ketchup
4oz (100gm) button mushrooms, washed, trimmed and sliced

1. Preheat oven to moderate, 350 deg F or gas 4 (180 deg C).
2. Trim meat and cut into cubes.
3. Heat butter and oil in a flameproof casserole and fry meat until browned all over. Transfer to a plate using a draining spoon.
4. Add carrots and onion to fat remaining in the casserole and fry gently together for about 5 minutes, or until lightly browned.
5. Sprinkle in the flour and stir over gentle heat for 1 minute.
6. Remove casserole from heat and gradually blend in stock and soy sauce. Add herbs.
7. Return to heat, bring to the boil and simmer for 2 minutes, stirring continuously. Season to taste with salt and pepper.
8. Return meat to casserole and stir well, then cover closely with lid or foil.
9. Cook in centre of oven for about 1½ hours, then stir in tomato ketchup and mushrooms and continue cooking for a further 20 minutes, or until meat is tender.

ROADHOUSE CASSEROLE
Serves 4–6

Steak and sausages make a satisfying meal.

1lb (½ kilo) stewing steak
1oz (25gm) dripping
1 onion, peeled and sliced
1 leek, washed, trimmed and sliced
1 large carrot, peeled and sliced
2 parsnips, peeled and sliced
salt and pepper
½ pint (250ml) beef stock
8oz (200gm) beef sausages
½oz (12gm) flour
1lb (½ kilo) potatoes

1. Preheat oven to cool, 300 deg F or gas 2 (150 deg C).
2. Trim meat and cut into small cubes.
3. Melt dripping in a flameproof casserole and fry meat until sealed all over.
4. Add vegetables and cook, turning with a metal spoon, for 2–3 minutes. Sprinkle with a little salt and pepper and add stock.
5. Cover closely with lid or foil and cook in centre of oven for about 1 hour.
6. Add sausages cut into small pieces and tossed in flour. Add potatoes, peeled and cut into quarters.
7. Replace cover and continue cooking for a further hour, or until meat and potatoes are tender.

RUSTIC CASSEROLE
Serves 4–6

1½lb (¾ kilo) stewing steak
2oz (50gm) dripping or lard
1 large onion, peeled and sliced
2 large carrots, peeled and sliced
2 sticks celery, washed, trimmed and sliced
1oz (25gm) flour
1 pint (approximately ½ litre) beef stock
1 tablespoon made mustard
1 tablespoon finely chopped parsley
1 can (11½oz or 326gm) sweetcorn kernels, drained
salt and pepper

1. Preheat oven to very moderate, 325 deg F or gas 3 (170 deg C).
2. Trim meat and cut into cubes.
3. Melt dripping or lard in a large

pan and fry meat and onion until meat is sealed all over.
4. Add carrots and celery and continue cooking for 2–3 minutes.
5. Sprinkle in flour and stir over gentle heat for 1 minute.
6. Remove pan from heat and gradually blend in stock and mustard. Stir in parsley.
7. Return to heat, bring to the boil and simmer for 2 minutes, stirring continuously.
8. Cover with lid or foil and cook in centre of oven for about 2 hours, then add sweetcorn and continue cooking for a further 30 minutes, or until meat is tender.
9. Add salt and pepper if necessary before serving.

CHIDDINGLY HOTPOT
Serves 4–6

1½lb (¾ kilo) stewing steak
1 large onion, peeled and chopped
4oz (100gm) stoned green olives, chopped
8oz (200gm) celery, washed and chopped
pinch of ground allspice
ground black pepper
few cloves
1½lb (¾ kilo) potatoes, peeled and sliced
12oz (300gm) small onions, peeled
1 pint (approximately ½ litre) water
1 dessertspoon tarragon vinegar

1. Preheat oven to cool, 300 deg F or gas 2 (150 deg C).
2. Slice beef and cut into strips.
3. Cover the base of a large ovenproof casserole with chopped onion and sprinkle with some of the chopped olives and celery.
4. Cover with a layer of beef, sprinkle with allspice, pepper and add 2 cloves.
5. Cover with a layer of potatoes, olives, celery and whole onions.
6. Continue in layers till all the ingredients are used, seasoning with allspice, pepper and a clove between layers.
7. Mix water with vinegar and pour into casserole. (No salt is required because of the vinegar.)
8. Cover closely with lid or foil and cook in centre of oven for 3–4 hours, or until meat is tender.

TANGY BEEF CASSEROLE
Serves 6–8

This dish is at its best if it is made on one day and served the next.

2oz (50gm) butter or dripping
1lb (½ kilo) onions, peeled and sliced
2lb (1 kilo) stewing steak
2 level tablespoons flour
salt and pepper
dry mustard
½ pint (250ml) hot water
1 tablespoon tomato purée
1 tablespoon French mustard
¼ teaspoon caraway seeds
¼ pint (125ml) red wine

1. Preheat oven to very moderate, 325 deg F or gas 3 (170 deg C).
2. Melt butter or dripping in a pan and fry onions for 2–3 minutes, then transfer to a casserole using a draining spoon.
3. Cut meat into cubes and toss in flour seasoned with salt, pepper and dry mustard.
4. Brown meat in fat remaining in the pan and add to onions in casserole.
5. Sprinkle any remaining flour into pan and stir over gentle heat for 1 minute. Remove pan from heat.
6. Blend hot water with tomato purée, French mustard, 1 teaspoon salt, caraway seeds and wine. Pour into pan and stir well.
7. Return to heat and bring to the boil, stirring. Pour over meat in casserole.
8. Cover closely with lid or foil and cook in centre of oven for about 2 hours, or until meat is tender.
9. Serve with boiled rice and salad.

Slow Cooker Method
1. Proceed as stages 2–6 above, inclusive, using a preheated slow cooker instead of a casserole.
2. Cook on High for 30 minutes and on Low for 6–8 hours.

Pressure Cooker Method
(15lb or H)
1. Fry onions and meat seasoned with salt, pepper and dry mustard in hot fat in pan of pressure cooker until browned.
2. Proceed as stage 6 above.
3. Cover, bring to pressure: lower heat and cook for 20 minutes. Reduce the pressure and remove lid.
4. Adjust seasoning. Thicken, if liked, in open pressure cooker.

EMPIRE STEW
Serves 4–6

1½lb (¾ kilo) stewing steak
1oz (25gm) flour
salt and pepper
1 level teaspoon dry mustard
1oz (25gm) beef dripping
1 medium onion, peeled and
sliced
1 small can (3oz or 75gm)
tomato purée
1 pint (approximately ½ litre)
beef stock
2oz (50gm) button mushrooms,
washed and trimmed
1 bayleaf
pinch of dried mixed herbs
1 tablespoon French mustard
1 can (7¾oz or 220gm) baked
beans in tomato sauce

1. Preheat oven to very moderate,
325 deg F or gas 3 (170 deg C).
2. Trim meat, cut into cubes,
then toss in flour seasoned with
salt, pepper and mustard.
3. Melt dripping in a flameproof
casserole and fry onion gently
for 2–3 minutes.
4. Add meat and fry until brown
all over. Sprinkle in any
remaining flour and stir over
gentle heat for 1 minute.
Remove heat for 1 minute.
Remove casserole from heat.
5. Mix tomato purée with stock
and pour over meat. Add
mushrooms, bayleaf and mixed
herbs. Stir well, then return to
heat and bring to the boil.
6. Cover closely with lid or foil
and cook in centre of oven for
2–2½ hours, or until meat is
tender.
7. Remove bayleaf, stir in French
mustard and baked beans and
return to oven for a further 15
minutes.

Slow Cooker Method
1. Proceed as stages 2–5 above,
inclusive, but using a saucepan.
2. Transfer to a preheated slow
cooker and cook on High for
30 minutes and on Low for 6–8
hours.
3. Remove bay leaf, stir in French
mustard and baked beans and
continue cooking for 30 minutes.

INNKEEPERS' CASSEROLE
Serves 4–6

1½lb (¾ kilo) stewing steak
2oz (50gm) butter
1 large onion, peeled and
chopped
1 stick celery, washed and
chopped
1oz (25gm) flour
1 small can (2oz or 50gm)
tomato purée
¾ pint (375ml) brown ale
1 bayleaf
pinch of dry mustard
pinch of ground mace
salt and pepper
2 level teaspoons sugar

1. Preheat oven to very moderate,
325 deg F or gas 3 (170 deg C).
2. Trim meat and cut into cubes.
3. Melt butter in a flameproof
casserole and fry meat until
browned all over. Transfer to a
plate using a draining spoon.
4. Add onion and celery to fat
remaining in the casserole and
fry gently together for about
5 minutes, or until tender.
5. Sprinkle in flour and stir over
gentle heat for 1 minute.
6. Remove casserole from heat
and gradually blend in tomato
purée and ale.
7. Return to heat, bring to the
boil and simmer for 2 minutes,
stirring continuously.
8. Add bayleaf, mustard and
mace, season well with salt and
pepper and add sugar.
9. Return meat to pan and cover
closely with lid or foil.
10. Cook in centre of oven for
about 2 hours, or until meat is
tender.

Slow Cooker Method
1. Proceed as stages 2–8 above,
inclusive, but using a saucepan.
2. Transfer to a preheated slow
cooker and cook on High for 30
minutes and on Low for 6–8 hours.

Pressure Cooker Method
(15lb or H)
1. Fry meat, onion and celery in
butter in pan of pressure cooker
until browned.
2. Remove from heat and blend in
tomato purée and ale.
3. Add seasoning as in stage 8
above.
4. Cover, bring to pressure: lower
heat and cook for 15–20 minutes.
Reduce the pressure and remove
lid.
5. Adjust seasoning. Thicken, if
liked, in open pressure cooker.

FESTIVE CASSEROLE
Serves 4

1lb (½ kilo) stewing steak
1oz (25gm) flour
salt and pepper
1oz (25gm) dripping or lard
8oz (200gm) onions, peeled and
sliced
8oz (200gm) carrots, peeled and
sliced
4oz (100gm) mushrooms
¾ pint (375ml) beef stock
1 tablespoon creamed
horseradish
1 bayleaf
1 small packet frozen peas
1 small can (3½oz or 87gm)
pimentos, drained and cut
into strips

1. Preheat oven to very
moderate, 325 deg F or gas 3
(170 deg C).
2. Trim meat, cut into cubes and
toss in flour seasoned with salt
and pepper.
3. Melt dripping or lard in a
frying pan and fry onions gently
for 2–3 minutes, then transfer to
a casserole using a draining
spoon.
4. Add meat to fat remaining in
the pan and fry until brown all
over. Add to onions in casserole
using a draining spoon.
5. Add carrots and mushrooms
to casserole.
6. Sprinkle any remaining flour
into the frying pan and stir over
gentle heat for 1 minute.
7. Remove pan from heat and
gradually blend in stock and
creamed horseradish.
8. Return to heat, bring to the
boil and simmer for 2 minutes,
stirring continuously. Pour over
ingredients in casserole, stir well
together and add bayleaf.
9. Cover closely with lid or foil
and cook in centre of oven for
about 2 hours.
10. Add frozen peas and strips of
pimento and continue cooking
for a further 30 minutes, or until
meat is tender.

THATCHERS' CASSEROLE
Serves 6

2lb (1 kilo) stewing steak
2oz (50gm) dripping or lard
8oz (200gm) button onions,
peeled
1lb (½ kilo) carrots, peeled and
sliced
1 garlic clove, peeled and
crushed
1 bayleaf
2oz (50gm) flour
2 level teaspoons dried
marjoram
½ pint (250ml) red wine
1 pint (approximately ½ litre)
water
salt and pepper
8oz (200gm) self-raising flour
3oz (75gm) shredded suet
2 level teaspoons mixed herbs
1 tablespoon finely grated
horseradish
cold water to mix

1. Preheat oven to very moderate,
325 deg F or gas 3 (170 deg C).
2. Trim meat and cut into large
cubes.
3. Melt dripping or lard in a pan
and add onions, carrots, garlic
and bayleaf and fry for 2–3
minutes. Transfer to a casserole
using a draining spoon.
4. Fry meat in fat remaining in
the pan until brown all over.
5. Sprinkle in flour and marjoram
and stir over gentle heat for 1
minute.
6. Remove pan from heat and
gradually blend in red wine and
water.
7. Return to heat, bring to the
boil and add to ingredients in
casserole. Season to taste with
salt and pepper.
8. Cover closely with lid or foil
and cook in centre of oven for
2–2½ hours, or until meat is
tender.
9. Meanwhile, sift flour into a
bowl. Add shredded suet, salt,
pepper, mixed herbs and grated
horseradish.
10. Mix to a soft but not sticky
dough with water. Divide mixture
into small pieces and roll into
balls with floured hands.
11. Increase oven temperature to
hot, 425 deg F or gas 7 (220 deg C)
and place dumplings on top of
meat.
12. Replace lid and return to
oven for a further 30 minutes,
removing the lid for the last 5
minutes to allow dumpling to
brown.

FAMILY FILLER
Serves 6

1½–2lb (¾–1 kilo) stewing steak
1½oz (37gm) dripping or lard
1lb (½ kilo) onions, peeled and
sliced
1lb (½ kilo) carrots, peeled and
sliced
3-4 sticks celery, trimmed,
washed and cut into small
pieces
1oz (25gm) flour
1 pint (½ litre) beef stock
2 tablespoons sweet chutney,
finely chopped
salt and pepper
2lb (1 kilo) potatoes, peeled and
cut into small pieces
1 packet (4 servings) instant
peas

1. Preheat oven to very moderate,
325 deg F or gas 3 (170 deg C).
2. Trim meat and cut into neat
cubes.
3. Melt dripping or lard in a large
pan and fry meat and onions
until meat is sealed all over.
4. Add carrots and celery and
continue cooking for 2–3 minutes.
5. Sprinkle in flour and stir over
gentle heat for 1 minute.
6. Remove pan from heat and
gradually blend in stock and
chutney.
7. Return to heat, bring to the
boil and simmer for 2 minutes,
stirring continuously. Season well
to taste with salt and pepper.
8. Transfer to a large casserole
and cover closely with lid or foil.
9. Cook in centre of oven for
about 2 hours, then add potatoes
and peas and continue cooking
for a further 35–40 minutes, or
until potatoes are cooked through
and meat is tender.

GIPSY BEEF
Serves 4–6

2lb (1 kilo) chuck steak
1oz (25gm) flour
salt and pepper
1oz (25gm) beef dripping
1 can (14oz or 397gm) peeled
tomatoes
1 rounded tablespoon made
English mustard
¼ pint (125ml) beef stock
1 tablespoon sweet chutney
1 tablespoon honey
1 tablespoon blackcurrant jam
1 garlic clove, peeled and
crushed
8-10 small onions, peeled

1. Preheat oven to very moderate,
325 deg F or gas 3 (170 deg C).
2. Trim meat and cut into large
cubes, then toss in flour seasoned
with salt and pepper.
3. Heat dripping in a large pan,
add meat and fry until browned
all over.
4. Add tomatoes with their juice
and mustard and blend well
together.
5. Sprinkle in any remaining
flour and stir over gentle heat for
1 minute. Remove pan from heat
and gradually blend in stock.
Return pan to heat and simmer
for 2 minutes, stirring
continuously.
6. Stir in chutney, honey, jam,
garlic and onions, adding more
seasoning if necessary.
7. Transfer to a casserole and
cover closely with lid or foil.
8. Cook in centre of oven for
2–2½ hours, or until meat is
tender.
9. Skim fat from surface before
serving.

SPICED STEAK
Serves 4–6

1½lb (¾ kilo) chuck steak
1oz (25gm) flour
1 level teaspoon salt
1 level teaspoon sugar
1 level teaspoon ground ginger
pinch of nutmeg
¾ pint (375ml) beef stock
2 tablespoons tomato ketchup
1 tablespoon vinegar
1 onion, peeled and finely
chopped
1 tablespoon drained capers

1. Preheat oven to very moderate,
325 deg F or gas 3 (170 deg C).
2. Trim meat, cut into cubes and
toss in flour seasoned with salt,
sugar, ginger and nutmeg.
3. Place prepared meat in a
casserole with any remaining
flour.
4. Blend stock with tomato
ketchup and vinegar, add onion,
then pour over meat in the
casserole.
5. Cover closely with lid or foil
and cook in centre of oven for
about 1½–2 hours, or until meat
is tender.
6. Stir in capers and adjust
seasoning, if necessary, just
before serving.

SAVOURY MEATBALLS
Serves 4

1lb (½ kilo) minced beef
salt and pepper
pinch of nutmeg
1oz (25gm) flour
½oz (12gm) dripping or lard
1 packet (1½ pints or
approximately ¾ litre)
Florida soup mix
1 pint (approximately ½ litre)
water

1. Preheat oven to moderate,
350 deg F or gas 4 (180 deg C).
2. Mix minced beef with salt,
pepper and nutmeg and divide
into 12 pieces. Shape into neat
balls with floured hands.
3. Melt dripping or lard in a pan
and fry prepared meatballs until
browned all over. Transfer to a
casserole using a draining spoon.
4. Stir soup mix into fat
remaining in pan together with
any remaining flour and stir
over gentle heat for 1 minute.
5. Remove pan from heat and

gradually blend in water. Return
to heat, bring to the boil and
simmer gently for 2 minutes,
stirring continuously. Pour over
meatballs in casserole.
6. Cover closely with lid or foil
and cook in centre of oven for
about 45 minutes, or until meat
is tender.
7. Serve with freshly boiled rice
or creamed potatoes.

BEEF AND BARLEY
Serves 6–8

A good, old-fashioned way of
serving brisket.

1oz (25gm) dripping or lard
3lb (1½ kilo) brisket, boned and
rolled
2 medium onions, peeled and
chopped
½ pint (250ml) beef stock
1oz (25gm) pearl barley
1lb (½ kilo) carrots, peeled and
cut into strips lengthways
1 level teaspoon made mustard
salt and pepper

1. Preheat oven to cool, 300 deg F
or gas 2 (150 deg C).
2. Heat dripping or lard in a
flameproof casserole and brown
meat quickly all over. Drain well
over casserole and keep on one
side.
3. Add onions to fat remaining in
the casserole and fry for 3–4
minutes, or until tender and
lightly browned. Add stock and
return meat to casserole.
4. Cover closely with lid or foil
and cook below centre of oven for
2 hours.
5. Add barley and carrots and
cook for a further hour, or until
meat, barley and vegetables are
tender.
6. Lift meat out on to a serving
dish.
7. Add mustard to vegetable
mixture, season well with salt and
pepper and place around meat to
serve.

Slow Cooker Method
1. Brown meat all over in fat in a
saucepan. Drain well.
2. Place onions, boiling stock,
carrots and barley in a preheated
slow cooker. Add meat. Cook on
High for 30 minutes and on Low
for about 8 hours.
3. Complete recipe as in stage 7
above.

HADRIAN'S CASSEROLE
Serves 4

1lb (½ kilo) buttock steak,
thinly sliced
1oz (25gm) flour
salt and pepper
1oz (25gm) dripping or lard
2 carrots, peeled and grated
1 onion, peeled and finely
chopped
2oz (50gm) mushrooms, washed,
trimmed and chopped
¼ pint (125ml) beef stock
1 teaspoon Worcestershire
sauce
1lb (½ kilo) spring greens,
washed and trimmed
½oz (12gm) butter

1. Preheat oven to moderate, 350
deg F or gas 4 (180 deg C).
2. Coat meat in flour seasoned
with salt and pepper.
3. Melt dripping or lard in a pan
and fry meat until browned all
over. Drain well and keep on one
side.
4. Add carrots, onion and
mushrooms to fat remaining in
the pan and cook gently for 3–4
minutes, or until tender.
5. Sprinkle in any remaining
flour and stir over gentle heat for
1 minute.
6. Remove pan from heat and
gradually blend in stock and
Worcestershire sauce.
7. Return to heat, bring to the
boil and simmer for 2 minutes,
stirring continuously.
8. Place prepared greens in
boiling, salted water and cook for
4–5 minutes, then strain
thoroughly.
9. Grease a casserole with a little
butter, then line the casserole
with cooked cabbage leaves.
Arrange meat slices and vegetable
mixture in centre and cover with
remaining cabbage.
10. Dot with remaining butter.
11. Cover with lid or foil and
cook in centre of oven for 1–1½
hours, or until meat is tender.

Slow Cooker Method
1. Proceed as stages 2–8 above,
inclusive, but using a saucepan.
2. Continue with stages 9 and 10
using a preheated slow cooker.
3. Cook on Low for 4–6 hours.

JUGGED BEEF
Serves 4–6

1½lb (¾ kilo) shin of beef
1oz (25gm) flour
salt and pepper
4oz (100gm) streaky bacon,
trimmed and chopped
2 medium onions, peeled
4 cloves
¾ pint (375ml) beef stock
finely grated rind of half a
lemon
¼ level teaspoon mixed dried
herbs
1 bayleaf
2 level teaspoons made mustard
2 level teaspoons redcurrant
jelly

1. Preheat oven to cool, 300 deg F
or gas 2 (150 deg C).
2. Trim beef, cut into 2-inch
chunky pieces and toss in flour
seasoned with salt and pepper.
3. Fry bacon in a large pan until
fat begins to run.
4. Add meat and continue cooking
until browned all over.
5. Stick onions with cloves and
add to the pan. Sprinkle in any
remaining flour and stir over
gentle heat for 1 minute.
6. Remove pan from heat and add
stock, lemon rind, herbs and
bayleaf.
7. Return to heat, bring to the
boil, stirring, then transfer to a
casserole.
8. Cover closely with lid or foil
and cook in centre of oven for
2½–3 hours, or until meat is
tender.
9. Remove onions and bayleaf
and stir in mustard and
redcurrant jelly before serving.

Slow Cooker Method
1. Proceed as stages 2–6 above,
inclusive, but using a saucepan.
2. Return to heat, bring to the
boil, stirring, then transfer to a
preheated slow cooker.
3. Cook on High for 30 minutes
and on Low for 6–8 hours.
4. Complete recipe as in stage 9.

Pressure Cooker Method
(15lb or H)
1. Proceed as stages 2–7 above,
inclusive, using pan of pressure
cooker and omitting the flour.
2. Cover, bring to pressure: lower
heat and cook for 20 minutes.
Reduce the pressure and remove
lid.
3. Thicken, if liked, in the open
pressure cooker.
4. Complete recipe as in stage 9.

BRAISED BEEF
Serves 6–8

2 leeks, trimmed, washed and
sliced
1 onion, peeled and sliced
1 can (14oz or 397gm) peeled
tomatoes
2 large carrots, peeled and
sliced
bouquet garni
salt and pepper
3–3½lb (1½–1¾ kilo) silverside
4 streaky bacon rashers
1 packet (8oz or 200gm) frozen
whole green beans

1. Preheat oven to cool, 300 deg F
or gas 2 (150 deg C).
2. Arrange leeks in the base of a
deep casserole. Add onion and
tomatoes together with the
juice, carrots and bouquet garni.
Season with salt and pepper.
3. Place meat on top of vegetables
and cover top with bacon rashers.
4. Cover closely with lid or foil
and cook below centre of oven for
about 3½ hours.
5. Remove lid, add frozen beans
and continue cooking, uncovered,
for a further 30 minutes, or until
meat is tender.
6. Arrange meat on a serving dish
and keep hot.
7. Strain vegetables, reserving
the stock, and arrange around
meat. Remove bouquet garni.
8. Serve stock separately as it is
or, if preferred, thickened with a
little cornflour blended with
water.

HUNTERS' STEW
Serves 4

A traditional Dutch way of using
up leftover roast meat.

2½oz (62gm) butter
8oz (200gm) onions, peeled and
chopped
8oz (200gm) cooked beef or
other roast meat, finely
chopped
½ pint (250ml) beef stock
salt and pepper
nutmeg
8oz (200gm) apples, peeled,
cored and chopped
1lb (½ kilo) mashed potatoes
1 tablespoon breadcrumbs

1. Preheat oven to moderate to
moderately hot, 375 deg F or gas 5
(190 deg C).
2. Melt 1½oz (37gm) butter in a

pan and fry onions until lightly
browned.
3. Add meat and stock and season
with salt, pepper and a little
nutmeg.
4. Grease a shallow casserole
with ½oz (12gm) butter and cover
with alternate layers of meat
mixture, apples and potato,
finishing with a layer of potato.
5. Dot surface with remaining
butter and sprinkle with
breadcrumbs.
6. Cook, uncovered, above centre
of oven for about 20 minutes, or
until cooked through and top is
golden brown.

CHILLI CON CARNE
(Illustrated on page 17)
Serves 4–6

A hot and spicy Mexican
speciality.

6oz (150gm) red kidney beans
1 tablespoon corn oil
1½lb (¾ kilo) minced beef
2 medium onions, peeled and
chopped
1 garlic clove, peeled and
crushed
1 can (15oz or 425gm) peeled
tomatoes
1 level dessertspoon mild chilli
powder
good pinch of sugar
1 tablespoon vinegar
dash of Tabasco sauce
salt and pepper

1. Soak beans overnight in cold
water to cover.
2. Preheat oven to very moderate,
325 deg F or gas 3 (170 deg C).
3. Heat oil in a heavy saucepan
and fry the minced beef until
lightly browned. Add onions and
garlic and continue cooking
gently for a further 5 minutes.
4. Stir in drained beans, tomatoes
with their juice, chilli powder
and sugar blended with vinegar.
Add Tabasco sauce and season
to taste with salt and pepper.
Transfer to a casserole.
5. Cover closely with lid or foil
and cook in centre of oven for
about 2 hours, or until meat is
tender.
6. Serve with boiled rice.

SCANDINAVIAN MEATBALLS
Serves 4

1lb (½ kilo) minced beef
1 small onion, peeled and chopped
2oz (50gm) fresh white breadcrumbs
2 tablespoons dry white wine or cider
1 tablespoon finely chopped parsley
salt and pepper
½ level teaspoon thyme
½ level teaspoon finely grated lemon rind
1 small egg, lightly beaten
1 tablespoon flour
2 tablespoons oil
1 packet (½ pint or 250ml) onion sauce mix
½ pint (250ml) milk

1. Preheat oven to moderate, 350 deg F or gas 4 (180 deg C).
2. Mix together meat, onion, breadcrumbs soaked in wine or cider, parsley, salt, pepper, thyme and lemon rind.
3. Bind together with beaten egg and form into eight balls with floured hands.
4. Heat oil in a pan and fry meatballs until browned all over, then drain well over pan and transfer to a casserole.
5. Make up onion sauce according to packet directions with milk, then pour over meatballs.
6. Cover with lid or foil and cook in centre of oven for about 45 minutes, or until cooked through.

BEEF AND PEACH PAPRIKA
Serves 4

1 can (15½oz or 439gm) cling peach slices
1lb (½ kilo) stewing steak
1oz (25gm) flour
2 level teaspoons paprika pepper
½ level teaspoon salt
¼ level teaspoon pepper
2 tablespoons salad oil
1 can (8oz or 200gm) tomatoes
1 level teaspoon caraway seeds (optional)

1. Preheat oven to very moderate, 325 deg F or gas 3 (170 deg C).
2. Drain the peaches, reserving syrup.
3. Trim steak and cut into cubes.
4. Combine the flour, paprika

pepper, salt and pepper.
5. Heat oil in a heavy pan.
6. Toss the meat in the seasoned flour and brown in the oil.
7. Sprinkle in any remaining flour and stir well over gentle heat for 1 minute.
8. Remove pan from heat and gradually blend in reserved peach syrup, tomatoes and caraway seeds (if used). Return to heat and bring to the boil.
9. Transfer to a casserole, cover closely with lid or foil and cook in centre of oven for about 1½ hours, or until meat is tender.
10. Add peaches and heat through.

BOEUF ROUSSY
(Illustrated on page 17)
Serves 4–6

A French country casserole, sweet in flavour because of the high proportion of carrots.

1½lb (¾ kilo) stewing steak
6 tablespoons oil
1oz (25gm) butter
3–4 shallots or very small onions
2lb (1 kilo) carrots, peeled and cut into strips lengthways
salt and pepper
pinch of nutmeg

1. Preheat oven to very moderate, 325 deg F or gas 3 (170 deg C).
2. Trim meat and cut into individual portions.
3. Heat oil and butter together in a flameproof casserole and fry shallots or onions until lightly browned.
4. Add meat and brown on all sides.
5. Add carrots and season well with salt, pepper and nutmeg.
6. Cover closely with lid or foil and cook in centre of oven for 2 hours, or until meat is tender.
7. Serve with creamed potatoes and a green vegetable.

Slow Cooker Method
1. Proceed as stages 2–5 above, inclusive, but using a saucepan.
2. Transfer to a preheated slow cooker. Cook on High for 30 minutes and on Low for 6–8 hours.

CARBONNADE OF BEEF
Serves 4–6

The beer gives this traditional Flemish stew a very full flavour.

2lb (1 kilo) lean stewing steak
2oz (50gm) butter
1lb (½ kilo) onions, peeled and sliced
1oz (25gm) flour
1 pint (approximately ½ litre) beer
salt and pepper
good pinch of thyme
2 bayleaves
1 garlic clove, peeled and crushed (optional)
4 lumps sugar
2 tablespoons wine vinegar

1. Preheat oven to very moderate, 325 deg F or gas 3 (170 deg C).
2. Trim meat and cut into oblong strips about 3 inches by 1 inch.
3. Melt butter in a frying pan and fry meat, turning with a metal spoon, until brown all over, then transfer with a draining spoon to a casserole.
4. Add onions to fat remaining in the pan and cook for 5–10 minutes, or until tender. Add to meat in the casserole.
5. Sprinkle flour into the frying pan and stir over gentle heat for 1 minute.
6. Remove pan from heat and gradually blend in beer to make a smooth sauce. Return to heat, bring to the boil and simmer gently for 2 minutes, stirring continuously.
7. Season with salt and pepper, add thyme, bayleaves and garlic, if used, and pour over meat in casserole.
8. Cover closely with lid or foil and cook towards base of oven for about 2–2½ hours, or until meat is tender.
9. Stir sugar and wine vinegar into the casserole just before serving.

Pressure Cooker Method
(15lb or H)
1. Brown onions and meat in butter in pan of pressure cooker.
2. Remove from heat and stir in ¾ pint (375ml) beer. Season with salt and pepper. Add thyme, 1 bay leaf and garlic, if used.
3. Cover, bring to pressure: lower heat and cook for 15–20 minutes. Reduce the pressure and remove lid.
4. Stir in sugar and wine vinegar and, if liked, thicken in the open pressure cooker.

HUNGARIAN GOULASH
Serves 4–6

No stock or water should be added. The long, slow cooking produces a rich and spicy sauce.

2 red or green peppers
2lb (1 kilo) stewing steak
2oz (50gm) dripping or lard
1lb (½ kilo) onions, peeled and chopped
2 rounded tablespoons mild paprika pepper
1lb (½ kilo) tomatoes, peeled and sliced
salt and pepper
1 carton soured cream

1. Preheat oven to very moderate, 325 deg F or gas 3 (170 deg C).
2. Discard stalk and seeds from peppers, wash, then chop flesh into small pieces.
3. Trim meat and cut into cubes.
4. Melt dripping or lard in a pan and fry onions until golden brown.
5. Add meat and stir with a metal spoon until brown all over.
6. Stir in paprika pepper, tomatoes and chopped peppers and season well with salt and pepper.
7. Bring to the boil, then transfer to a casserole.
8. Cover closely with lid or foil and cook in centre of oven for about 2 hours, or until meat is tender.
9. Spoon soured cream into centre of goulash just before serving.

BISTRO CASSEROLE
Serves 4–6

1½lb (¾ kilo) stewing steak
1oz (25gm) flour
salt and pepper
2oz (50gm) dripping or lard
2 onions, peeled and thinly sliced
1 garlic clove, peeled and crushed
½ pint (250ml) beef stock
½ pint (250ml) brown ale
bouquet garni
pinch of nutmeg
¼ teaspoon sugar
5 slices French bread
2 tablespoons French mustard
parsley

1. Preheat oven to moderate, 350 deg F or gas 4 (180 deg C).
2. Cut the meat into 2-inch cubes

and coat in flour well seasoned with salt and pepper.
3. Melt dripping or lard in a pan and fry meat until brown on all sides. Drain and place in a casserole.
4. Fry onions and garlic in fat remaining in the pan, then add to the casserole.
5. Sprinkle any remaining flour into pan and stir over gentle heat for 1 minute.
6. Remove pan from heat and pour in stock and ale, and add bouquet garni, salt, pepper, nutmeg and sugar.
7. Return to heat and bring to the boil, stirring.
8. Cover closely with lid or foil and cook in centre of oven for 2¼ hours.
9. Add French bread spread with mustard and return casserole to oven, uncovered, for a further 15 minutes, or until top is crisp and brown.
10. Garnish with parsley.

BEEF RIVIERA
Serves 6

1oz (25gm) dripping or lard
1 tablespoon oil
4 streaky bacon rashers, trimmed and cut into small pieces
1 onion, peeled and chopped
1 garlic clove, peeled and crushed
2lb (1 kilo) stewing steak
salt and pepper
½ level teaspoon oregano
¼ pint (125ml) dry red wine
1 small can (2¼oz or 56gm) tomato purée
½ pint (250ml) beef stock
1oz (25gm) flour
1 tablespoon water
4oz (100gm) button mushrooms, washed, trimmed and cut into quarters

1. Preheat oven to very moderate, 325 deg F or gas 3 (170 deg C).
2. Heat dripping or lard and oil in a flameproof casserole and fry bacon, onion and garlic until they begin to brown.
3. Trim meat, cut into cubes, sprinkle with salt, pepper and oregano and add to casserole. Cook for 3–4 minutes until sealed all over.
4. Pour in wine and simmer, uncovered, for 10 minutes.
5. Blend tomato purée with

stock, add to casserole and stir well.
6. Cover closely with lid or foil and cook in centre of oven for about 1½–2 hours.
7. Blend flour to a smooth paste with 1 tablespoon water and a little liquid from the casserole, then stir into the casserole, together with mushrooms, and return to oven for a further 30 minutes, or until meat is tender.

DIJON BEEF
Serves 4–6

2 tablespoons oil
1oz (25gm) butter
4oz (100gm) mushrooms, washed, trimmed and sliced
4oz (100gm) onions, peeled and chopped
1 small garlic clove, peeled and crushed
1½lb (¾ kilo) stewing steak
1oz (25gm) flour
¼ pint (125ml) red Burgundy or Beaujolais wine
½ pint (250ml) beef stock
1 level tablespoon Dijon mustard
salt and pepper
2 tablespoons chopped pickled gherkins

1. Preheat oven to very moderate, 325 deg F or gas 3 (170 deg C).
2. Heat oil and butter in a flameproof casserole and fry mushrooms, onions and garlic gently together for 2–3 minutes. Remove from casserole with a draining spoon and keep on one side.
3. Trim meat, cut into cubes and toss in flour.
4. Fry meat in fat remaining in the casserole until sealed all over.
5. Sprinkle in any remaining flour and stir over gentle heat for 1 minute.
6. Remove casserole from heat and gradually blend in wine, stock and mustard.
7. Return to heat, bring to the boil and simmer gently for 2 minutes, stirring continuously.
8. Add prepared mushrooms, onion and garlic, stir well and season to taste.
9. Cover closely with lid or foil and cook in centre of oven for about 2–2½ hours, or until meat is tender.
10. Stir chopped gherkin into casserole just before serving.

VALENCIA BEEF CASSEROLE
Serves 4

1½lb (¾ kilo) stewing steak
1½oz (37gm) cornflour
salt and pepper
2 tablespoons oil
2 onions, peeled and chopped
1 garlic clove, peeled and crushed
2 carrots, peeled and sliced
2 oranges
¼ pint (125ml) white wine or cider
1 beef stock cube
good pinch of mixed herbs

1. Preheat oven to moderate, 350 deg F or gas 4 (180 deg C).
2. Trim meat, cut into cubes and toss in cornflour seasoned with salt and pepper.
3. Heat oil in a flameproof casserole and fry onions and garlic for 2–3 minutes, or until tender.
4. Add meat to the casserole and brown all over.
5. Add carrots.
6. Peel 1 orange very finely, taking care not to remove any of the white pith. Place rind in boiling water for 1 minute, then drain and cut into thin strips.
7. Add half the orange rind to the casserole and reserve remainder for garnish.
8. Squeeze juice from both oranges and add to wine or cider. Make up to 1½ pints (approximately ¾ litre) with boiling water.
9. Add beef stock cube and herbs, stir well together and pour into casserole.
10. Cover closely with lid or foil and cook in centre of oven for about 1½–2 hours, or until meat is tender.
11. Skim excess fat from surface if necessary and sprinkle with remaining orange rind.

Pressure Cooker Method
(15lb or H)
1. Proceed as stages 2–9 above, inclusive, using pan of pressure cooker, but omit the cornflour in stage 2 and make liquid up to only ¾ pint (375ml) in stage 8.
2. Cover, bring to pressure: lower heat and cook for 20 minutes. Reduce the pressure and remove lid.
3. Thicken, if liked, in the open pressure cooker. Serve sprinkled with remaining orange rind.

RAGOUT OF BEEF WITH PRUNES
Serves 4–6

4oz (100gm) prunes
1oz (25gm) lard
4oz (100gm) streaky bacon, trimmed and chopped
1½lb (¾ kilo) stewing steak, cut into 1-inch cubes
1oz (25gm) flour
salt and pepper
1 onion, peeled and chopped
2 sticks celery, washed, trimmed and chopped
½ pint (250ml) beef stock
3 tablespoons HP sauce
finely grated rind and juice of 1 orange

1. Soak prunes overnight in cold water to cover, then drain well.
2. Preheat oven to very moderate, 325 deg F or gas 3 (170 deg C).
3. Melt lard in a pan and add bacon.
4. Toss meat in flour seasoned with salt and pepper. Add to pan and fry for 5 minutes, or until brown on all sides. Transfer meat and bacon to a casserole.
5. Add onion and celery to fat remaining in the pan and fry gently for 3 minutes.
6. Sprinkle in any remaining flour and stir well over gentle heat for 1 minute.
7. Remove pan from heat and gradually blend in stock, sauce, orange rind and juice, and prunes.
8. Return to heat, bring to the boil, stirring, and pour over meat.
9. Cover closely with lid or foil and cook in centre of oven for about 2 hours, or until meat is tender.

TIVOLI HOTPOT
Serves 4–6

8oz (200gm) belly of pork
1lb (½ kilo) chuck steak
salt and pepper
½ level teaspoon dried marjoram
1½lb (¾ kilo) potatoes
1lb (½ kilo) onions, peeled and sliced
8oz (200gm) carrots, peeled and sliced
¼ pint (125ml) lager or light ale
1oz (25gm) butter or margarine

1. Preheat oven to very moderate, 325 deg F or gas 3 (170 deg C).
2. Trim pork and steak, cut into

neat pieces and season well with salt, pepper and marjoram.
3. Peel potatoes, slice thinly and keep in cold water to avoid discoloration.
4. Place about one third of potatoes in the base of a deep casserole, cover with a layer of onions and carrots and season well.
5. Add meat, cover with a thin layer of potatoes, then arrange remaining onions and carrots on top.
6. Pour in lager or ale, then arrange neatly overlapping potatoes to completely cover top.
7. Dot with butter or margarine.
8. Cook, uncovered, above centre of oven for 15 minutes, then cover closely with lid or foil and continue cooking for 1½ hours, or until meat is tender.
9. Remove cover and cook for a further 15 minutes to brown the potatoes.

SWISS STEAK
Serves 3–4

1lb (½ kilo) blade or chuck steak, about 1 inch thick
1oz (25gm) flour
½ level teaspoon salt
pinch of pepper
¼ level teaspoon dry mustard
1oz (25gm) dripping or lard
1 large onion, peeled and sliced
¼ level teaspoon dried marjoram
¼ level teaspoon sugar
1 can (8oz or 200gm) tomato juice

1. Preheat oven to cool, 300 deg F or gas 2 (150 deg C).
2. Trim meat if necessary and cut into serving portions.
3. Coat meat thoroughly in flour seasoned with salt, pepper and mustard.
4. Melt dripping or lard in a flameproof casserole, add meat and onion and fry until lightly browned.
5. Sprinkle in any remaining flour and stir over gentle heat for 1 minute.
6. Remove casserole from heat, add marjoram and sugar to tomato juice and pour over steak in the casserole.
7. Return to heat and bring to the boil, stirring.
8. Cover with lid or foil and cook in centre of oven for about 2–2¼ hours, or until meat is tender.

BEEF BORDELAISE
Serves 4

1½lb (¾ kilo) braising steak, cut
in one piece, 1 inch thick
1oz (25gm) flour
salt and pepper
1½oz (37gm) lard
1 onion, peeled and chopped
1lb (½ kilo) tomatoes, peeled
and quartered
4 tablespoons water or red
wine

1. Preheat oven to cool, 300 deg F
or gas 2 (150 deg C).
2. Trim meat and coat with flour
seasoned with salt and pepper.
3. Heat 1oz (25gm) lard in a
flameproof casserole and fry meat
on both sides until brown. Drain
and keep on one side.
4. Add remaining lard to
casserole and fry onion for a few
minutes, then add tomatoes.
5. Return meat to pan and add
water or wine.
6. Cover closely with lid or foil
and cook in centre of oven for
about 2–2½ hours, or until meat is
tender.
7. Adjust seasoning and add a
little more liquid if necessary.
8. Serve with creamed or baked
potatoes and a green vegetable or
crisp green salad.

BOEUF PROVENÇAL
Serves 4–6

1½lb (¾ kilo) shin of beef
2oz (50gm) dripping or lard
4oz (100gm) salt belly of pork,
cut into small pieces
2 onions, peeled and thinly
sliced
8oz (200gm) tomatoes, peeled
and chopped
1 garlic clove, peeled and
crushed
1 bayleaf
½ pint (250ml) beef stock
1 large glass red wine
2 level tablespoons cornflour
2 tablespoons water
8-12 pimento-stuffed olives,
cut into slices

1. Trim beef and cut into neat
strips.
2. Melt dripping or lard in a
flameproof casserole and lightly
fry salt pork for 2–3 minutes.
Add onions and continue cooking
for a further 2–3 minutes. Place
meat on top.
3. Add tomatoes, garlic, bayleaf,

stock and wine. Cover with a lid
and allow to stand for about 1
hour.
4. Preheat oven to cool, 300 deg F
or gas 2 (150 deg C).
5. Blend cornflour with water
and stir into casserole.
6. Cover closely with lid or foil
and cook in centre of oven for 3–4
hours, or until meat is tender.
7. Stir in sliced olives a few
minutes before serving.

BOEUF EN DAUBE
Serves 6–8

Beef marinated in wine and
spices, then cooked until it is so
tender it could be eaten with a
spoon.

2lb (1 kilo) topside of beef
2 onions, peeled and sliced
2 carrots, peeled and sliced
1 bouquet garni
1 strip of orange rind
salt
freshly ground black pepper
½ pint (250ml) red wine
2 tablespoons brandy
2 tablespoons olive oil
4oz (100gm) lean bacon,
trimmed and cut into small
pieces
1 garlic clove, peeled and
crushed
½ pint (250ml) beef stock
4oz (100gm) stoned olives
8oz (200gm) tomatoes, peeled,
de-seeded and chopped

1. Trim meat, cut into cubes and
place in a large bowl.
2. Add onions, carrots, bouquet
garni, orange rind, salt, pepper,
red wine and brandy. Leave to
stand for 4–5 hours, stirring
occasionally.
3. Preheat oven to cool, 300 deg F
or gas 2 (150 deg C).
4. Heat olive oil in a frying pan
and lightly fry bacon.
5. Drain meat, reserving
marinade, then fry meat with
bacon until browned all over. Stir
in garlic. Transfer to a casserole.
6. Heat marinade until reduced
by half then pour over the meat.
Add stock.
7. Cover closely with lid or foil
and cook below centre of oven
for 3–4 hours, or until meat is
tender.
8. Skim fat from surface, add
olives and tomatoes and return to
oven for a further 30 minutes
before serving.

BOEUF BOURGUIGNONNE
Serves 6

Beef cooked in red wine – a
classic dish from the Burgundy
district of France.

2lb (1 kilo) topside of beef
2 tablespoons oil
4oz (100gm) streaky bacon
rashers, trimmed and cut into
small pieces
1 onion, peeled and chopped
1 garlic clove, peeled and
crushed
1 tablespoon flour
¼ pint (125ml) red Burgundy
wine
¼ pint (125ml) beef stock
salt and pepper
bouquet garni
1oz (25gm) butter
1lb (½ kilo) button or pickling
onions, peeled

1. Preheat oven to very moderate,
325 deg F or gas 3 (170 deg C).
2. Trim meat and cut into large
cubes.
3. Heat oil in a frying pan and
fry meat on all sides until well
sealed.
4. Transfer meat to a casserole.
5. Add bacon to fat remaining in
the pan and cook until opaque.
Add chopped onion and garlic and
continue cooking until lightly
golden.
6. Sprinkle in flour and stir over
gentle heat for 1 minute.
7. Remove pan from heat and
gradually blend in wine and beef
stock.
8. Return to heat, bring to the
boil, then simmer for 2 minutes,
stirring continuously.
9. Season well and add bouquet
garni, then pour over meat in
casserole.
10. Cover closely with lid or foil
and cook in centre of oven for 2
hours.
11. Melt butter in a small pan and
cook button or pickling onions
until browned.
12. Reduce oven temperature to
cool, 300 deg F or gas 2 (150 deg
C). Add onions to casserole and
continue cooking for a further
30 minutes, or until meat is tender
and onions cooked through.
13. Remove bouquet garni before
serving.

Veal

Casseroling is ideal for this versatile meat, and the delicate flavour blends happily with creamy sauces, as well as with fuller, spicier ingredients.

POT OF VEAL
Serves 4–6

3lb (1½ kilo) neck or breast of veal, boned
2 tablespoons oil
1 streaky bacon rasher, trimmed and cut into small pieces
8–12 button onions, peeled
4oz (100gm) mushrooms, washed, trimmed and cut into quarters
½oz (12gm) flour
½ pint (250ml) chicken stock
1 tablespoon lemon juice
1 tablespoon finely chopped parsley
salt and pepper

1. Preheat oven to moderate, 350 deg F or gas 4 (180 deg C).
2. Discard skin and bone from meat and cut veal into small pieces.
3. Heat oil in a pan and fry bacon until transparent, then add veal and brown lightly. Transfer with a draining spoon to a casserole and add onions and mushrooms.
4. Sprinkle flour into fat remaining in the pan and stir over gentle heat for 1 minute.
5. Remove pan from heat and gradually blend in stock, lemon juice and parsley.
6. Return to heat, bring to the boil and simmer for 2 minutes, stirring continuously. Season to taste with salt and pepper.
7. Pour prepared sauce over ingredients in the casserole.
8. Cover closely with lid or foil and cook in centre of oven for about 1½–2 hours, or until meat is tender.

BRAISED VEAL
Serves 4–6

1oz (25gm) butter
1 tablespoon oil
3lb (1½ kilo) neck of veal
2 streaky bacon rashers, trimmed and cut into small pieces
1lb (½ kilo) carrots, peeled and sliced
8oz (200gm) onions, peeled and sliced
1 leek, washed, trimmed and sliced
½ level teaspoon dried thyme
salt and pepper
¼ pint (125ml) stock or water
little finely grated lemon rind

1. Preheat oven to moderate, 350 deg F or gas 4 (180 deg C).
2. Heat butter and oil in a frying pan and fry meat and bacon together until lightly browned.
3. Arrange carrots, onions and leek in a casserole, sprinkle with thyme and season with salt and pepper.
4. Pour in stock or water to come half way up the vegetables.
5. Drain meat and bacon well and place on top of vegetables.
6. Cover with lid or foil and cook in centre of oven for about 1½–2 hours, or until meat is tender.
7. Cut meat into portions and arrange on a serving dish.
8. Drain vegetables, reserving liquid to serve separately. Arrange vegetables with meat on a serving dish and sprinkle with lemon rind.

VEAL WITH PARSLEY
Serves 4–6

1½lb (¾ kilo) stewing veal
2 tablespoons oil
1 packet (½ pint or 250ml) parsley sauce mix
½ pint (250ml) milk
1 tablespoon lemon juice
salt and pepper
2–3 tablespoons cream
lemon wedges to garnish

1. Preheat oven to moderate, 325 deg F or gas 3 (170 deg C).
2. Trim meat and cut into neat cubes.
3. Heat oil in a frying pan and fry veal until sealed all over. Drain well over pan and transfer to a casserole.
4. Make up sauce according to packet directions using milk.
5. Stir in lemon juice and add seasoning if necessary. Pour over veal in the casserole and stir together.
6. Cover with lid or foil and cook in centre of oven for about 1½–2 hours, or until meat is tender.
7. Stir in cream just before serving and garnish with lemon wedges.

Slow Cooker Method
1. Preheat slow cooker.
2. Trim meat, cut into neat cubes and add to cooker.
3. Proceed as stages 4 and 5 above.
4. Cook on High for 30 minutes and on Low for 6–8 hours.
5. Stir in cream just before serving and garnish with lemon wedges.

Chilli con carne (see page 11)   Boeuf Roussy (see page 12)

Paprika veal (see page 22)   Osso buco (see page 24)

Sweet September casserole (see page 30) Belgian chops (see page 32)

Lamb Genevieve (see page 32) Pork Peking (see page 43)

GRANGE CASSEROLE
Serves 4

1lb (½ kilo) stewing veal
¾oz (18gm) flour
1 small onion, peeled and chopped
2 sticks celery, washed and chopped
4 streaky bacon rashers, trimmed and cut into small pieces
salt and pepper
¾ pint (375ml) chicken stock
bouquet garni
strip of lemon rind
chopped parsley

1. Preheat oven to moderate, 350 deg F or gas 4 (180 deg C).
2. Trim veal, cut into cubes and toss in flour.
3. Place meat in a casserole, together with onion, celery and bacon. Season well with salt and pepper.
4. Pour in stock, add bouquet garni and lemon rind.
5. Cover closely with lid or foil and cook in centre of oven for about 1¼ hours, or until meat is tender.
6. Remove bouquet garni and strip of lemon rind and serve sprinkled with chopped parsley.

KENSINGTON CASSEROLE
Serves 4–6

1½lb (¾ kilo) lean stewing veal
3 streaky bacon rashers, trimmed and cut into small pieces
3 medium onions, peeled and sliced
salt
freshly ground black pepper
3 medium potatoes, peeled
3 tomatoes, peeled and cut into quarters
2 tablespoons tomato purée
½ pint (250ml) chicken stock
1 packet (8oz or 200gm) frozen peas

1. Preheat oven to very moderate, 325 deg F or gas 3 (170 deg C).
2. Trim meat and cut into neat cubes.
3. Fry bacon in a heavy pan until fat begins to run, then add veal and onions and fry until lightly browned.
4. Transfer with a draining spoon to a casserole. Season well with

salt and freshly ground black pepper.
5. Cut potatoes into chunky pieces, dry well on kitchen paper and add to fat remaining in the pan. Fry gently for 3–4 minutes, or until lightly browned.
6. Stir in tomatoes, tomato purée and stock, bring to the boil and pour into casserole.
7. Cover with lid or foil and cook in centre of oven for about 1 hour.
8. Add peas and continue cooking for a further 30 minutes, or until meat is tender.

GOLDEN CASSEROLE
Serves 4

1lb (½ kilo) stewing veal
1oz (25gm) butter
1oz (25gm) flour
2 oranges
¾ pint (375ml) chicken stock
1 tablespoon sweet white vermouth
salt and pepper
8oz (200gm) carrots, peeled and sliced
1 tablespoon finely chopped parsley

1. Preheat oven to very moderate, 325 deg F or gas 3 (170 deg C).
2. Trim meat if necessary and cut into neat cubes.
3. Melt butter in a flameproof casserole and fry veal until sealed all over. Remove from pan with a draining spoon and keep on one side.
4. Sprinkle flour into fat remaining in the pan and stir over gentle heat for 1 minute.
5. Remove pan from heat and gradually blend in finely grated rind of 1 orange and the juice of both oranges, chicken stock and sweet vermouth.
6. Return to heat, bring to the boil and simmer for 2 minutes, stirring continuously. Season well to taste with salt and pepper.
7. Return meat to casserole and stir in carrots.
8. Cover closely with lid or foil and cook just below centre of oven for about 1½ hours, or until meat is tender.
9. Serve sprinkled with parsley.

SAVOURY VEAL CASSEROLE
Serves 6

Breast or loin of veal filled with savoury stuffing and then gently braised.

2oz (50gm) butter
1 small onion, peeled and chopped
1lb (½ kilo) sausagemeat
1 level teaspoon mixed dried herbs
salt and pepper
3lb (1½ kilo) breast or loin of veal (ask the butcher to remove the bone)
2 streaky bacon rashers, trimmed and cut into small pieces
1 large onion, peeled and sliced
2 carrots, peeled and sliced
½ pint (250ml) chicken stock

1. Preheat oven to very moderate, 325 deg F or gas 3 (170 deg C).
2. Melt 1oz (25gm) butter in a pan and fry the small, chopped onion until softened. Add to sausagemeat and mix well together.
3. Add herbs, salt and pepper and blend stuffing well together.
4. Spread prepared stuffing over the meat, roll up and tie securely with string.
5. Melt the remaining butter in a flameproof casserole and fry the stuffed veal slowly until golden brown.
6. Remove meat from the pan, draining it well, and keep on one side.
7. Add bacon to casserole and cook for 2–3 minutes.
8. Add large, sliced onion and carrots, cover casserole and cook for a further 2–3 minutes.
9. Place prepared meat on top of vegetables and pour stock over.
10. Cover pan closely with lid or foil and cook in centre of oven for 2–2½ hours, or until cooked through.
11. Arrange meat and vegetables on a serving dish and keep warm.
12. Heat stock remaining in casserole until slightly reduced.
13. Check seasoning then spoon over the prepared meat.

VEAL ANGOSTURA
Serves 6–8

Aromatic bitters add their distinctive flavour to this dish.

2lb (1 kilo) lean stewing veal
1oz (25gm) flour
salt and pepper
4 tablespoons olive oil
1 onion, peeled and chopped
½ pint (250ml) chicken stock
¼ pint (125ml) fresh orange juice
2oz (50gm) sultanas
1 tablespoon Angostura bitters
1 tablespoon flaked almonds, lightly toasted

1. Preheat oven to moderate, 350 deg F or gas 4 (180 deg C).
2. Trim meat, cut into neat cubes and toss in flour seasoned with salt and pepper.
3. Heat oil in a flameproof casserole and fry onion until tender.
4. Add meat and cook for 2–3 minutes, or until sealed all over.
5. Sprinkle in any remaining flour and stir over gentle heat for 1 minute.
6. Remove casserole from heat and gradually blend in stock and orange juice.
7. Return to heat, bring to the boil and simmer for 2 minutes, stirring continuously.
8. Add sultanas and Angostura bitters, and adjust seasoning if necessary.
9. Cover closely with lid or foil and cook in centre of oven for about 1–1¼ hours, or until meat is tender.
10. Serve sprinkled with almonds.

Slow Cooker Method
1. Proceed as stages 2–8 above, inclusive, but using a saucepan.
2. Transfer to a preheated slow cooker and cook on High for 30 minutes and on Low for about 6 hours.

Pressure Cooker Method
(15lb or H)
1. Trim meat, cut into neat cubes and brown together with onion in hot oil in pan of pressure cooker.
2. Remove from heat and stir in stock, orange juice, sultanas and Angostura bitters.
3. Cover, bring to pressure: lower heat and cook for 12 minutes. Reduce the pressure and remove lid.
4. Adjust seasoning. Thicken, if liked, in open pressure cooker.

CHOPS WITH ROSEMARY
Serves 4

A very simply prepared dish of veal in tomatoes.

4 veal chops, ½ inch–1 inch thick
½oz (12gm) butter
¼ level teaspoon dried rosemary
1 can (14oz or 397gm) peeled tomatoes

1. Preheat oven to moderate to moderately hot, 375 deg F or gas 5 (190 deg C).
2. Trim chops if necessary.
3. Heat butter in a flameproof casserole and fry chops until golden brown on both sides.
4. Stir rosemary into tomatoes and pour over meat in the casserole.
5. Cover with lid or foil and cook in centre of oven for about 30–40 minutes, or until meat is tender.

LONDON VEAL ROLLS
Serves 4

A special occasion dish.

1lb (½ kilo) fillet of veal, thinly sliced
6oz (150gm) streaky bacon rashers, trimmed
1 tablespoon made English mustard
salt and pepper
2oz (50gm) butter
1 tablespoon oil
2 medium onions, peeled and cut into wedges
1oz (25gm) flour
½ pint (250ml) chicken stock
¼ pint (125ml) dry white wine or extra stock
1 tablespoon tomato purée
¼ level teaspoon crushed dried rosemary

1. Preheat oven to very moderate, 325 deg F or gas 3 (170 deg C).
2. Beat veal out thinly and cut into pieces about 2 inches by 1½ inches.
3. Stretch bacon on a board with the back of a knife and cut into 2-inch lengths.
4. Spread each piece of veal with mustard and season with salt and pepper. Roll up with a piece of bacon on the outside and secure with a wooden cocktail stick.
5. Heat butter and oil in a pan and fry prepared rolls until lightly browned. Drain well over pan and transfer to a casserole.
6. Fry onions in fat remaining in the pan till browned, then transfer to casserole with a draining spoon.
7. Sprinkle flour into fat remaining in the pan and stir over gentle heat for 1 minute.
8. Remove pan from heat and gradually blend in stock, wine or extra stock, tomato purée and rosemary.
9. Return to heat, bring to the boil and simmer for 2 minutes, stirring continuously. Season to taste, then pour over meat in casserole.
10. Cover with lid or foil and cook in centre of oven for 1 hour, or until meat is tender.

VEAL POLONAISE
Serves 4–6

1½lb (¾ kilo) lean stewing veal
½oz (12gm) flour
salt and pepper
3 level teaspoons paprika pepper
2oz (50gm) butter
8oz (200gm) onions, peeled and sliced
½ level teaspoon dried marjoram
8oz (200gm) tomatoes, peeled and sliced
¼ pint (125ml) tomato juice
2 tablespoons soured cream
finely chopped fresh parsley

1. Preheat oven to cool, 300 deg F or gas 2 (150 deg C).
2. Trim veal, cut into cubes and toss in flour seasoned with salt, pepper and paprika pepper.
3. Melt butter in a frying pan and lightly fry onions until tender. Add marjoram and mix well together.
4. Arrange layers of meat, onions and tomatoes in a casserole and pour tomato juice over the top.
5. Cover closely with lid or foil and cook in centre of oven for 2–3 hours, or until meat is tender.
6. Pour soured cream over the top and sprinkle with chopped parsley before serving.

SESAME VEAL
Serves 6–8

Veal cooked in white wine sauce.

2lb (1 kilo) stewing veal
1½oz (37gm) flour
salt and pepper
2oz (50gm) butter
1 tablespoon oil
2 medium onions, peeled and
chopped
4oz (100gm) mushrooms,
washed, trimmed and sliced
½ pint (250ml) dry white wine
½ pint (250ml) chicken stock
2 level tablespoons made
English mustard
1 carton soured cream
2–3 teaspoons sesame seeds,
lightly toasted

1. Preheat oven to very moderate,
325 deg F or gas 3 (170 deg C).
2. Trim meat and toss in flour
seasoned with salt and pepper.
3. Heat butter and oil together
in a frying pan and brown meat
all over.
4. Use a draining spoon to
transfer meat to a casserole.
5. Fry onions and mushrooms
in fat remaining in the pan for
4–5 minutes, then sprinkle in any
remaining flour and stir well
together over gentle heat for
1 minute.
6. Remove pan from heat and
gradually blend in wine, stock
and mustard.
7. Return to heat, bring to the
boil, and simmer for 2 minutes,
stirring continuously.
8. Cover closely with lid or foil
and cook in centre of oven for
about 1½ hours, or until meat is
tender.
9. Stir in soured cream and
return to oven for a further 5
minutes to heat through.
10. Sprinkle with toasted sesame
seeds before serving.

Slow Cooker Method
1. Proceed as stages 2–7 above,
inclusive, but using a saucepan.
2. Transfer to a preheated slow
cooker and cook on High for 30
minutes and on Low for 6 hours.
3. Sprinkle with toasted sesame
seeds before serving.

CHALET VEAL
Serves 4–6

1½lb (¾ kilo) stewing veal
1oz (25gm) flour
salt and pepper
2oz (50gm) dripping or lard
8 button onions or shallots,
peeled
2 sticks celery, washed,
trimmed and chopped
8oz (200gm) carrots, peeled and
sliced
1 pint (approximately ½ litre)
stock made from veal bones
1 bouquet garni
4oz (100gm) self-raising flour
2oz (50gm) shredded suet
1 level teaspoon caraway seeds
cold water to mix
4oz (100gm) button mushrooms
finely grated rind and juice of
1 lemon

1. Preheat oven to very moderate,
325 deg F or gas 3 (170 deg C).
2. Trim meat, cut into cubes and
toss in flour seasoned with salt
and pepper.
3. Heat dripping or lard in a large
pan and fry veal gently until
sealed all over. Remove from pan
with a draining spoon and keep
on one side.
4. Add onions or shallots, celery
and carrots to fat remaining in
the pan and cook gently for about
7–8 minutes.
5. Sprinkle in any remaining
flour and stir over gentle heat
for 1 minute.
6. Remove pan from heat and
gradually blend in stock.
7. Return to heat, bring to the
boil and simmer for 2 minutes,
stirring continuously. Add
bouquet garni.
8. Cover with lid or foil and cook
in centre of oven for about 1
hour.
9. Meanwhile, prepare dumplings.
Place self-raising flour, suet and
caraway seeds in a bowl and mix
well together.
10. Bind to a soft but not sticky
dough with water, then shape into
six to eight small balls with
floured hands.
11. Stir mushrooms and lemon
rind and juice into the casserole,
then add prepared dumplings.
12. Continue cooking for a
further 30 minutes, removing
lid or foil for the last 10 minutes
so that dumplings cook through.

VEAL GOULASH
Serves 4

4oz (100gm) fat salt pork or
bacon pieces, cut into small
pieces
1lb (½ kilo) stewing veal
1 large onion, peeled and
chopped
1oz (25gm) flour
1 level dessertspoon mild
paprika pepper
¾ pint (375ml) chicken stock
4 small potatoes, peeled and
thinly sliced
4 button onions, peeled
1 can (4oz or 100gm) pimentos,
drained and cut into small
pieces
1 bayleaf
1 carton natural yogurt

1. Preheat oven to very moderate,
325 deg F or gas 3 (170 deg C).
2. Fry pork or bacon pieces in a
heavy frying pan until the fat
begins to run.
3. Discard pork or bacon and fry
veal, cut into neat pieces, in the
pan until sealed all over.
4. Stir in large, chopped onion
and continue cooking for 2–3
minutes. Transfer with a draining
spoon to a casserole.
5. Sprinkle flour and paprika
pepper into fat remaining in the
pan and stir over gentle heat for
1 minute.
6. Remove pan from heat and
gradually blend in stock.
7. Return to heat, bring to the
boil and simmer for 2 minutes,
stirring continuously. Pour over
meat in casserole.
8. Add potatoes, button onions,
pimentos and bayleaf to
casserole and stir together.
9. Cover with lid or foil and cook
below centre of oven for 2–3
hours, or until meat is tender.
10. Remove bayleaf and adjust
seasoning if necessary. Stir in
yogurt before serving.

Slow Cooker Method
1. Proceed as stages 2–8 above,
inclusive, using a preheated slow
cooker instead of a casserole.
2. Cook on High for 30 minutes
and on Low for 6 hours.
3. Complete recipe as in stage 10.

VEAL SOMBRERO
Serves 4–6

1½lb (¾ kilo) stewing veal
½oz (12gm) butter
1 tablespoon oil
2 medium onions, peeled and
chopped
1 level dessertspoon mild
paprika pepper
1 level tablespoon flour
1 level tablespoon tomato
purée
½ pint (250ml) chicken stock
small strip of lemon rind
1 bayleaf
1 can (11½oz or 326gm)
sweetcorn kernels
1 packet (8oz or 200gm) frozen
peas

1. Preheat oven to moderate,
350 deg F or gas 4 (180 deg C).
2. Trim meat and cut into neat
cubes.
3. Heat butter and oil in a
flameproof casserole and fry veal
until browned all over.
4. Add onions and paprika pepper
to pan and continue cooking
for 1 minute.
5. Sprinkle in flour and stir over
gentle heat for 1 minute.
6. Remove casserole from heat
and gradually blend in tomato
purée and stock.
7. Return to heat, bring to the
boil and simmer for 2 minutes,
stirring continuously.
8. Add lemon rind and bayleaf.
9. Cover closely with lid or foil
and cook in centre of oven for
about 1 hour, then remove
bayleaf and lemon rind.
10. Stir in drained sweetcorn
and frozen peas and continue
cooking for a further 15 minutes,
or until meat is tender.

Pressure Cooker Method
(15lb or H)
1. Proceed as stages 2–8 above,
omitting stage 5 and using pan of
pressure cooker.
2. Cover, bring to pressure: lower
heat and cook for 10 minutes.
Reduce the pressure and remove
lid.
3. Stir in drained sweetcorn and
frozen peas. Bring back to
simmering point in open pan,
lower heat and continue cooking
for 5–8 minutes until tender.
4. Adjust seasoning. Thicken, if
liked, in open pressure cooker.

PAPRIKA VEAL
(Illustrated on page 17)
Serves 4

1lb (½ kilo) stewing veal
1oz (25gm) butter
1 large onion, peeled and
chopped
1–2 level teaspoons mild
paprika pepper
1 level tablespoon tomato
purée
¾ pint (375ml) chicken stock
salt
freshly ground black pepper
6oz (150gm) long-grain rice
1 small carton yogurt or
soured cream
chopped parsley
finely grated rind of half a
lemon

1. Preheat oven to very moderate,
325 deg F or gas 3 (170 deg C).
2. Trim meat and cut into neat
cubes.
3. Melt butter in a frying pan
and fry meat until golden brown
all over. Transfer to a casserole,
using a draining spoon.
4. Add onion to fat remaining in
the pan and fry gently until
tender.
5. Stir in paprika pepper and
tomato purée, then gradually
blend in the stock. Season with
salt and pepper, then pour over
veal in casserole.
6. Cover closely with lid or foil
and cook in centre of oven for
about 1 hour, then stir in the
rice.
7. Replace lid or foil and
continue cooking for a further
30 minutes, or until rice is cooked
and meat is tender.
8. Stir in yogurt or soured cream,
reserving a little.
9. Pour rest of yogurt or soured
cream on top and serve sprinkled
with a little chopped parsley and
finely grated lemon rind.

Slow Cooker Method
1. Proceed as stages 2–5 above,
inclusive, using a preheated slow
cooker instead of a casserole.
2. Cook on High for 30 minutes
and on Low for 6 hours.
3. Cook rice in separate saucepan.
Drain, add to slow cooker and
cook on Low for further 15
minutes.
4. Complete recipe as in stages 8
and 9.

MARYNKA
Serves 6

2lb (1 kilo) stewing veal
1oz (25gm) flour
salt and pepper
1oz (25gm) butter
2 tablespoons olive oil
1 garlic clove, peeled and
crushed
2 tablespoons tomato purée
1 pint (approximately ½ litre)
beef stock
1 bayleaf
good pinch of dried thyme
good pinch of dried sweet basil
4oz (100gm) mushrooms,
washed, trimmed and sliced

1. Preheat oven to moderate,
350 deg F or gas 4 (180 deg C).
2. Trim the meat, cut into cubes
and toss in flour well seasoned
with salt and pepper.
3. Heat butter and oil in a
flameproof casserole and fry the
meat until golden brown all over.
4. Stir in garlic, tomato purée
and any remaining flour, and stir
over gentle heat for 1 minute.
5. Remove casserole from heat,
gradually blend in stock and add
bayleaf and herbs.
6. Return to heat, bring to the
boil and simmer for 2 minutes,
stirring continuously.
7. Cover closely with lid or foil
and cook in centre of oven for
1 hour.
8. Add mushrooms, replace lid
and continue cooking for a
further 20–30 minutes, or until
meat is tender and mushrooms
cooked.

VEAL CHASSEUR
Serves 4–6

1½lb (¾ kilo) stewing veal
2 tablespoons oil
1oz (25gm) butter
4oz (100gm) mushrooms,
washed, trimmed and sliced
4 shallots, peeled
1oz (25gm) flour
¾ pint (375ml) chicken stock
1–2 wine glasses white wine
1 dessertspoon tomato purée
1 bayleaf
good pinch of sugar
salt and pepper

1. Preheat oven to very moderate,
325 deg F or gas 3 (170 deg C).
2. Trim meat if necessary and cut
into neat cubes.
3. Heat oil and butter in a

flameproof casserole and fry veal until sealed all over. Remove from casserole with a draining spoon and keep on one side.
4. Add mushrooms and shallots to fat remaining in the casserole and fry gently for 3–4 minutes.
5. Sprinkle in flour and stir over gentle heat for 1 minute.
6. Remove casserole from heat and gradually blend in stock, white wine and tomato purée. Add bayleaf and sugar and season well with salt and pepper.
7. Return to heat, bring to the boil and simmer for 2 minutes, stirring continuously.
8. Return meat to pan and cover closely with lid or foil.
9. Cook just below centre of oven for about 1½ hours, or until meat is tender.

VIENNA CASSEROLE
Serves 4–6

1½lb (¾ kilo) lean stewing veal
2oz (50gm) butter
1 large onion, peeled and chopped
1 garlic clove, peeled and crushed
2 carrots, peeled and sliced
1oz (25gm) flour
1 tablespoon tomato ketchup
¾ pint (375ml) veal stock made from bones
1 green pepper, de-seeded and sliced
3 tomatoes, peeled, de-seeded and chopped

1. Preheat oven to very moderate, 325 deg F or gas 3 (170 deg C).
2. Trim veal and cut into neat cubes.
3. Melt butter in a pan and fry veal until sealed all over. Drain meat well and transfer to a casserole.
4. Add onion and garlic to fat remaining in the pan and cook gently for 2–3 minutes, or until tender.
5. Add carrots and continue cooking for 1 minute.
6. Sprinkle in flour and stir well over gentle heat for 1 minute.
7. Remove pan from heat and gradually blend in tomato ketchup and stock.
8. Return to heat, bring to the

boil and simmer for 2 minutes, stirring continuously. Add green pepper.
9. Pour prepared sauce over meat in the casserole and mix well together.
10. Cover with lid or foil and cook in centre of oven for about 1½ hours, or until meat is tender, then stir in tomatoes and return to oven for 5 minutes.
11. Check seasoning before serving.

CURRIED VEAL
Serves 4

1lb (½ kilo) lean stewing veal
1 level tablespoon curry powder
1oz (25gm) flour
salt and pepper
2oz (50gm) butter
2 onions, peeled and sliced
1 dessert apple
1 pint (approximately ½ litre) chicken stock
1–2 level teaspoons curry paste
1 tablespoon lemon juice
1 tablespoon apricot jam, sieved
4 cocktail gherkins, chopped
2 tablespoons single cream

1. Preheat oven to very moderate, 325 deg F or gas 3 (170 deg C).
2. Trim meat, cut into small pieces and toss in a mixture of curry powder, flour, salt and pepper.
3. Heat butter in a flameproof casserole and fry onions until tender. Remove from pan with a draining spoon and keep on one side.
4. Add meat to fat remaining in the pan and fry until sealed all over. Stir in any remaining curry powder and flour and add peeled, cored and diced apple.
5. Remove pan from heat and gradually blend in stock, curry paste, lemon juice and apricot jam. Stir in fried onions.
6. Return to heat, bring to the boil and simmer for 2 minutes, stirring continuously.
7. Cover with lid or foil and cook in centre of oven for about 1–1½ hours, or until meat is tender.
8. Stir in gherkins and cream and return to oven for 5 minutes.
9. Check seasoning before serving with freshly boiled rice.

FRICASSEE OF VEAL
Serves 4–6

A smooth, creamy sauce complements the delicate flavour of the veal.

1½lb (¾ kilo) lean veal (from shoulder or knuckle)
1½oz (37gm) butter or margarine
2 medium onions, peeled and chopped
¼ pint (125ml) milk
¼ pint (125ml) water
1 bayleaf
1 blade of mace
salt and pepper
small strip of lemon rind
2 level tablespoons cornflour
1 egg yolk
3 tablespoons single cream
lemon wedges
small sprigs of parsley to garnish

1. Preheat oven to very moderate, 325 deg F or gas 3 (170 deg C).
2. Cut veal into small cubes.
3. Melt butter or margarine in a flameproof casserole and lightly fry veal for 3–4 minutes without browning.
4. Add onions, milk, water, bayleaf, mace, salt, pepper and lemon rind.
5. Bring to the boil, then cover closely with lid or foil.
6. Cook in centre of oven for 1½–2 hours, or until meat is tender.
7. Remove bayleaf, mace and lemon rind.
8. Blend the cornflour with 3–4 tablespoons water and gradually blend into the pan. Bring to the boil and cook for 2–3 minutes, stirring continuously.
9. Remove from heat and add egg yolk beaten together with cream. Reheat without boiling.
10. Garnish with wedges of lemon and sprigs of parsley and serve with freshly cooked, buttered noodles.

Pressure Cooker Method
(15lb or H)
1. Proceed as stages 2–4 above, inclusive, using pan of pressure cooker.
2. Cover, bring to pressure: lower heat and cook for 12 minutes. Reduce the pressure and remove lid.
3. Complete recipe as in stages 7–10 inclusive.

OSSO BUCO
(Illustrated on page 17)
Serves 4

This is a colourful, classic dish
from Italy.

**2lb (1 kilo) shin of veal, cut
into four pieces
1oz (25gm) flour
salt
freshly ground black pepper
4 tablespoons olive oil
1 garlic clove, peeled and
crushed
1 medium onion, peeled and
chopped
2 carrots, peeled and sliced
¼ pint (125ml) dry white wine
¼ pint (125ml) stock or water
2–3 tablespoons tomato purée
1 bouquet garni
grated rind of half a lemon
finely chopped parsley**

1. Preheat oven to moderate,
350 deg F or gas 4 (180 deg C).
2. Toss pieces of veal in flour
seasoned with salt and pepper.
3. Heat olive oil in a flameproof
casserole, add meat and cook
until browned all over.
4. Stir in garlic, onion, carrots,
wine and stock or water. Blend in
tomato purée and add bouquet
garni.
5. Cover closely with lid or foil
and cook in centre of oven for
about 1½ hours, or until meat is
tender.
6. Remove bouquet garni and
serve sprinkled with lemon rind
and finely chopped parsley.

Slow Cooker Method
1. Proceed as stages 2–4 above,
inclusive, but using a saucepan.
2. Transfer to a preheated slow
cooker. Cook on High for 30
minutes and on Low for about
6 hours.
3. Complete recipe as in stage 6.

Pressure Cooker Method
(15lb or H)
1. Proceed as stages 3 and 4 above
using pan of pressure cooker.
2. Cover, bring to pressure: lower
heat and cook for 15 minutes.
Reduce the pressure and remove
lid.
3. Remove bouquet garni, thicken,
if liked, in the open pressure
cooker and serve sprinkled with
lemon rind and finely chopped
parsley.

VEAL SORRENTO
Serves 4

**4 veal escalopes
little made mustard
4 thin slices ham (the same size
as veal escalopes)
1 egg, beaten with 1
tablespoon milk
4 tablespoons fresh white
breadcrumbs
pinch of oregano
1 tablespoon grated Parmesan
or sharp, dry Cheddar cheese
2–3 tablespoons oil
½oz (12gm) butter
3–4 tablespoons tomato juice**

1. Preheat oven to moderate,
350 deg F or gas 4 (180 deg C).
2. Pound escalopes until thin
and spread lightly with mustard.
3. Place a slice of ham on each
escalope.
4. Dip in egg beaten with milk
and then in a mixture of
breadcrumbs, oregano and cheese.
Pat coating on firmly.
5. Heat oil in a frying pan and
fry meat until brown on both
sides.
6. Grease a shallow casserole
with butter and place veal in it.
Sprinkle lightly with tomato
juice.
7. Cook, uncovered, in centre of
oven for about 20 minutes, or
until meat is tender.
8. Serve with sauté potatoes and
salad.

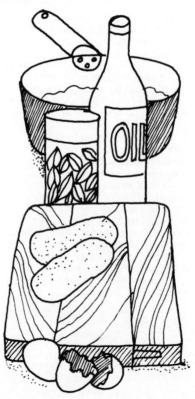

VEAL BALALAIKA
Serves 6

Soured cream and toasted
almonds give a party finish to
this dish.

**2lb (1 kilo) boned shoulder of
veal
1oz (25gm) flour
salt
freshly ground black pepper
1oz (25gm) butter
2 tablespoons olive oil
1 large onion, peeled and
chopped
1 can (4oz or 100gm) button
mushrooms, washed and sliced
½ pint (250ml) chicken stock
2 level tablespoons mild
paprika pepper
1 carton soured cream
1oz (25gm) almonds, blanched
and lightly toasted**

1. Preheat oven to moderate,
350 deg F or gas 4 (180 deg C).
2. Trim meat, cut into 1-inch
cubes and toss in flour seasoned
with salt and pepper.
3. Heat butter and oil in a large
frying pan and brown meat all
over.
4. Use a draining spoon to
transfer meat to a casserole.
5. Fry onion and mushrooms in
fat remaining in the pan for 4–5
minutes. Sprinkle in any
remaining flour and stir over
gentle heat for 1 minute.
6. Remove pan from heat and
gradually blend in stock.
7. Return to heat and bring to the
boil, stirring. Add paprika pepper,
check seasoning, then pour into
casserole.
8. Cover closely with lid or foil
and cook in centre of oven for
about 1–1½ hours, or until meat
is tender.
9. Stir in soured cream and
scatter toasted almonds over
before serving.

Slow Cooker Method
1. Proceed as stages 2–7 above,
inclusive, using a preheated slow
cooker instead of a casserole.
2. Cook on High for 30 minutes
and on Low for about 6 hours.
3. Complete recipe as in stage 9.

Lamb

You will find here recipes which include many classic and traditional dishes, together with a number using wine and spices for those with more exotic tastes.

HERBY HOTPOT
Serves 4

Lamb well flavoured with herbs and topped with browned potatoes.

2lb (1 kilo) middle neck of lamb
1½oz (37gm) dripping or lard
1lb (½ kilo) onions, peeled and quartered
1lb (½ kilo) carrots, peeled and quartered
1oz (25gm) flour
1 pint (approximately ½ litre) stock
1 level teaspoon mixed dried herbs
1 level tablespoon finely chopped fresh mint
2 tablespoons tomato purée
salt and pepper
1 bayleaf
2lb (1 kilo) potatoes, peeled and sliced
½oz (12gm) butter

1. Preheat oven to very moderate, 325 deg F or gas 3 (170 deg C).
2. Trim meat and cut into neat pieces.
3. Melt dripping or lard in a pan and fry meat until browned on both sides. Drain well over the pan and transfer to a plate.
4. Fry onions and carrots in fat remaining in the pan for 2–3 minutes, then drain well over pan and put on the plate with the meat.
5. Sprinkle flour into pan and stir over gentle heat for 1 minute.
6. Remove pan from heat and gradually blend in the stock to make a thin gravy.
7. Add mixed herbs, mint and tomato purée and blend well together. Season to taste with salt and pepper, and add bayleaf.
8. Return to heat and bring to the boil.
9. Arrange half the potato slices in the base of a casserole. Place lamb and vegetables on top and pour prepared sauce over. Arrange remaining potato slices neatly on top and brush with melted butter.
10. Cover closely with lid or foil and cook in centre of oven for about 2–2½ hours. About 20 minutes before serving, remove lid or foil and turn up oven temperature to moderately hot, 400 deg F or gas 6 (200 deg C) to brown potatoes.

IRISH STEW
Serves 4

This is the simplest and cheapest of all lamb stews.

2lb (1 kilo) middle neck of lamb
2lb (1 kilo) potatoes, peeled and sliced
2 large onions, peeled and sliced
salt and pepper
1 pint (approximately ½ litre) water

1. Preheat oven to very moderate, 325 deg F or gas 3 (170 deg C).
2. Trim excess fat from meat and divide into neat pieces.
3. Arrange layers of meat, potatoes and onion in a deep casserole, seasoning well between each layer. Add water to come about threequarters of the way up the pot.
4. Cover closely with lid or foil and cook in centre of oven for about 2–2½ hours, or until meat and potatoes are tender.

LAMB AND BUTTER BEANS
Serves 4

2lb (1 kilo) middle neck of lamb
1oz (25gm) flour
salt and pepper
1oz (25gm) dripping or lard
1 rounded dessertspoon tomato purée
¾ pint (375ml) water
1 can (8oz or 200gm) butter beans
1 large carrot, peeled and sliced
1 leek, washed, trimmed and sliced
1 parsnip, peeled and sliced

1. Preheat oven to very moderate, 325 deg F or gas 3 (170 deg C).
2. Trim lamb, cut into convenient serving portions, then toss in flour well seasoned with salt and pepper.
3. Melt dripping or lard in a large pan and fry meat for 2–3 minutes, or until golden brown. Remove with a draining spoon and transfer to a casserole.
4. Sprinkle remaining flour into fat in the pan and stir over gentle heat for 1 minute.
5. Remove pan from heat and gradually blend in tomato purée, water and liquid strained from butter beans.
6. Return to heat, bring to the boil and simmer for 2 minutes, stirring continuously. Season to taste with salt and pepper.
7. Add carrot, leek and parsnip to casserole and pour prepared sauce over.
8. Cover closely with lid or foil and cook in centre of oven for about 1½ hours, then add butter beans and continue cooking for a further 15 minutes, or until meat and vegetables are tender.

HIGH DAYS HOTPOT
Serves 4

2lb (1 kilo) potatoes
salt and pepper
2lb (1 kilo) middle neck of lamb
2 lamb's kidneys
2oz (50gm) dripping or cooking
fat
1 large onion, peeled and sliced
1 swede or turnip, peeled and
diced
4oz (100gm) mushrooms,
washed and trimmed
1oz (25gm) flour
¾ pint (375ml) stock
2 tablespoons mint jelly
1 bayleaf

1. Preheat oven to very moderate,
325 deg F or gas 3 (170 deg C).
2. Peel and slice potatoes and
arrange half of them in the base of
a large casserole. Season well
with salt and pepper.
3. Trim lamb and cut into neat
pieces.
4. Skin and core kidneys and cut
into small pieces.
5. Melt 1oz (25gm) dripping or
cooking fat in a large frying pan
and fry lamb and kidneys until
browned all over. Drain well over
pan and transfer to casserole.
6. Add onion, swede or turnip
and mushrooms to fat remaining
in the pan and cook for 3–4
minutes. Use a draining spoon to
transfer to casserole.
7. Add remaining fat to frying
pan and sprinkle in flour. Stir well
together over gentle heat for
1 minute.
8. Remove pan from heat and
gradually blend in stock and mint
jelly. Add bayleaf.
9. Return to heat, bring to the
boil and simmer gently for 2
minutes, stirring continuously.
Season with salt and pepper.
10. Pour prepared sauce into the
casserole and top with remaining
potatoes arranged in a neat layer.
11. Cover with lid or foil and
cook in centre of oven for about
2–2½ hours, removing the cover
for the last 20 minutes to brown
the potatoes.

VILLAGE CASSEROLE
Serves 4

2lb (1 kilo) middle neck of lamb
2 onions, peeled and sliced
1½lb (¾ kilo) potatoes, peeled
and sliced
salt
freshly ground black pepper
1 level teaspoon dried mint
2 tablespoons lentils
1 pint (approximately ½ litre)
stock

1. Preheat oven to moderate,
350 deg F or gas 4 (180 deg C).
2. Trim lamb and cut into neat
pieces.
3. Arrange a layer each of meat,
onions and potatoes in a
casserole, sprinkling with salt,
pepper and a little dried mint
between each layer.
4. Add lentils, then continue in
layers, finishing with a final
topping of potatoes.
5. Pour stock into casserole.
6. Cover closely with lid or foil
and cook in centre of oven for
1½ hours, then remove lid and
continue cooking for a further
30 minutes to brown top.

STRATFORD CASSEROLE
Serves 4

3oz (75gm) dripping
2lb (1 kilo) neck of lamb, cut
into 4 pieces
1 medium onion, peeled and
sliced
1 large carrot, peeled and
sliced
8oz (200gm) mushrooms,
washed, trimmed and sliced
salt and pepper
½ pint (250ml) dry cider
1lb (½ kilo) chestnuts

1. Preheat oven to very
moderate, 325 deg F or gas 3
(170 deg C).
2. Heat dripping in a pan and
brown the meat on all sides.
Transfer to a casserole using a
draining spoon.
3. Fry the vegetables in fat
remaining in pan, then add to
casserole.
4. Season with salt and pepper
and pour in the cider.
5. Cover closely with lid or foil
and cook in centre of oven for
about 2 hours.
6. Meanwhile, wash chestnuts
and make a split in both ends

with a knife. Boil in water for 10
minutes, then peel away both the
outside and inside skins, taking
only a few chestnuts at a time
from the pan.
7. Place the peeled nuts in a
saucepan and cover with a little
stock or water. Bring to the boil,
then reduce heat and simmer for
35–40 minutes, or until tender.
8. Add chestnuts to casserole and
cook for a further 20 minutes.

WINTER CASSEROLE
Serves 3–4

Small turnips can be used instead
of swedes – sprinkle them with
2 teaspoons white sugar.

1 best end neck of lamb, boned
and rolled
½oz (12gm) flour
salt and pepper
1oz (25gm) dripping or lard
1½lb (¾ kilo) swedes, peeled and
cut into slices
½ pint (250ml) beef stock
2 tablespoons finely chopped
parsley

1. Preheat oven to moderate,
350 deg F or gas 4 (180 deg C).
2. Dust the meat with flour well
seasoned with salt and pepper.
3. Melt dripping or lard in a pan
and fry meat until browned all
over.
4. Arrange swedes in the base of
a casserole and sprinkle well with
salt and pepper.
5. Place meat on top of swedes,
fat side uppermost and pour
stock around.
6. Cook uncovered, in centre of
oven for about 1 hour, or until
meat and vegetables are tender.
7. Remove meat, cut into thick
slices then replace in casserole.
8. Sprinkle with parsley to serve.

Pressure Cooker Method
(15lb or H)
1. Brown meat in hot fat in pan
of pressure cooker. Drain well and
keep on one side.
2. Arrange swedes in base of
pressure cooker and season. Place
meat on top, fat side uppermost,
and pour stock around.
3. Cover, bring to pressure: lower
heat and cook for 12 minutes.
Reduce the pressure and remove
lid.
4. Remove meat, cut into thick
slices and arrange on top of
swedes on serving dish. Sprinkle
with parsley.

LAMB ORLANDO
Serves 4

1½lb (¾ kilo) best end neck of
lamb
1oz (25gm) flour
salt and pepper
1 onion, peeled and sliced
2 carrots, peeled and sliced
8oz (200gm) courgettes,
trimmed and cut into ½-inch
slices
¾ pint (375ml) chicken stock
1–2 teaspoons Worcestershire
sauce
bouquet garni

1. Preheat oven to moderate,
350 deg F or gas 4 (180 deg C).
2. Trim meat, cut into portions
and toss in flour seasoned with
salt and pepper.
3. Arrange meat and prepared
vegetables in layers in a
casserole.
4. Pour in stock and
Worcestershire sauce and add
bouquet garni.
5. Cover closely with lid or foil
and cook in centre of oven for
1½ hours, or until meat is tender.
6. Remove bouquet garni before
serving.

LANCASHIRE HOTPOT
Serves 4–6

2lb (1 kilo) potatoes, peeled and
thinly sliced
2lb (1 kilo) middle neck of
mutton
2 lamb's kidneys
2oz (50gm) dripping or lard
1 onion, peeled and thinly
sliced
1oz (25gm) flour
1 pint (approximately ½ litre)
stock
salt and pepper
1 teaspoon caster sugar
chopped parsley

1. Preheat oven to very moderate,
325 deg F or gas 3 (170 deg C).
2. Cover base of a large casserole
with potatoes.
3. Trim and cut mutton into even-
sized chops.
4. Skin and core kidneys and
cut into small pieces.
5. Melt 1oz (25gm) dripping or
lard in a pan and fry chops until
brown all over. Transfer to a
casserole with a draining spoon.
6. Fry kidneys in fat remaining
in the pan until brown, and place

on top of mutton.
7. Add remaining fat to the pan
and fry onion until tender.
8. Sprinkle in flour and stir over
gentle heat for 1 minute.
9. Remove pan from heat and
gradually add stock, stirring well.
10. Return pan to heat and bring
to the boil. Season well and add
sugar.
11. Pour over meat and potatoes
in casserole.
12. Arrange remaining potato
to completely cover the surface.
13. Cover closely with lid or foil
and cook in centre of oven for
1¾ hours.
14. Remove cover, return to
oven and cook for a further
15–20 minutes, or until potato is
brown and crisp.
15. Sprinkle with chopped
parsley and serve with pickled
red cabbage.

WELSH CASSEROLE
Serves 4

2lb (1 kilo) neck of lamb
1oz (25gm) dripping or lard
1 onion, peeled and chopped
1 leek, washed, trimmed and
sliced
4 tomatoes, peeled and sliced
1lb (½ kilo) potatoes, peeled and
sliced
½ pint (250ml) stock or water
salt and pepper
1 dessertspoon finely chopped
parsley

1. Preheat oven to moderate,
350 deg F or gas 4 (180 deg C).
2. Trim meat and cut into neat
pieces.
3. Melt dripping or lard in a
flameproof casserole and fry meat
until browned all over. Drain
well over pan and keep on one
side.
4. Add onion and leek to fat
remaining in pan and cook gently
for 2–3 minutes.
5. Add tomatoes, potatoes, stock
or water, salt and pepper and
parsley.
6. Return meat to casserole and
bring to the boil, stirring
continuously.
7. Cover closely with lid or foil
and cook in centre of oven for
1½–2 hours, or until meat is
tender.
8. Skim fat from surface before
serving.

LAMB CHOP POT
Serves 4

1½lb (¾ kilo) neck of mutton
1oz (25gm) dripping or lard
2 onions, peeled and sliced
2 carrots, peeled and sliced
1 garlic clove, peeled and
crushed (optional)
1oz (25gm) flour
¾ pint (375ml) stock
salt and pepper
1lb (½ kilo) potatoes, peeled and
quartered
1 packet (4oz or 100gm) frozen
peas

1. Preheat oven to moderate,
350 deg F or gas 4 (180 deg C).
2. Trim meat and divide into
serving portions.
3. Melt dripping or lard in a pan
and fry meat until brown all over.
Remove with a draining spoon
to a plate.
4. Add onions, carrots and garlic
(if used) to fat remaining in the
pan and fry gently for 2–3
minutes.
5. Sprinkle in flour and stir over
gentle heat for 1 minute.
6. Remove pan from heat and
gradually blend in stock.
7. Return to heat, bring to the
boil and simmer for 2 minutes,
stirring constantly.
8. Add salt, pepper, potatoes and
peas.
9. Turn into a casserole, cover
closely with lid or foil and cook
in centre of oven for about 1½
hours, or until meat is tender.

Slow Cooker Method
1. Proceed as stages 2–8 above,
inclusive.
2. Transfer to a preheated slow
cooker. Cook on High for 30
minutes and on Low for 5–6 hours.

Pressure Cooker Method
(15lb or H)
1. Proceed as stages 2–4 above,
inclusive, using pan of pressure
cooker.
2. Remove from heat and stir in
stock. Place prepared meat on
top. Season with salt and pepper.
3. Cover, bring to pressure: lower
heat and cook for 10 minutes.
Reduce the pressure and remove
lid.
4. Add potatoes and peas. Replace
lid, bring back to pressure: lower
heat and continue cooking 4
minutes.

LAMB WOODSTOCK
Serves 4

Stuffed breast of lamb on a bed of savoury potatoes.

4oz (100gm) dried apricots
2 breasts of lamb, boned
1 small onion, peeled and finely chopped
8oz (200gm) pork sausagemeat
1 level tablespoon finely chopped fresh mint
2oz (50gm) fresh white breadcrumbs
salt and pepper
2lb (1 kilo) potatoes
2 level teaspoons flour
2 level teaspoons chopped chives
½ pint (250ml) chicken stock
little chopped fresh mint to garnish

1. Soak apricots overnight in cold water to cover.
2. Preheat oven to moderate to moderately hot, 375 deg F or gas 5 (190 deg C).
3. Trim excess fat from meat.
4. Drain apricots and cut into small pieces, then mix together with onion, sausagemeat, mint and breadcrumbs. Season with salt and pepper.
5. Spread boned side of each breast of lamb with the prepared mixture. Roll up neatly and tie each roll three times with string at even intervals. Cut between each piece of string to form four rolls from each joint.
6. Peel and thinly slice potatoes, place in a pan of boiling, salted water and simmer for 5 minutes. Drain well.
7. Arrange potatoes in a large shallow casserole, sprinkling each layer with flour and chopped chives. Pour in the stock.
8. Arrange lamb rolls on top.
9. Cover with lid or foil and cook in centre of oven for 40 minutes, then remove cover and cook for a further 40 minutes, or until meat and potatoes are tender.
10. Remove string from lamb and sprinkle with chopped fresh mint before serving.

COUNTY LAMB
Serves 4

4 lamb chops
2oz (50gm) butter
2 cooking apples
1 onion, peeled and chopped
1oz (25gm) flour
¼ pint (125ml) apple juice
¼ pint (125ml) water
2oz (50gm) sultanas
½ level teaspoon mixed dried herbs
salt and pepper
2 tablespoons single cream

1. Preheat oven to moderate, 350 deg F or gas 4 (180 deg C).
2. Trim chops if necessary.
3. Melt 1oz (25gm) butter in a frying pan and fry chops until browned on both sides. Drain well over pan and transfer to a casserole.
4. Peel, core and slice apples and add to fat remaining in the pan, together with onion. Cook over gentle heat, turning with a metal spoon, for 3–4 minutes, then add to casserole.
5. Melt remaining butter in the frying pan, sprinkle in flour and stir over gentle heat for 1 minute.
6. Remove pan from heat and gradually blend in apple juice and water. Stir in sultanas and herbs.
7. Return to heat, bring to the boil and simmer for 2 minutes, stirring continuously. Season with salt and pepper.
8. Pour into casserole.
9. Cover with lid or foil and cook in centre of oven for about 45 minutes–1 hour, or until meat is tender.
10. Stir cream into casserole just before serving.

Slow Cooker Method
1. Proceed as stages 2–7 above, inclusive, using a preheated slow cooker instead of a casserole.
2. Cook on High for 30 minutes and on Low for 5–6 hours.
3. Complete recipe as in stage 10.

LAMB WITH SAVOURY DUMPLINGS
Serves 4

1oz (25gm) dripping or lard
1 medium onion, peeled and thinly sliced
2 carrots, peeled and thinly sliced
2 sticks celery, washed, trimmed and sliced
8 best end or middle neck of lamb chops
½oz (12gm) flour
1 can (14oz or 397gm) peeled tomatoes
¼ pint (125ml) plus 2–3 tablespoons cold water
1 level teaspoon mixed dried herbs
salt and pepper
½ level teaspoon sugar
4oz (100gm) self-raising flour
½ level teaspoon dry mustard
1½oz (37gm) shredded suet
few poppy seeds

1. Preheat oven to moderate, 350 deg F or gas 4 (180 deg C).
2. Melt dripping or lard in a frying pan, add onion, carrots and celery and fry for 2–3 minutes. Transfer with a draining spoon to a shallow casserole.
3. Trim chops and toss in flour, then add to fat remaining in the pan and brown on both sides. Arrange on top of vegetables.
4. Pour tomatoes into the frying pan, stir in ¼ pint (250ml) water and the herbs. Bring to the boil, stirring, then season with salt, pepper and sugar and pour over lamb in casserole.
5. Cover with lid or foil and cook in centre of oven for 1–1½ hours, or until meat is tender.
6. Place self-raising flour in a bowl, season with mustard, ¼ teaspoon salt, and pepper and stir in suet.
7. Mix to a soft but not sticky dough with 2–3 tablespoons water. Form into eight balls and place on top of casserole.
8. Scatter tops with poppy seeds and return to oven for a further 20–30 minutes, removing the lid for the last 5 minutes to allow dumplings to brown.

WEALDEN CASSEROLE
Serves 4

4 lamb chump chops
salt and pepper
2 small onions, peeled and sliced
3 medium carrots, peeled and sliced
1 medium turnip, peeled and sliced
8oz (200gm) courgettes, trimmed and sliced
½ pint (250ml) stock
finely chopped fresh mint

1. Preheat oven to moderate to moderately hot, 375 deg F or gas 5 (190 deg C).
2. Sprinkle meat with salt and pepper.
3. Arrange half the vegetables in a casserole and sprinkle with salt and pepper.
4. Place lamb on top, cover with rest of vegetables and sprinkle with salt and pepper.
5. Pour in stock.
6. Cover closely with lid or foil and cook in centre of oven for 30 minutes.
7. Reduce oven temperature to very moderate, 325 deg F or gas 3 (170 deg C) and cook for a further hour, or until meat is tender.
8. Sprinkle a little mint over the top before serving.

COUNTRY HOTPOT
Serves 4

1oz (25gm) butter
1 medium onion, peeled and chopped
12oz (300gm) cold roast lamb, sliced
1 can (14oz or 397gm) peeled tomatoes
salt
freshly ground black pepper
1 level teaspoon sugar
3–4 medium potatoes

1. Preheat oven to moderate, 350 deg F or gas 4 (180 deg C).
2. Grease a deep casserole with a little of the butter.
3. Place a little onion in the base of casserole, then arrange half the lamb on top.
4. Drain tomatoes, reserving juice, and place on top of lamb. Season with salt, pepper and sugar.
5. Arrange rest of lamb on top

and sprinkle with remaining onion.
6. Peel and very thinly slice potatoes and arrange neatly overlapping to completely cover top.
7. Pour reserved tomato juice over and dot with remaining butter.
8. Cover with lid or foil and cook in centre of oven for about 45 minutes, then remove lid and cook for about 15 minutes longer, or until potatoes are tender and browned.

MONDAY FAVOURITE
Serves 3–4

8oz (200gm) cold, cooked lamb
1oz (25gm) butter or dripping
1 large onion, peeled and chopped
1oz (25gm) flour
½ pint (250ml) chicken stock
1 tablespoon tomato ketchup
1 tablespoon Worcestershire sauce
1 level teaspoon made mustard
1lb (½ kilo) parsnips, peeled and thinly sliced
1 bayleaf
1 small strip orange rind

1. Preheat oven to moderate to moderately hot, 375 deg F or gas 5 (190 deg C).
2. Trim meat if necessary and cut into cubes.
3. Melt butter or dripping in a pan and fry onion until tender.
4. Add meat and cook over gentle heat for 2 minutes.
5. Sprinkle in flour and stir over gentle heat for 1 minute.
6. Remove pan from heat and gradually blend in stock, tomato ketchup, Worcestershire sauce and mustard.
7. Return to heat, gradually bring to the boil and simmer for 2 minutes, stirring continuously.
8. Add parsnips, bayleaf and orange rind.
9. Cover closely with lid or foil and cook in centre of oven for about 45 minutes, or until parsnips are tender.
10. Remove bayleaf and orange rind before serving.

LAMB WITH MARJORAM
Serves 6

2lb (1 kilo) lean stewing lamb
1½oz (37gm) flour
salt and pepper
1¼oz (37gm) dripping
2 onions, peeled and sliced
½ pint (250ml) stock
1 can (15oz or 425gm) peeled tomatoes
2 level teaspoons dried marjoram
juice and grated rind of half a lemon

1. Preheat oven to very moderate, 325 deg F or gas 3 (170 deg C).
2. Trim meat and cut into neat pieces. Toss in flour well seasoned with salt and pepper.
3. Heat dripping in a frying pan, add onions and cook for 2–3 minutes. Drain well over pan and transfer to a casserole.
4. Fry lamb in fat remaining in the pan until browned on both sides, then place on top of onions.
5. Sprinkle any remaining flour into frying pan and stir over gentle heat for 1 minute.
6. Remove pan from heat, gradually blend in stock, then stir in tomatoes, marjoram and lemon juice.
7. Return to heat, bring to the boil and simmer for 2–3 minutes, stirring continuously. Season well to taste.
8. Pour sauce into casserole and cover closely with lid or foil.
9. Cook in centre of oven for 1½–2 hours, or until lamb is tender.
10. Serve sprinkled with grated lemon rind.

Pressure Cooker Method
(15lb or H)
1. Trim meat and cut into neat pieces. Season with salt and pepper.
2. Fry onions and meat in hot dripping in pan of pressure cooker. Stir until meat is browned.
3. Remove from heat and stir in stock, tomatoes, marjoram and lemon juice.
4. Cover, bring to pressure: lower heat and cook for 15 minutes. Reduce the pressure and remove lid.
5. Adjust seasoning. Thicken, if liked, in open pressure cooker.
6. Complete recipe as in stage 10 above.

SWEET SEPTEMBER CASSEROLE
(Illustrated on page 18)
Serves 6

1½lb (¾ kilo) lean stewing lamb
2–3 tablespoons salad oil
1 onion, peeled and sliced
1oz (25gm) flour
salt and pepper
½ pint (250ml) chicken stock
½ pint (250ml) dry cider
8oz (200gm) fresh or canned
plums or greengages
4oz (100gm) carrots

1. Preheat oven to very moderate,
325 deg F or gas 3 (170 deg C).
2. Trim meat and cut into small
pieces.
3. Heat oil in a flameproof
casserole and fry onion gently for
2–3 minutes, or until lightly
browned. Remove onion with a
draining spoon and keep on one
side.
4. Toss meat in flour seasoned
with salt and pepper until coated
all over.
5. Add meat to oil remaining in
the casserole and stir over gentle
heat until browned all over.
Sprinkle in any remaining flour
and stir over gentle heat for 1
minute.
6. Remove casserole from heat
and gradually stir in stock,
together with the cider.
7. Return to heat, add prepared
onion and bring to the boil,
stirring. Cover closely with lid
or foil and cook in centre of oven
for about 1½ hours.
8. Add washed, halved and stoned
plums or greengages and return
to oven for a further 20–30
minutes, or until fruit is tender.
9. Stir in grated carrot just
before serving.

Slow Cooker Method
1. Proceed as stages 2–6 above,
inclusive, but using a saucepan.
2. Return to heat, add prepared
onion and bring to the boil,
stirring.
3. Transfer to a preheated slow
cooker. Cook on High for 30
minutes and on Low for 5 hours.
Add washed, halved and stoned
plums or greengages and continue
cooking 1–2 hours. Stir in grated
carrot just before serving.

LAMB WITH LENTILS
Serves 4

½ small shoulder lamb (about
2lb or 1 kilo), boned
4 streaky bacon rashers, cut in
half
salt and pepper
½ level teaspoon dried thyme
4oz (100gm) brown lentils
2 small onions, peeled and
finely chopped
½ pint (250ml) beef stock
1 tablespoon finely chopped
parsley

1. Preheat oven to moderate,
350 deg F or gas 4 (180 deg C).
2. Open meat out flat and cover
with bacon rashers.
3. Season with salt and pepper
and sprinkle with thyme.
4. Roll up firmly and tie securely
about three times with string.
5. Place lentils and onions in the
base of a casserole and pour in
the stock.
6. Place meat on top.
7. Cover closely with lid or foil
and cook in centre of oven for
about 2 hours, or until meat and
vegetables are tender.
8. Take out meat, cut into slices,
removing string, and arrange on
a serving dish.
9. Spoon lentils around the meat
or, if liked, pass through a sieve
or liquidizer and serve as a sauce.
10. Serve sprinkled with parsley.

TRANSATLANTIC CASSEROLE
Serves 4

3oz (75gm) prunes
1oz (25gm) dried apricots
1½lb (¾ kilo) middle neck of
lamb
1oz (25gm) dripping or lard
1 medium onion, peeled and
thinly sliced
1 large cooking apple
salt and pepper
½ level teaspoon mixed spice
½ pint (250ml) chicken stock

1. Soak prunes and apricots
overnight in cold water to cover.
2. Preheat oven to moderate,
350 deg F or gas 4 (180 deg C).
3. Drain fruit and cut into small
pieces, discarding stones.
4. Trim meat and cut into neat
pieces.
5. Melt dripping or lard in a
frying pan and brown meat on
both sides. Remove from pan and
drain well on kitchen paper.
6. Arrange alternate layers of
prunes and apricots, lamb and
onion, peeled, cored and sliced
apple in a casserole, seasoning
between each layer with salt,
pepper and mixed spice.
7. Add stock, then cover closely
with lid or foil.
8. Cook in centre of oven for
about 2 hours, or until meat is
tender.
9. If necessary, skim excess fat
from surface before serving.

LAMB VERSAILLES
Serves 4

2lb (1 kilo) lean shoulder of
lamb, boned
1oz (25gm) flour
salt
freshly ground black pepper
2oz (50gm) butter
1 tablespoon oil
1 pint (approximately ½ litre)
stock
1 bayleaf
½ level teaspoon crushed dried
rosemary
8 small carrots, peeled
12 button onions, peeled
2oz (50gm) sultanas
1 tablespoon redcurrant jelly
freshly chopped parsley

1. Preheat oven to moderate,
350 deg F or gas 4 (180 deg C).
2. Trim meat, cut into neat cubes
and toss in flour seasoned with
salt and pepper.
3. Heat butter and oil in a large,
heavy frying pan and fry lamb
until browned and sealed all
over. Use a draining spoon to
transfer to a casserole.
4. Sprinkle any remaining flour
into frying pan and stir over
gentle heat for 1 minute.
5. Remove pan from heat and
gradually blend in stock.
6. Return to heat, bring to the
boil and simmer for 2 minutes,
stirring continuously. Add bayleaf
and rosemary.
7. Pour prepared sauce over lamb
and cover casserole closely with
lid or foil.
8. Cook in centre of oven for
about 1 hour, then stir in carrots,
onions, sultanas and redcurrant
jelly.
9. Continue cooking for about
45 minutes–1 hour, or until meat
and vegetables are tender.
10. Check seasoning and sprinkle
with parsley before serving.

COONAWARRA CASSEROLE
Serves 8

Australian lamb stew with wine and herbs.

2lb (1 kilo) lean lamb from shoulder or leg
2oz (50gm) butter
1 tablespoon oil
1 large onion, peeled and sliced
salt and pepper
1 level teaspoon dried mixed herbs
½ pint (250ml) dry red wine
½ pint (250ml) chicken stock
8oz (200gm) small white onions, peeled and left whole
1lb (½ kilo) carrots, peeled and cut into strips
6oz (150gm) button mushrooms, washed and trimmed
2 tablespoon cornflour
2 tablespoons water

1. Preheat oven to cool, 300 deg F or gas 2 (150 deg C).
2. Trim lamb and cut into cubes.
3. Heat butter and oil in a flameproof casserole and fry meat until browned all over. Transfer to a plate using a draining spoon.
4. Add sliced onion to fat remaining in the pan and fry gently until soft.
5. Return meat to pan, add salt and pepper and herbs and pour in wine and stock.
6. Bring to the boil, then cover with lid or foil.
7. Cook in centre of oven for about 2 hours, then add small onions and carrots and cook for a further 30 minutes.
8. Add mushrooms and cook for a further 30 minutes.
9. Blend cornflour with water, stir in a little of the hot stock from the casserole, then stir into the casserole until well blended.
10. Either return casserole to oven for a further 15 minutes or stir over gentle heat on top of cooker until thickened.

LAMB ROCHELLE
Serves 4

½ shoulder lamb (about 2lb or 1 kilo)
3 level tablespoons flour
salt and pepper
2oz (50gm) butter
½ pint (250ml) stock
1 bayleaf
¼ level teaspoon crushed rosemary
1lb (½ kilo) potatoes, peeled and quartered
¼ pint (125ml) single cream
paprika pepper

1. Preheat oven to very moderate, 325 deg F or gas 3 (170 deg C).
2. Remove meat from bone, trim, cut into cubes and toss in flour seasoned with salt and pepper.
3. Melt butter in a flameproof casserole and fry meat until golden brown all over.
4. Sprinkle in any remaining flour and stir over gentle heat for 1 minute.
5. Remove casserole from heat and gradually blend in stock. Add bayleaf and crushed rosemary.
6. Return to heat, bring to the boil and simmer for 2 minutes, stirring continuously.
7. Cover closely with lid or foil and cook in centre of oven for 45 minutes–1 hour, then add potatoes and continue cooking for a further 1 hour, or until potatoes are cooked and lamb is tender.
8. Allow to cool slightly, then stir in cream. Return casserole to heat on top of cooker, but do not allow to boil.
9. Serve sprinkled with a little paprika pepper.

LAMB BRETONNE
Serves 6

1 tablespoon dripping or lard
1 leg of lamb (about 3–4lb or 1½–2 kilo)
8oz (200gm) tomatoes, peeled, de-seeded and chopped
1 garlic clove, peeled and crushed
salt and pepper
¼ pint (125ml) dry white wine
1 bayleaf

1. Preheat oven to very moderate, 325 deg F or gas 3 (170 deg C).
2. Melt dripping or lard in a deep, flameproof casserole and fry lamb, turning as necessary, until golden brown all over.
3. Arrange tomatoes and garlic around the meat in the casserole. Season with salt and pepper.
4. Pour wine over meat and add bayleaf.
5. Cover with lid or foil and cook in centre of oven for about 2½ hours, or until meat is tender.
6. Add a little stock to the sauce if it is too thick and check seasoning before serving.

ITALIAN CASSEROLE OF LAMB
Serves 6

4lb (2 kilo) lean shoulder of lamb, boned
1oz (25gm) flour
salt and pepper
2 tablespoons oil
4 streaky bacon rashers, trimmed and cut into small pieces
1 garlic clove, peeled and crushed
1 medium onion, peeled and chopped
1 can (8oz or 200gm) peeled tomatoes
¼ pint (125ml) white wine
¾ pint (375ml) stock
1 bouquet garni
½ level teaspoon dried basil
¼ level teaspoon finely grated lemon rind

1. Preheat oven to moderate, 350 deg F or gas 4 (180 deg C).
2. Trim meat, cut into neat cubes and toss in flour seasoned with salt and pepper.
3. Heat oil in a large, heavy frying pan and fry bacon for 2–3 minutes, then add meat and stir until sealed all over.
4. Add garlic and onion and continue cooking for 2–3 minutes, or until lightly browned.
5. Sprinkle in any remaining flour and stir over gentle heat for 1 minute.
6. Remove pan from heat and gradually blend in tomatoes, wine and stock.
7. Return to heat, bring to the boil and simmer gently, stirring continuously.
8. Add bouquet garni, basil and lemon rind and stir well together.
9. Cover closely with lid or foil and cook in centre of oven for 1½–2 hours, or until meat is tender.

LAMB CREOLE
Serves 4

4 chump chops
1oz (25gm) flour
salt and pepper
2oz (50gm) dripping or lard
½ pint (250ml) stock
2 tablespoons tomato ketchup
2 teaspoons Worcestershire sauce
1 teaspoon vinegar
1 level tablespoon demerara sugar
½ teaspoon Tabasco sauce
1 green pepper, de-seeded and cut into small strips

1. Preheat oven to moderate, 350 deg F or gas 4 (180 deg C).
2. Trim chops if necessary then coat in flour seasoned with salt and pepper.
3. Melt dripping or lard in a large frying pan and fry chops until golden brown on both sides. Drain well over pan and transfer to a casserole.
4. Sprinkle any remaining flour into pan and stir over gentle heat for 1 minute.
5. Remove pan from heat and gradually blend in stock, tomato ketchup, Worcestershire sauce, vinegar, sugar and Tabasco sauce. Add green pepper.
6. Return to heat, bring to the boil and simmer for 2 minutes, stirring continuously.
7. Pour prepared sauce over chops in casserole.
8. Cover with lid or foil and cook in centre of oven for about 45 minutes–1 hour, or until meat is tender.

BELGIAN CHOPS
(Illustrated on page 18)
Serves 6

8oz (200gm) pork sausagemeat
6 lamb chops
2 oranges, peeled and thinly sliced
salt
freshly ground black pepper
¼ pint (125ml) cider
watercress and fesh orange slices to garnish

1. Preheat oven to moderate, 350 deg F or gas 4 (180 deg C).
2. Divide sausagemeat into six pieces. Fill cavity of each chop with sausagemeat and fasten

with a wooden cocktail stick.
3. Brown very quickly on both sides under a hot grill.
4. Arrange orange slices in a casserole, season well and arrange chops on top. Add cider.
5. Cover closely with lid or foil and cook in centre of oven for about 1 hour, or until meat is tender, removing the lid for the last 10 minutes of cooking time.
6. Serve garnished with watercress and fresh orange slices.

NAVARIN OF LAMB
Serves 4

A very simple but classic way of cooking neck of lamb.

2lb (1 kilo) middle neck of lamb
2oz (50gm) dripping or lard
1oz (25gm) flour
2 level teaspoons salt
½ level teaspoon pepper
4 level tablespoons tomato paste
1 pint (approximately ½ litre) hot water
good pinch of sugar
bouquet garni
1 garlic clove
8 small onions
1½lb (¾ kilo) small new potatoes

1. Preheat oven to moderate, 350 deg F or gas 4 (180 deg C).
2. Trim meat and cut into serving pieces.
3. Melt 1oz (25gm) dripping or lard in a saucepan and brown the meat a few pieces at a time.
4. Season flour with salt and pepper, sprinkle it over meat and continue cooking for 2–3 minutes.
5. Remove pan from heat. Blend tomato paste with hot water and sugar and gradually stir into pan.
6. Add bouquet garni and cut garlic clove. Return to heat and bring to the boil.
7. Transfer to a casserole, cover with lid or foil and cook in centre of oven for 1 hour.
8. Peel onions and fry in remaining dripping or lard until brown all over. Drain well on kitchen paper, then add to casserole.
9. Peel potatoes, add to casserole and continue cooking for 30–45 minutes, or until tender.
10. Skim off any surplus fat and adjust seasoning before serving.

LAMB GENEVIEVE
(Illustrated on page 18)
Serves 4

2lb (1 kilo) middle neck of lamb
1 large onion, peeled and chopped
1½lb (¾ kilo) potatoes, peeled and diced
8oz (200gm) tomatoes, sliced
1 pint (approximately ½ litre) stock
salt and pepper
1 small can pimentos, cut into strips
1 small packet (8oz or 200gm) frozen green beans
fresh mint if available

1. Preheat oven to very moderate, 325 deg F or gas 3 (170 deg C).
2. Trim meat, cut into chops and place in a casserole.
3. Add onion, potatoes and tomatoes, pour in stock and season with salt and pepper.
4. Cover closely with lid or foil and cook in centre of oven for about 2 hours, or until meat is tender.
5. Stir in pimento and frozen beans, cover with lid again and continue cooking for a further 30 minutes.
6. Serve sprinkled with chopped mint if available.

LAMB POMPEY
Serves 4

2lb (1 kilo) middle neck of lamb
1 large onion, peeled and sliced
8oz (200gm) carrots, peeled and sliced
2 sticks celery, washed, trimmed and sliced
2 level teaspoons dry mustard
1 teaspoon Worcestershire sauce
1 tablespoon tomato ketchup
2 level teaspoons sugar
¼ pint (125ml) stock
2 tablespoons cider vinegar
2 level teaspoons capers, drained and chopped
½ level teaspoon dried tarragon

1. Preheat oven to very moderate, 325 deg F or gas 3 (170 deg C).
2. Trim meat, cut into neat pieces and arrange in layers, together with vegetables, in a casserole.
3. Mix mustard with

Worcestershire sauce, tomato ketchup and sugar, then gradually blend in stock and cider vinegar. Stir in capers and tarragon and pour over ingredients in casserole.
4. Cover closely with lid or foil and cook in centre of oven for 1½–2 hours, or until meat is tender.

LAMB SHANGHAI
Serves 4–6

3lb (1½ kilo) lean shoulder of lamb, boned
2 tablespoons oil
1 onion, peeled and sliced
1oz (25gm) flour
salt and pepper
1 level teaspoon ground ginger
½ pint (250ml) chicken stock
1 can (8oz or 200gm) pineapple pieces
1 green pepper, de-seeded and cut into strips
1–2 pieces preserved ginger, chopped
1 tablespoon vinegar
little soy sauce
2 tomatoes, peeled, de-seeded and cut into strips

1. Preheat oven to very moderate, 325 deg F or gas 3 (170 deg C).
2. Trim meat and cut into cubes.
3. Heat oil in a flameproof casserole and fry onion for 3–4 minutes, or until lightly browned. Remove from pan with a draining spoon and keep on one side.
4. Toss meat in flour seasoned with salt, pepper and ground ginger and fry in fat remaining in the pan until browned all over.
5. Sprinkle in any remaining flour and stir over gentle heat for 1 minute.
6. Remove casserole from heat and gradually blend in stock and syrup drained from pineapple.
7. Return onions to pan and add green pepper, preserved ginger, vinegar and a few drops of soy sauce.
8. Return to heat, bring to the boil and simmer for 2 minutes, stirring continuously. Season if necessary.
9. Cover closely with lid or foil and cook in centre of oven for about 1½ hours.
10. Add pineapple pieces and tomato strips, and continue cooking for a further 15–20 minutes, or until meat is tender.

MARINADED LAMB
Serves 6

4lb (2 kilo) lean shoulder of lamb, boned
2 medium onions, peeled and sliced
1 garlic clove, peeled and crushed
2 level teaspoons powdered cumin
½ pint (250ml) dry white wine
2 tablespoons oil
1oz (25gm) flour
salt and pepper
¼ pint (125ml) stock or water
1 level dessertspoon chopped parsley

1. Trim the meat, cut into neat cubes and place in a deep bowl.
2. Add onions, garlic and cumin and mix well together.
3. Pour wine over meat and cover bowl with a plate. Leave to stand for about 2 hours or leave overnight in refrigerator.
4. Preheat oven to very moderate, 325 deg F or gas 3 (170 deg C).
5. Drain meat well, reserving the marinade, then pat dry on kitchen paper.
6. Heat oil in a flameproof casserole and fry meat until sealed all over.
7. Sprinkle in flour, salt and pepper and stir over gentle heat for 1 minute.
8. Remove casserole from heat and gradually blend in stock or water and marinade.
9. Return to heat, bring to the boil and simmer for 2 minutes, stirring continuously.
10. Stir in parsley and add extra seasoning if necessary.
11. Cover with lid or foil and cook in centre of oven for about 1½ hours, or until meat is tender.

GREEK GRATINE
Serves 4–6

4oz (100gm) butter
1½lb (¾ kilo) potatoes, peeled and thinly sliced
1 medium onion, peeled and chopped
1½lb (¾ kilo) cooked lamb, minced
5 tablespoons tomato ketchup
1 tablespoon Worcestershire sauce
1 garlic clove, peeled and crushed
1 tablespoon finely chopped parsley
salt and pepper
4 large tomatoes, peeled and sliced
2 tablespoons finely grated cheese
2 tablespoons fresh white breadcrumbs

1. Preheat oven to moderately hot, 400 deg F or gas 6 (200 deg C).
2. Melt 3oz (75gm) butter in a heavy frying pan and fry potatoes until crisp and golden. Drain well on absorbent kitchen paper.
3. Place half the prepared potatoes in a deep casserole.
4. Fry onion in remaining butter until transparent, then stir in minced lamb, tomato ketchup, Worcestershire sauce, garlic and chopped parsley. Season to taste with salt and pepper.
5. Add mixture to casserole and cover with sliced tomatoes.
6. Arrange rest of potatoes, neatly overlapping, to cover top and sprinkle with cheese and breadcrumbs.
7. Cook, uncovered, in centre of oven for 20–30 minutes, or until golden brown and crisp.

LAMB DJUVEC
Serves 4

A traditional dish from
Yugoslavia.

4 loin lamb chops
salt
freshly ground black pepper
¼ level teaspoon dried thyme
1oz (25gm) dripping or lard
1 tablespoon oil
1lb (½ kilo) onions, peeled and
sliced
1 garlic clove, peeled and
crushed
1½lb (¾ kilo) potatoes, peeled
and thinly sliced
2 large green peppers,
de-seeded and sliced into rings
1½lb (¾ kilo) tomatoes, peeled
and sliced
2 small bayleaves
6 tablespoons chicken stock

1. Preheat oven to moderate,
350 deg F or gas 4 (180 deg C).
2. Trim the lamb chops if
necessary, then season with salt,
pepper and thyme.
3. Heat dripping or lard and oil
in a frying pan and fry the chops
until browned on both sides.
Drain well over pan and keep on
one side.
4. Add onions and garlic to fat
remaining in the pan and cook
gently for 2–3 minutes, or until
tender.
5. Use a draining spoon to
transfer half the onion mixture to
a casserole.
6. Arrange potatoes in a layer
over the onions in the casserole,
then top with green peppers.
7. Cover with half the tomatoes
and season well with salt and
pepper. Add remaining well
drained onion mixture, remaining
tomatoes and the bayleaves.
8. Pour stock into the casserole
and arrange lamb chops on top of
vegetables.
9. Cover closely with lid or foil
and cook in centre of oven for
about 45 minutes.
10. Remove cover and continue
cooking for a further 15–20
minutes, or until meat is tender
and vegetables cooked through.
11. Remove bayleaves before
serving.

GINGERED LAMB CHOPS
Serves 4

2oz (50gm) butter
2 medium onions, peeled and
chopped
8 small lamb chops
1oz (25gm) flour
2 level teaspoons ground ginger
salt and pepper
1 tablespoon tomato purée
½ pint (250ml) stock or water
1 packet (4oz or 100gm) frozen
peas

1. Preheat oven to moderate, 350
deg F or gas 4 (180 deg C).
2. Melt 1oz (25gm) butter in a
frying pan and fry onions until
transparent, then transfer to a
casserole.
3. Trim meat if necessary, then
coat in flour mixed with ginger,
salt and pepper.
4. Fry meat in remaining butter
until browned on both sides, then
place on top of onions in
casserole.
5. Sprinkle any remaining flour
into frying pan and stir over
gentle heat for 1 minute.
6. Remove pan from heat and
gradually blend in tomato purée
and stock or water.
7. Return to heat, bring to the
boil and simmer for 2 minutes,
stirring continuously.
8. Pour prepared sauce over
chops.
9. Cover closely with lid or foil
and cook in centre of oven for
about 45 minutes.
10. Add frozen peas and continue
cooking for a further 20–30
minutes, or until meat is tender.

Pressure Cooker Method
(15lb or H)
1. Melt 1oz (25gm) butter in a
frying pan and fry onions until
transparent, then transfer to pan
of pressure cooker.
2. Trim meat if necessary, then
fry in remaining butter until
browned on both sides. Place on
top of onions.
3. Blend together ground ginger,
tomato purée and stock. Season
well with salt and pepper and add
to pan (off heat).
4. Cover, bring to pressure: lower
heat and cook for 10 minutes.
Reduce the pressure and remove
lid.
5. Add frozen peas and continue
cooking in open pan for 5–8
minutes until tender.
6. Adjust seasoning. Thicken, if
liked, in open pressure cooker.

PAPRIKA LAMB
Serves 4

2lb (1 kilo) middle neck of
lamb
1½oz (37gm) flour
1½oz (37gm) dripping
3 onions, peeled and
quartered
1 level tablespoon made mild
mustard
2–3 level teaspoons mild
paprika pepper
¼ level teaspoon dried basil or
mixed herbs
1 pint (approximately ½ litre)
stock
salt and pepper
4oz (100gm) mushrooms,
washed, trimmed and sliced
2 tablespoons soured cream or
yogurt (optional)

1. Preheat oven to very moderate,
325 deg F or gas 3 (170 deg C).
2. Trim meat, cut into neat pieces
and toss in flour.
3. Melt dripping in a frying pan,
add onions and cook for 2–3
minutes. Drain well over the pan
and transfer to a casserole.
4. Fry lamb in fat remaining in
the pan until browned on both
sides, then place on top of onions.
5. Sprinkle any remaining flour
into frying pan and stir over
gentle heat for 1 minute.
6. Remove pan from heat, stir in
mustard, paprika pepper and
herbs, then gradually blend in
stock.
7. Return to heat, bring to the
boil and simmer for 2 minutes,
stirring continuously. Season to
taste with salt and pepper.
8. Pour prepared sauce into the
casserole and cover closely with
lid or foil.
9. Cook in centre of oven for
about 1½ hours, or until meat is
tender, adding sliced mushrooms
15 minutes before the end of
cooking time.
10. If liked, stir soured cream or
yogurt into the casserole just
before serving.

Slow Cooker Method
1. Proceed as stages 2–8 above,
inclusive, using a preheated slow
cooker instead of a casserole.
2. Cook on High for 30 minutes
and on Low for 5–6 hours. Add
sliced mushrooms and continue
cooking for 1–2 hours.
3. Complete recipe as in stage 10.

Pork vindaloo (see page 44)

Californian platter (see page 45)

Riviera casserole (see page 46)

Sausage capers (see page 48)

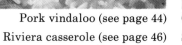

Old English casserole (see page 52)

Kidney and onion stew (see page 52)

Family casserole (see page 57)

Poulet basque (see page 64)

LAMB GOULASH
Serves 4–6

8 lamb chops
salt and pepper
2oz (50gm) dripping
2 large onions, peeled and
thinly sliced
4 level dessertspoons mild
paprika pepper
1oz (25gm) plain flour
1 tablespoon tomato purée
1 garlic clove, peeled and
crushed
1 pint (approximately ½ litre)
stock or water
1 bayleaf
2 large tomatoes, peeled and
quartered
1 small carton soured cream or
yogurt
chopped parsley to garnish

1. Preheat oven to moderate, 350
deg F or gas 4 (180 deg C).
2. Trim the meat and season with
salt and pepper.
3. Heat dripping in a flameproof
casserole and fry meat until
sealed on both sides.
4. Add onions and continue
cooking for a further 4–5 minutes.
5. Stir in paprika pepper, flour,
tomato purée and garlic.
6. Remove casserole from heat
and gradually blend in stock or
water. Add bayleaf.
7. Return to heat, bring to the
boil and simmer for 2–3 minutes,
stirring continuously.
8. Cover closely with lid or foil
and cook in centre of oven for
about 1 hour or until meat is
tender, then stir in tomatoes and
return to oven for a further 5–10
minutes.
9. Spoon soured cream or yogurt
over the surface and sprinkle well
with chopped parsley before
serving.

Pressure Cooker Method
(15lb or H)
1. Proceed as stages 2–6 above,
inclusive, using pan of pressure
cooker but omit the flour in stage
5 and add only ¾ pint (375ml)
stock in stage 6.
2. Cover, bring to pressure: lower
heat and cook for 10 minutes.
Reduce the pressure and remove
lid.
3. Add tomatoes and continue
cooking without lid for 5 minutes.
4. Adjust seasoning. Thicken, if
liked, in open pressure cooker.
5. Turn into heated serving dish
and complete recipe as in stage 9.

MUTTON CURRY
Serves 4–6

2lb (1 kilo) breast, neck or
scrag of mutton (without bone)
2oz (50gm) cooking fat
8oz (200gm) onions, peeled and
sliced
1 garlic clove, peeled and
finely chopped
1 level tablespoon curry
powder
1 level teaspoon salt
1 can (14oz or 397gm) peeled
tomatoes
2 tablespoons mango chutney
2oz (50gm) sultanas

1. Preheat oven to very moderate,
325 deg F or gas 3 (170 deg C).
2. Cut the meat into small pieces.
3. Melt fat in a flameproof
casserole and fry onions and
garlic till tender.
4. Mix in the curry powder and
salt, then add the meat. Continue
cooking till meat is well browned.
5. Stir in tomatoes, mango
chutney and sultanas, and bring
to the boil, stirring.
6. Cover with a lid or foil and
cook in centre of oven for 1½–2
hours, or until meat is tender.
7. Serve with freshly boiled rice
and, if liked, small bowls of
chutney, coconut, sultanas and
peanuts.

CREAMED LAMB CURRY
Serves 4–6

1½lb (¾ kilo) lean lamb from
shoulder or leg
2 tablespoons oil
1 packet (½ pint or 250ml)
onion sauce mix
½ pint (250ml) milk
1 level tablespoon curry
powder
½ level teaspoon mixed spice
1 tablespoon lemon juice
1 can (8oz or 200gm) peeled
tomatoes
1 dessert apple
2oz (50gm) sultanas
2 tablespoons soured cream or
yogurt
1 tablespoon desiccated
coconut

1. Preheat oven to moderate,
350 deg F or gas 4 (180 deg C).
2. Trim meat and cut into neat
cubes.
3. Heat oil in a flameproof

casserole and fry meat for 2–3
minutes, or until sealed all over.
4. Make up onion sauce,
according to packet directions,
using the milk.
5. Blend curry powder, mixed
spice, lemon juice and tomatoes
into the onion sauce and simmer
gently for 2–3 minutes.
6. Stir in peeled, cored and diced
apple and the sultanas, then pour
over lamb in casserole.
7. Cover with lid or foil and cook
in centre of oven for about 1½–2
hours, or until meat is tender.
8. Stir in soured cream or
yogurt and sprinkle with
desiccated coconut before serving.

ARABIAN LAMB
Serves 4–6

A touch of sweetness and a
touch of spiciness combine to
give an exotic touch to this dish.

4oz (100gm) dried apricots
2lb (1 kilo) lean lamb
(preferably from the leg)
2–3 tablespoons salad oil
1 onion, peeled and chopped
2 level teaspoons ground
ginger
½ level teaspoon ground
cinnamon
¾ pint (375ml) chicken stock
1 tablespoon clear honey

1. Soak apricots overnight in
cold water to cover.
2. Preheat oven to very moderate,
325 deg F or gas 3 (170 deg C).
3. Trim meat and cut into cubes.
4. Heat oil in a pan and fry onion
for 2–3 minutes, or until tender
but not browned.
5. Add meat and turn with a
metal spoon until sealed all over.
6. Sprinkle in ginger and
cinnamon and stir well together.
7. Stir in stock and bring to the
boil. Transfer to a casserole and
cover closely with lid or foil.
8. Cook in centre of oven for
1½ hours, or until meat is tender.
9. Stir in drained and chopped
apricots and the honey and return
to the oven for a further 20–30
minutes.
10. Skim fat from surface, add
more seasoning if necessary and
thicken, if liked, before serving.

Pork

There are recipes here which make use of the traditional combination of pork and apples, plus plenty of other favourites from my collection.

THURSDAY CASSEROLE
Serves 4

¾oz (18gm) butter
4 thick rashers lean belly of pork
½oz (12gm) flour
½ pint (250ml) chicken stock
1 dessertspoon tomato purée
1 heaped tablespoon mustard pickle, finely chopped
salt and pepper

1. Preheat oven to very moderate, 325 deg F or gas 3 (170 deg C).
2. Grease a shallow casserole with a little butter and arrange rashers in the base.
3. Melt remaining butter in a saucepan, sprinkle in flour and cook over gentle heat for 1 minute.
4. Remove pan from heat and gradually blend in stock.
5. Return to heat, bring to the boil and simmer for 2 minutes, stirring continuously.
6. Stir in tomato purée and mustard pickle and season with salt and pepper.
7. Pour prepared sauce over meat in the casserole.
8. Cover closely with lid or foil and cook in centre of oven for 1 hour, or until meat is tender.

PORK CHARLOTTE
Serves 3–4

1oz (25gm) butter
6oz (150gm) fresh white breadcrumbs
1lb (½ kilo) lean belly of pork
8oz (200gm) tomatoes
2 medium onions, peeled and sliced
salt and pepper
1 level teaspoon dried sage
1 can (10½oz or 298gm) condensed tomato soup
½ soup can water

1. Preheat oven to moderately hot, 400 deg F or gas 6 (200 deg C).
2. Well grease a shallow, ovenproof dish with butter and sprinkle in about 2oz (50gm) breadcrumbs.
3. Trim meat and cut into small pieces.
4. Arrange half the pork, tomatoes and onions in the dish, seasoning well with salt, pepper and sage.
5. Scatter a further 2oz (50gm) breadcrumbs over the top, then cover with remaining pork, tomatoes and onions, seasoning well as before.
6. Blend soup with water and pour into the casserole.
7. Sprinkle remaining breadcrumbs over top.
8. Cover with lid or foil and cook in centre of oven for about 1 hour, or until meat is tender, then remove lid and cook for a further 10–15 minutes to brown the top.

PORK AND APPLE HOTPOT
Serves 4

1lb (½ kilo) lean hand or belly of pork
1 pig's kidney
2 cooking apples, peeled, cored and sliced
4 large potatoes, peeled and sliced
salt and pepper
1 level teaspoon dried sage
½ pint (250ml) stock
little dripping

1. Preheat oven to moderate, 350 deg F or gas 4 (180 deg C).
2. Trim pork and cut into cubes.
3. Skin, halve and core kidney and cut into small pieces.
4. Arrange pork, kidney, apples and potatoes in a casserole, sprinkling each layer with salt, pepper and sage and finishing with a layer of potatoes.
5. Pour stock over and dot top with dripping.
6. Cover closely with lid or foil and cook in centre of oven for about 1 hour.
7. Remove lid or foil and continue cooking for a further 30–45 minutes, or until meat is cooked and potatoes are golden brown.

HOMESTEAD CASSEROLE
Serves 4

1 tablespoon oil
1oz (25gm) butter
1 large leek, trimmed, washed
and sliced
1lb (½ kilo) lean pork
1oz (25gm) flour
salt
freshly ground black pepper
1 level teaspoon dried sage
¾ pint (375ml) chicken stock
2 large carrots, peeled and
sliced
1 large cooking apple
2 level teaspoons capers,
drained and chopped

1. Preheat oven to moderate,
350 deg F or gas 4 (180 deg C).
2. Heat oil and butter in a pan
and fry leek for 3–4 minutes, or
until lightly browned. Transfer
to a casserole using a draining
spoon.
3. Trim meat, cut into neat cubes
and toss in flour seasoned with
salt, pepper and sage.
4. Fry in fat remaining in the
pan until sealed all over. Transfer
to a casserole using a draining
spoon.
5. Sprinkle any remaining flour
into the pan and stir over gentle
heat for 1 minute.
6. Remove pan from heat and
gradually blend in stock.
7. Return to heat, bring to the
boil and simmer gently for 2
minutes, stirring continuously.
Pour over ingredients in the
casserole.
8. Add carrots and peeled, cored
and sliced apple to casserole and
stir together.
9. Cover closely with lid or foil
and cook in centre of oven for
about 1½–2 hours, or until meat
is tender.
10. Add capers and stir well
before serving, so that the cooked
apple blends into the sauce.

PORK SURPRISE
Serves 4–6

1½lb (¾ kilo) lean pork
2oz (50gm) butter
1 onion, peeled and chopped
1 garlic clove, peeled and
crushed
1oz (25gm) flour
1 pint (approximately ½ litre)
chicken stock
1 teaspoon tomato purée
good pinch of cinnamon
salt and pepper
2 firm pears, peeled, cored and
sliced
½ small cucumber, cut into dice
1 dessertspoon vinegar
1 level dessertspoon sugar

1. Preheat oven to very moderate,
325 deg F or gas 3 (170 deg C).
2. Trim meat and cut into cubes.
3. Melt butter in a flameproof
casserole and fry pork until
sealed all over.
4. Add onion and garlic and
continue cooking gently for 3–4
minutes.
5. Sprinkle in flour and stir
over gentle heat for 1 minute.
6. Remove casserole from heat
and gradually blend in stock and
tomato purée.
7. Return to heat, bring to the
boil and simmer for 2 minutes,
stirring continuously. Add
cinnamon and season well to taste
with salt and pepper.
8. Cover closely with lid or foil
and cook in centre of oven for
1½ hours, then add pears and
cucumber. Continue cooking for a
further 30 minutes, or until meat
and pears are tender.
9. Stir in vinegar and sugar
before serving.

PORK AND CELERY
CASSEROLE
Serves 4–6

1½lb (¾ kilo) lean shoulder pork
2 pig's kidneys
½oz (12gm) flour
salt and pepper
8oz (200gm) celery, washed,
trimmed and chopped
4oz (100gm) onions, peeled and
chopped
1 level teaspoon dried thyme
½ pint (250ml) stock or water

1. Preheat oven to very moderate,
325 deg F or gas 3 (170 deg C).
2. Trim pork and cut into neat

cubes.
3. Skin, halve and core kidneys
and cut into small pieces.
4. Toss pork and kidneys in flour
seasoned with salt and pepper.
Place in a casserole and add
celery and onions.
5. Stir well together and add
thyme and stock or water.
6. Cover with lid or foil and cook
in centre of oven for about 1½
hours, or until meat is tender.

GRENDON CASSEROLE
Serves 4–6

2oz (50gm) dripping or lard
1 onion, peeled and chopped
1 large leek, washed, trimmed
and chopped
1 green pepper, de-seeded and
cut into strips
4oz (100gm) mushrooms,
washed, trimmed and sliced
1½lb (¾ kilo) lean pork
½oz (12gm) flour
salt and pepper
2 level teaspoons curry powder
1 can (8oz or 200gm) peeled
tomatoes
¼ pint (125ml) water
1 dessertspoon dry sherry

1. Preheat oven to very moderate,
325 deg F or gas 3 (170 deg C).
2. Melt dripping or lard in a
frying pan and gently cook onion,
leek, green pepper and
mushrooms for 2–3 minutes, or
until tender. Drain well over
pan and transfer to a casserole.
3. Trim pork and cut into neat
pieces, then toss in flour
seasoned with salt, pepper and
curry powder.
4. Fry pork in fat remaining in
the pan until browned all over,
then add to vegetables in the
casserole.
5. Sprinkle any remaining flour
into frying pan and stir over
gentle heat for 1 minute.
6. Remove pan from heat and
gradually blend in tomatoes,
water and sherry.
7. Return to heat, bring to the
boil and simmer for 2 minutes,
stirring continuously. Pour into
the casserole.
8. Cover closely with lid or foil
and cook in centre of oven for
1½–2 hours, or until meat is
tender.

COOK'S FAVOURITE
Serves 4–6

Pork and tomatoes cooked in light ale.

1¼lb (¾ kilo) lean pork
1oz (25gm) cooking fat
12oz (300gm) small onions, peeled
1oz (25gm) flour
½ pint (250ml) light ale
2 tablespoons tarragon vinegar
3 level tablespoons demerara sugar
salt and pepper
1 dessertspoon Worcestershire sauce
12oz (300gm) carrots, peeled and cut into strips lengthways
8oz (200gm) tomatoes, peeled

1. Preheat oven to very moderate, 325 deg F or gas 3 (170 deg C).
2. Trim pork and cut into neat cubes.
3. Heat fat in a flameproof casserole and fry pork until sealed all over. Remove from casserole with a draining spoon and keep on one side.
4. Add onions to fat remaining in the casserole and brown lightly.
5. Sprinkle in flour and stir over gentle heat for 1 minute.
6. Remove casserole from heat and gradually blend in light ale and vinegar.
7. Return to heat, bring to the boil and simmer for 2 minutes, stirring continuously. Return meat to casserole and stir in sugar. Season with salt and pepper and add Worcestershire sauce, carrots and tomatoes.
8. Cover with lid or foil and cook in centre of oven for about 1½–2 hours, or until meat is tender.
9. Check seasoning before serving.

HANDY CASSEROLE
Serves 6

6 lean pork chops
½oz (12gm) butter
3oz (75gm) fresh white breadcrumbs
1 level teaspoon salt
pepper
2 level teaspoons dried sage
1 small egg, beaten
1 can (15oz or 425gm) asparagus soup

1. Preheat oven to moderately hot, 400 deg F or gas 6 (200 deg C).
2. Trim excess fat from chops.
3. Grease a shallow casserole with butter and arrange pork chops in the base.
4. Mix together breadcrumbs, salt, pepper and sage and bind together with beaten egg.
5. Spread top of each chop with this mixture. Pour asparagus soup over.
6. Cover closely with lid or foil and cook in centre of oven for about 45 minutes–1 hour, or until meat is tender.

HAMPTON CASSEROLE
Serves 4

6 tablespoons long-grain rice
2 cooking apples
4 pork chops or 1lb (½ kilo) pork fillet
salt and pepper
1 level tablespoon dried sage
1 can (14oz or 397gm) peeled tomatoes
½ pint (250ml) stock

1. Preheat oven to very moderate, 325 deg F or gas 3 (170 deg C).
2. Wash rice. Peel, core and slice apples. Trim pork chops or cut fillet into slices.
3. Arrange in layers in a casserole, seasoning well with salt, pepper and sage.
4. Pour tomatoes and stock over.
5. Cover with lid or foil and cook in centre of oven for about 2 hours, or until meat is tender.

PORK 'N APPLE
Serves 4

8oz (200gm) tomatoes, sliced
salt
freshly ground black pepper
1lb (½ kilo) cooking apples
¼ level teaspoon dried chervil or parsley
¼ level teaspoon dried sweet basil
4 tablespoons water
1 level dessertspoon water
4 lean pork chops

1. Preheat oven to moderate, 350 deg F or gas 4 (180 deg C).
2. Arrange tomatoes in base of a shallow casserole and season well with salt and pepper.
3. Peel, core and slice apples and arrange on top of tomatoes. Season as before and sprinkle with chervil or parsley and basil.
4. Add water to casserole and arrange pork chops on top of apples.
5. Cover closely with lid or foil and cook above centre of oven for 1 hour, then remove cover and cook for a further 15–20 minutes to brown chops.

PORK CHOPS WITH ORANGE
Serves 4

3oz (75gm) butter
12oz (300gm) onions, peeled and sliced
salt and pepper
1 level teaspoon dry mustard
2 level teaspoons demerara sugar
4 pork chops, trimmed of excess fat
1 level teaspoon cornflour
3 large oranges
¼ pint (125ml) dry white wine

1. Preheat oven to moderate, 350 deg F or gas 4 (180 deg C).
2. Melt half the butter in a frying pan and fry onions until light brown. Transfer to a casserole using a draining spoon.
3. Mix together salt, pepper, mustard, sugar and remaining butter and spread on each chop.
4. Fry chops in fat remaining in pan until golden brown on both sides, then place on top of onions in casserole.
5. Sprinkle cornflour into the frying pan and stir over gentle heat for 1 minute.
6. Remove pan from heat and

blend in finely grated rind and juice of 2 oranges, and the wine.

7. Return to heat, bring to the boil and simmer for 2 minutes, stirring continuously. Pour into casserole.

8. Cover closely with lid or foil and cook in centre of oven for about 1 hour.

9. Peel remaining orange, cut into segments, removing any pith or pips, and arrange on top of chops. Return to oven and cook, uncovered, for a further 10–15 minutes.

PORK CHOPS IN MUSHROOM SAUCE
Serves 4

Pork chops cooked in individual parcels of foil.

4 lean pork chops
2oz (50gm) butter
8oz (200gm) mushrooms, washed, trimmed and chopped
1 tablespoon lemon juice
1oz (25gm) flour
salt
freshly ground black pepper
¼ level teaspoon dried sage
4 tablespoons double cream
paprika pepper

1. Preheat oven to very moderate, 325 deg F or gas 3 (170 deg C).
2. Trim excess fat from chops.
3. Melt butter in a pan and fry chops until golden brown on both sides. Drain well over pan and keep on one side.
4. Add mushrooms to fat remaining in the pan and cook gently until tender. Stir in lemon juice, sprinkle in flour and stir over gentle heat for 1 minute. Add seasoning to taste and stir in sage.
5. Arrange each pork chop on a square of foil large enough to wrap round it completely, then top each chop with mushroom mixture and 1 tablespoon cream. Sprinkle with paprika pepper.
6. Fold foil over chops, sealing all edges well together and place in a shallow casserole.
7. Cook in centre of oven for about 45 minutes–1 hour, or until meat is tender.

BRAISED PORK CHOPS
Serves 4

4 thick pork chops
salt and pepper
1 level teaspoon dried sage
2oz (50gm) butter or dripping
1 carrot, peeled and thinly sliced
1 large leek, washed, trimmed and sliced
2 sticks celery, washed, trimmed and sliced
1 can (8oz or 200gm) peeled tomatoes

1. Preheat oven to moderate, 350 deg F or gas 4 (180 deg C).
2. Trim chops, season with salt and pepper and sprinkle with a little sage.
3. Melt butter or dripping in a pan and fry meat until brown all over. Drain and keep on one side.
4. Add carrot, leek and celery to fat remaining in the pan and cook over gentle heat, turning with a metal spoon, for 3–4 minutes. Transfer to a casserole and pour tomatoes over.
5. Arrange pork chops on top.
6. Cover with lid or foil and cook in centre of oven for about 1 hour, or until meat is tender.

PORK CHOPS SAVANNAH
Serves 4

½oz (12gm) butter
1 large onion, peeled and thinly sliced
4 pork chops
4 lemon slices
4 orange slices
4 tablespoons mango chutney, chopped
4 level dessertspoons soft brown sugar
2 tablespoons water

1. Preheat oven to moderate, 350 deg F or gas 4 (180 deg C).
2. Grease a shallow casserole with butter and cover with onion.
3. Place pork chops on top and place a slice of lemon and orange on each chop. Spoon mango chutney over top and sprinkle with sugar.
4. Pour water into casserole.
5. Cover closely with lid or foil and cook in centre of oven for about 1 hour, or until meat is tender.

DUTCH CASSEROLE
Serves 4–6

1oz (25gm) butter
1 large onion, peeled and thinly sliced
1 garlic clove, peeled and crushed
2 small pork fillets (about 1¼lb or ¾ kilo)
1 can (15oz or 425gm) peeled tomatoes
1 tablespoon tomato purée
4oz (100gm) button mushrooms
salt and pepper
4oz (100gm) self-raising flour
1 level teaspoon dry mustard
2oz (50gm) Gouda cheese, finely grated
2oz (50gm) shredded suet
water

1. Preheat oven to moderate, 350 deg F or gas 4 (180 deg C).
2. Melt butter in a flameproof casserole and fry onion and garlic until soft.
3. Add pork, cut into cubes, and stir over gentle heat until pork is sealed all over.
4. Stir in tomatoes, tomato purée and mushrooms. Bring to the boil and season to taste with salt and pepper.
5. Cover with lid or foil and cook in centre of oven for about 30 minutes.
6. Meanwhile, prepare dumplings. Place flour, mustard, cheese and suet in a bowl, season with salt and pepper and mix well together.
7. Bind to a soft but not sticky dough with water and shape into eight small balls with floured hands.
8. Add dumplings to casserole and continue cooking for a further 30 minutes, or until meat is tender and dumplings cooked through.

PORK CHOPS MACON
Serves 6

6 pork loin chops
salt and pepper
3 level tablespoons mild
mustard
3oz (75gm) butter
¼ pint (125ml) white Macon
wine
3 tablespoons soured cream
3 tablespoons browned
breadcrumbs
2 tablespoons chopped fresh
parsley

1. Season chops both sides with salt and pepper. Spread with mustard and set aside in refrigerator or cool place for several hours.
2. Preheat oven to very moderate, 325 deg F or gas 3 (170 deg C).
3. Melt butter in a flameproof casserole and brown chops on both sides.
4. Add wine, cover closely with lid or foil and cook in centre of oven for about 45 minutes, or until meat is tender, basting twice during the last 15 minutes with soured cream.
5. Sprinkle with breadcrumbs and parsley before serving.

COLONIAL PORK CASSEROLE
Serves 4–6

Pork and beans, American style.

4oz (100gm) haricot beans
1½lb (¾ kilo) lean pork
1oz (25gm) butter
1 medium onion, peeled and
sliced
1oz (25gm) flour
1 pint (approximately ½ litre)
stock
2 level tablespoons tomato
purée
salt and pepper

1. Soak beans overnight in cold water to cover.
2. Preheat oven to moderate, 350 deg F or gas 4 (180 deg C).
3. Trim meat and cut into neat cubes.
4. Melt butter in a pan and fry onion for 2–3 minutes, or until tender.
5. Add pork and fry until browned all over.
6. Sprinkle in flour and stir over

gentle heat for 1 minute.
7. Remove pan from heat and gradually stir in stock.
8. Return to heat, bring to the boil, stirring continuously.
9. Stir in drained beans and tomato purée and season well to taste with salt and pepper.
10. Transfer to a casserole, cover with lid or foil and cook in centre of oven for about 1½–1¾ hours, or until meat is tender.

MEXICANA PORK
Serves 6

8oz (200gm) red kidney beans
2 tablespoons oil
1 large onion, peeled and sliced
2 carrots, peeled and sliced
2 green peppers, de-seeded
and cut into strips
2lb (1 kilo) lean pork
3 teaspoons tomato purée
2 garlic cloves, peeled and
crushed
1 bayleaf
1 can (14oz or 397gm) peeled
tomatoes
½ pint (250ml) chicken stock
salt and pepper
good dash of Tabasco sauce
little grated lemon rind

1. Soak beans overnight in cold water to cover.
2. Drain well, put into a saucepan, cover with fresh cold water and cook gently for 1 hour. Drain.
3. Preheat oven to moderate, 350 deg F or gas 4 (180 deg C).
4. Heat oil in a saucepan and add onion, carrots and green peppers. Cook gently, stirring occasionally, for 8–10 minutes.
5. Trim pork, cut into 1-inch cubes and add to pan. Continue cooking, stirring from time to time, until meat is lightly browned.
6. Stir in drained, cooked beans, tomato purée, garlic, bayleaf, tomatoes and stock. Season well with salt and pepper and add Tabasco sauce.
7. Transfer to a casserole, cover closely with lid or foil and cook in centre of oven for 1½–2 hours, or until meat and beans are tender.
8. Remove bayleaf and sprinkle with a little grated lemon rind before serving.

CARELIAN HOTPOT
Serves 8–10

A traditional spiced mixed meat dish from Finland.

1lb (½ kilo) lean stewing pork
1lb (½ kilo) stewing lamb
1lb (½ kilo) stewing steak
6oz (150gm) ox kidney
water to cover
salt
1–2 rounded tablespoons whole
black peppercorns
1–2 rounded tablespoons whole
white peppercorns

1. Preheat oven to cool, 275 deg F or gas 1 (140 deg C).
2. Trim meats, cut into chunky pieces and place in a deep casserole together with any bones.
3. Add cold water to just cover, season well with salt and add black and white peppercorns.
4. Cover closely with lid or foil and cook in centre of oven for about 6 hours, or until meat is tender.
5. Skim excess fat from surface then serve, without thickening, with freshly cooked rice, grated raw carrot and green salad.

SWEET PORK CASSEROLE
Serves 4–6

Apricots and green beans make this a colourful as well as tasty dish.

1½lb (¾ kilo) lean hand or belly of pork
3 tablespoons oil
1 onion, peeled and chopped
1 garlic clove, peeled and crushed (optional)
1oz (25gm) flour
salt and pepper
½ pint (250ml) chicken stock
1 can (15½oz or 439gm) apricot halves
1 tablespoon vinegar
1 tablespoon soy sauce
1 packet (8oz or 200gm) frozen green beans

1. Preheat oven to very moderate, 325 deg F or gas 3 (170 deg C).
2. Trim meat and cut into cubes.
3. Heat oil in a flameproof casserole and fry onion and garlic for 2–3 minutes, or until transparent.
4. Toss meat in flour seasoned with salt and pepper.
5. Add meat to casserole and continue cooking for a further 4–5 minutes.
6. Sprinkle in any remaining flour and stir over gentle heat for 1 minute.
7. Remove casserole from heat and gradually blend in stock and juice drained from apricots.
8. Return to heat, bring to the boil and simmer for 2–3 minutes, stirring continuously. Stir in vinegar and soy sauce and add more salt and pepper if necessary.
9. Cover closely with lid or foil and cook in centre of oven for about 1½ hours, then add apricot halves and green beans and continue cooking for a further 15–20 minutes, or until meat is tender.

PORK PEKING
(Illustrated on page 18)
Serves 4–6

Pork with a piquant sweet and sour sauce.

1½lb (¾ kilo) lean stewing pork
3 tablespoons oil
2 onions, peeled and sliced
1oz (25gm) flour
salt and pepper
½ pint (250ml) water
1 green pepper, de-seeded and sliced
1 small can mandarin oranges
1 tablespoon vinegar
little soy sauce
1 chicken stock cube
1 can (3½oz or 87gm) pimento, drained and cut into strips

1. Preheat oven to very moderate, 325 deg F or gas 3 (170 deg C).
2. Trim meat and cut into cubes.
3. Heat oil in a flameproof casserole and fry onions until lightly browned. Remove from pan with a draining spoon and keep on one side.
4. Toss meat in flour seasoned with salt and pepper and fry in fat remaining in the casserole, until brown all over.
5. Sprinkle in any remaining flour and stir over gentle heat for 1 minute.
6. Remove casserole from heat and gradually blend in water. Add cooked onion, green pepper, liquid drained from mandarin oranges, vinegar, soy sauce and chicken stock cube.
7. Return to heat, bring to the boil and simmer gently for 2 minutes, stirring continuously.
8. Cover closely with lid or foil and cook in centre of oven for about 1½ hours.
9. Add mandarin oranges and pimento and continue cooking for a further 10–15 minutes, or until meat is tender.

TAIPAN PORK
Serves 6

2lb (1 kilo) lean pork
3 tablespoons clear honey
2 tablespoons malt vinegar
2 tablespoons soy sauce
1 can (8oz or 200gm) pineapple pieces
½ chicken stock cube
1 garlic clove, peeled and crushed
1 small green pepper, trimmed, de-seeded and cut into small strips
½oz (12gm) cornflour
2 tablespoons water

1. Trim meat and cut into small cubes.
2. Mix together honey, vinegar and soy sauce, then blend in ¼ pint (125ml) syrup drained from pineapple, making up the quantity with water if necessary. Add crumbled stock cube and garlic.
3. Add meat to prepared sauce, stir well together and leave to stand several hours or overnight.
4. Preheat oven to very moderate, 325 deg F or gas 3 (170 deg C).
5. Transfer meat and sauce to a flameproof casserole and cover closely with lid or foil.
6. Cook in centre of oven for about 1 hour, then add green pepper and drained pineapple pieces. Cook for a further 30 minutes, or until meat is tender.
7. Blend cornflour with water, pour into the casserole and stir over gentle heat until thickened. Simmer gently for 2 minutes.

PORK WITH BARBECUE SAUCE
Serves 4

1oz (25gm) dripping or lard
4 spare rib pork chops
1 level dessertspoon cornflour
4 tablespoons vinegar
4 tablespoons tomato ketchup
¼ level teaspoon sugar
salt and pepper
dash of Worcestershire sauce
¼ pint (125ml) chicken stock
1 bayleaf

1. Preheat oven to moderate,
350 deg F or gas 4 (180 deg C).
2. Melt dripping or lard in a pan
and fry chops until browned on
both sides. Drain well and
transfer to a casserole.
3. Place cornflour in a basin and
gradually blend in vinegar,
tomato ketchup, sugar, salt,
pepper, Worcestershire sauce
and stock. Pour into a small pan
and bring to the boil, stirring.
4. Pour prepared sauce into
casserole and add bayleaf.
5. Cover closely with lid or foil
and cook in centre of oven for
about 1 hour, or until meat is
cooked through.
6. Remove bayleaf and serve pork
with freshly boiled rice.

PORK VINDALOO
(Illustrated on page 35)
Serves 4

A spicy and colourful dish.

1lb (½ kilo) lean pork
1 rounded dessertspoon
demerara sugar
2 tablespoons vinegar
1oz (25gm) dripping or lard
1 large onion, peeled and
chopped
2 level dessertspoons curry
powder
1 bayleaf
3 tomatoes, peeled and
chopped
salt and pepper

1. Trim and cut pork into small
cubes, place in a bowl and
sprinkle with sugar and vinegar.
2. Leave for about 2 hours,
turning occasionally with a
metal spoon.
3. Preheat oven to very moderate,
325 deg F or gas 3 (170 deg C).
4. Melt dripping or lard in a pan,
and fry onion lightly for 2–3
minutes.
5. Stir in prepared pork together
with juices. Add curry powder,
bayleaf, tomatoes, salt and pepper.
6. Bring to the boil, then transfer
to a casserole and cover closely
with lid or foil.
7. Cook in centre of oven for
1½–2 hours, or until meat is
tender.
8. Serve with boiled rice and
sliced bananas tossed in lemon
juice.

PORK MADRAS
Serves 4

1½lb (¾ kilo) spare rib pork
chops
1oz (25gm) flour
½oz (12gm) curry powder
2oz (50gm) dripping or lard
2oz (50gm) sultanas
1 onion, peeled and finely
chopped
4oz (100gm) long-grain rice
1 pint (approximately ½ litre)
stock
salt and pepper

1. Preheat oven to moderate,
350 deg F or gas 4 (180 deg C).
2. Trim chops if necessary, then
coat in a mixture of flour and
curry powder.
3. Heat dripping or lard in a pan
and fry meat until browned on
both sides, adding sultanas to
the pan for last few moments.
4. Place onion and washed rice
in a casserole, together with
remaining flour and curry powder.
Stir well together.
5. Add meat and sultanas and
any fat from pan.
6. Pour stock into casserole and
stir well together. Add salt and
pepper if necessary.
7. Cover pan with lid or foil and
cook in centre of oven for 1 hour.
8. Reduce heat to very moderate,
325 deg F or gas 3 (170 deg C)
and cook for about a further hour,
or until meat is tender, stirring
once or twice during cooking.

Bacon, ham and sausages

All these are excellent for casseroling and make delicious lunch and supper dishes to tempt the family.

BACON CHOP POT
Serves 4

1½lb (¾ kilo) potatoes, peeled and thinly sliced
8oz (200gm) onions, peeled and thinly sliced
salt
freshly ground black pepper
2oz (50gm) butter
¼ pint (125ml) chicken stock
1 tablespoon Fruity sauce
4 bacon chops, rind removed

1. Preheat oven to moderate, 350 deg F or gas 4 (180 deg C).
2. Arrange potatoes and onions in layers in a shallow casserole, seasoning well between layers with salt and pepper.
3. Heat butter, stock and Fruity sauce together in a pan until butter has melted, then spoon over ingredients in casserole.
4. Cover closely with lid or foil and cook in centre of oven for 1¼ hours.
5. Remove cover and arrange bacon chops on top. Continue cooking for 20–25 minutes, or until bacon is cooked.

CALIFORNIAN PLATTER
(Illustrated on page 35)
Serves 6

6 bacon chops
3 red dessert apples
1 can (1lb 14oz or 850gm) fruit cocktail
1 lemon, thinly sliced
1 level tablespoon cornflour
1 tablespoon water

1. Preheat oven to moderate, 350 deg F or gas 4 (180 deg C).
2. Trim a little fat from the bacon chops and heat it gently in a pan until it begins to run.
3. Remove the pieces of fat and fry bacon chops until golden brown on both sides. Drain well and transfer to a shallow casserole.
4. Wash, core and halve apples and place half an apple on top of each chop.
5. Cover closely with lid or foil and cook in centre of oven for about 45 minutes.
6. Meanwhile, drain fruit cocktail and pour the syrup into the pan in which the chops were cooked. Add sliced lemon and boil until liquid is reduced to about a teacupful.
7. Stir in cornflour blended with water and simmer gently until thick and clear, stirring continuously. Stir in the fruit.
8. Remove cover from casserole and pour fruit sauce over chops. Leave uncovered and continue cooking for a further 15 minutes, or until heated through.
9. Serve with freshly boiled rice.

CHILTERN CASSEROLE
Serves 6

4oz (100gm) butter beans
2lb (1 kilo) forehock bacon joint, boned
1oz (25gm) butter
2 leeks, washed, trimmed and sliced
2 large carrots, peeled and sliced
2 sticks celery, washed, trimmed and chopped
1 level tablespoon finely chopped parsley
freshly ground black pepper
1 pint (approximately ½ litre) water
1 bouquet garni

1. Soak butter beans overnight in cold water to cover.
2. Soak bacon for 3–4 hours in cold water to cover.
3. Preheat oven to very moderate, 325 deg F or gas 3 (170 deg C).
4. Melt butter in a flameproof casserole and fry leeks, carrots and celery for 3–4 minutes.
5. Add drained butter beans, sprinkle with parsley and season with pepper.
6. Place drained bacon on top and pour in water. Add bouquet garni.
7. Cover with lid or foil and cook in centre of oven for about 1½ hours, or until bacon is tender.

DANISH CASSEROLE
Serves 6

2½lb (1¼ kilo) collar bacon joint
4 peppercorns
1 bayleaf
3 leeks, washed and halved
1lb (½ kilo) carrots, peeled and
halved
1 small onion, peeled and
quartered
pinch of mixed herbs

1. Place bacon joint in a pan of
cold water, bring slowly to the
boil, then drain off hot water and
cover with fresh, cold water.
2. Add peppercorns and
bayleaf, bring slowly to the boil
and simmer for 35 minutes.
3. Drain the joint, reserving the
cooking liquid, and strip off the
rind.
4. Preheat oven to moderate,
350 deg F or gas 4 (180 deg C).
5. Place bacon in a casserole
together with vegetables. Add
½ pint (250ml) reserved liquid
and mixed herbs.
6. Cover closely with lid or foil
and cook in centre of oven for
20 minutes, then remove cover
and continue cooking for a
further 15–20 minutes, or until
bacon is tender.

BACON POT AU FEU
Serves 4–6

1½lb (¾ kilo) bacon joint
1 large onion, peeled and
chopped
1 garlic clove, peeled and
crushed
1lb (½ kilo) cabbage, washed,
trimmed and cut into quarters
1lb (½ kilo) carrots, peeled and
cut into quarters
1 bouquet garni
2 pints (approximately 1 litre)
stock or water
1 tablespoon finely chopped
parsley

1. Soak bacon for 2–3 hours in
cold water to cover.
2. Preheat oven to moderate,
350 deg F or gas 4 (180 deg C).
3. Drain bacon and cut into 4–6
chunky pieces.
4. Arrange bacon and prepared
vegetables in a deep casserole,
add bouquet garni and stock
or water to cover.
5. Cover closely with lid or foil
and cook in centre of oven for

about 1½ hours, or until bacon
and carrots are tender.
6. Remove bouquet garni.
Arrange bacon on a serving dish
together with strained vegetables
and sprinkle with parsley.
7. Use the stock as a basis for
making soup.

RIVIERA CASSEROLE
(Illustrated on page 35)
Serves 6–8

Smoked bacon joint casseroled
whole in Continental style.

3lb (1½ kilo) smoked bacon joint
4 black peppercorns
1 bayleaf
whole cloves
2 tablespoons honey
2oz (50gm) butter
8oz (200gm) onions, peeled and
chopped
1lb (½ kilo) tomatoes, peeled
and sliced
2 garlic cloves, peeled and
crushed
1 level teaspoon sweet basil
salt and pepper

1. Soak bacon overnight in cold
water to cover.
2. Drain joint and place in a
saucepan with fresh, cold water
to cover. Add peppercorns and
bayleaf. Bring to the boil and
simmer gently for 1 hour.
3. Preheat oven to moderate to
moderately hot, 375 deg F or gas 5
(190 deg C).
4. Remove bacon joint from the
saucepan, carefully strip off skin,
score fat and stud with cloves.
Place in a casserole and pour
honey over top.
5. Melt butter in a frying pan
and fry onions gently until tender,
then stir in tomatoes, garlic and
basil. Season well to taste with
salt and pepper, then pour
around bacon in the casserole.
6. Cover closely with lid or foil
and cook in centre of oven for
25 minutes. Remove lid or foil
and continue cooking for a
further 15 minutes, or until bacon
is tender.

HAM TAORMINA
Serves 6

2lb (1 kilo) lean gammon joint
8 tablespoons Marsala
1oz (25gm) butter
1 tablespoon oil
1 large onion, peeled and sliced
1 large carrot, peeled and
sliced
2 sticks celery, washed,
trimmed and sliced
4 tomatoes, sliced
bouquet garni
½ pint (250ml) stock or water
salt and pepper

1. Soak gammon for 3–4 hours in
cold water to cover.
2. Drain well and place in a bowl.
Pour Marsala over and leave to
soak for 3–4 hours, turning from
time to time.
3. Preheat oven to cool, 300 deg F
or gas 2 (150 deg C).
4. Heat butter and oil in a
flameproof casserole and fry
onion for 2–3 minutes, or until
tender.
5. Add carrot, celery and
tomatoes and continue cooking
for 2–3 minutes, stirring with a
metal spoon.
6. Drain gammon, reserving
Marsala, and arrange on top of
vegetables. Add bouquet garni
and stock or water.
7. Cover closely with lid or foil
and cook in centre of oven for
about 1½ hours, or until gammon is
tender.
8. Peel skin from gammon, cut
into slices, arrange on a serving
dish and keep hot.
9. Sieve vegetables and stock or
pass through a liquidizer, then
add reserved Marsala and boil
together for 2–3 minutes, or until
slightly reduced. Season to taste
with salt and pepper and pour
over gammon slices.

GAMMON RAREBIT
Serves 4

2lb (1 kilo) potatoes
1½oz (37gm) butter
1oz (25gm) flour
¼ pint (250ml) milk
¼ level teaspoon made English
mustard
3oz (75gm) Cheddar cheese,
finely grated
salt and pepper
4 gammon slices
¼ pint (125ml) lager or light ale

1. Preheat oven to very moderate,
325 deg F or gas 3 (170 deg C).
2. Peel and slice potatoes. Grease
a shallow casserole with ½oz
(12gm) butter and arrange
potato slices over the base.
3. Melt remaining butter in a
saucepan, sprinkle in flour and
stir over gentle heat for 1 minute.
4. Remove pan from heat and
gradually beat in milk.
5. Return to heat, bring to the
boil and simmer for 2 minutes,
stirring continuously.
6. Remove from heat and beat in
mustard and cheese until well
blended. Season to taste with salt
and pepper.
7. Pour prepared cheese sauce
over potatoes.
8. Cover closely with lid or foil
and cook in centre of oven for
about 1 hour.
9. Remove dish from oven.
Arrange gammon slices on top
and moisten with a little lager or
light ale.
10. Cover with lid or foil, return
to oven and cook for a further
30–45 minutes, or until gammon
is tender, basting from time to
time with remaining lager or light
ale.

GAMMON AND PEACHES
Serves 4

4 thick gammon slices
8 cloves
1 can (15oz or 425gm) peach
slices
4 teaspoons demerara sugar
¼ level teaspoon powdered
cinnamon
1oz (25gm) butter

1. Preheat oven to moderate to
moderately hot, 375 deg F or gas 5
(190 deg C).
2. Trim rind from gammon slices
and snip fat two or three times

with scissors. Press two cloves
into fat on each slice and place
gammon slices in a shallow
casserole.
3. Drain peaches, reserving
syrup, and arrange on top of
gammon.
4. Pour 4–6 tablespoons reserved
syrup around the gammon.
5. Mix sugar with cinnamon and
sprinkle over the top.
6. Dot with butter and cook,
uncovered, just above centre of
oven for about 35–40 minutes,
or until gammon is tender,
basting from time to time with
the syrup.

HAM AND PINEAPPLE
CRUNCH
Serves 4

4oz (100gm) mushrooms,
washed, trimmed and chopped
4 gammon slices, trimmed
1 can (8oz or 200gm) pineapple
rings
1 tablespoon demerara sugar
good pinch of cinnamon
1oz (25gm) walnuts, roughly
chopped

1. Preheat oven to moderate,
350 deg F or gas 4 (180 deg C).
2. Arrange mushrooms in the
base of a shallow casserole.
3. Snip fat of each gammon
slice several times and place on
top of mushrooms.
4. Drain pineapple rings,
reserving syrup, and arrange one
ring on top of each gammon
slice.
5. Pour 4 tablespoons reserved
syrup into dish.
6. Mix demerara sugar with
cinnamon and sprinkle over
gammon and pineapple.
7. Cover with lid or foil and cook
in centre of oven for 30 minutes.
Scatter walnuts over top and
continue cooking for about a
further 10 minutes, or until
cooked through.

HAM AND BANANA ROLLS
Serves 4

4 bananas
1½oz (37gm) butter
4 slices lean, boiled ham
made English mustard
tomato ketchup
½oz (12gm) flour
¼ pint (250ml) cold milk
4oz (100gm) Cheddar cheese,
finely grated
¼ level teaspoon mustard
salt and pepper
1 tablespoon walnuts, roughly
chopped
2 firm tomatoes, sliced

1. Preheat oven to moderate,
350 deg F or gas 4 (180 deg C).
2. Peel bananas and brush with
½oz (12gm) melted butter.
3. Spread ham slices with a little
made mustard and tomato
ketchup, then roll each banana
in a ham slice.
4. Grease a shallow casserole
with ½oz (12gm) butter and
arrange ham and banana rolls
in the base.
5. Melt remaining butter in a
saucepan over gentle heat. Stir
in flour and cook, without
browning, for 2 minutes, stirring
continuously.
6. Remove pan from heat and
gradually beat in the milk.
7. Return to heat and bring to the
boil, stirring.
8. Remove from heat and beat in
3oz (75gm) cheese and the
mustard and stir sauce over
gentle heat until cheese melts.
Season to taste with salt and
pepper.
9. Pour cheese sauce over top
of ham and banana rolls and
sprinkle with remaining cheese
and the chopped walnuts.
Decorate with slices of tomato.
10. Cook, uncovered, in centre
of oven for about 30 minutes, or
until heated through and golden
brown on top.

HOT BANGERS AND BEANS
Serves 4

½oz (12gm) butter
1lb (½ kilo) pork or beef
sausages
1 large onion, peeled and
chopped
1 garlic clove, peeled and
crushed
¼–½ level teaspoon crushed
dried chillies
1 level teaspoon paprika pepper
1 can (8oz or 200gm) peeled
tomatoes
1 can (15¾oz or 447gm) baked
beans in tomato sauce

1. Preheat oven to moderate,
350 deg F or gas 4 (180 deg C).
2. Melt butter in a frying pan
and fry sausages until browned
all over. Drain well over pan and
transfer to a casserole.
3. Fry onion and garlic in fat
remaining in the pan for 2–3
minutes, or until tender.
4. Stir in chillies, paprika pepper,
peeled tomatoes and baked
beans. Pour over sausages in
casserole.
5. Cover closely with lid or foil
and cook in centre of oven for
20–30 minutes, or until cooked
through.
6. Skim fat from surface if
necessary before serving.

SAUSAGE CAPERS
(Illustrated on page 35)
Serves 4

Serve with mashed potatoes to
mop up the delicious sauce.

8oz (200gm) onions, peeled and
thinly sliced
4 large tomatoes, peeled and
sliced
1 rounded tablespoon capers
salt
freshly ground black pepper
½ pint (250ml) chicken stock
1lb (½ kilo) pork sausages

1. Preheat oven to moderate to
moderately hot, 375 deg F or gas 5
(190 deg C).
2. Arrange onions in the base of
a shallow casserole.
3. Cover with tomatoes.
4. Sprinkle capers over top and
season with salt and pepper. Add
stock.
5. Arrange sausages on top, cover
closely with lid or foil and cook

in centre of oven for about 30–40
minutes, or until onions are
tender.
6. Remove lid and continue
cooking for a further 10–15
minutes to brown sausages.

SWEET CURRIED SAUSAGES
Serves 4

1oz (25gm) lard
1lb (½ kilo) pork sausages
1 medium onion, peeled and
chopped
½oz (12gm) curry powder
¾oz (18gm) flour
1 can (8oz or 200gm) apricot
halves
1 medium cooking apple,
peeled, cored and chopped
1 green pepper, de-seeded and
cut into small strips
1 dessertspoon lemon juice
1 level dessertspoon mango
chutney
salt and pepper
1 dessertspoon desiccated
coconut

1. Preheat oven to very moderate,
325 deg F or gas 3 (170 deg C).
2. Melt lard in a flameproof
casserole and brown sausages
all over. Drain well over pan and
keep on one side.
3. Add onion to fat remaining in
the pan and fry for 2–3 minutes,
or until soft.
4. Sprinkle in curry powder and
flour and stir over gentle heat for
2–3 minutes.
5. Remove casserole from heat.
Strain juice from apricots, make
up to ¾ pint (375ml) with water,
then gradually blend into pan.
6. Return to heat, bring sauce to
the boil and simmer for 2 minutes,
stirring continuously.
7. Return sausages to pan
together with apple, green pepper,
lemon juice and chutney. Season
to taste with salt and pepper.
8. Cover closely with lid or foil
and cook in centre of oven for
about 35 minutes. Add apricots
cut into quarters and return to
oven for a further 5 minutes, or
until heated through.
9. Sprinkle with desiccated
coconut and serve with freshly
boiled rice.

SMOTHERED SAUSAGES
Serves 3–4

1lb (½ kilo) pork sausages
8 streaky bacon rashers,
trimmed
made English mustard
2 large cooking apples
¼ level teaspoon dried sage
finely grated rind of half an
orange
¼ pint (125ml) stock
2 teaspoons demerara sugar

1. Preheat oven to moderate to
moderately hot, 375 deg F or gas 5
(190 deg C).
2. Grill sausages quickly under a
hot grill until browned all over.
3. Spread bacon rashers lightly
with made mustard, wrap a
rasher round each sausage and
pack closely together in a
shallow casserole.
4. Peel and core apples, cut into
rings and arrange over top of
sausages.
5. Sprinkle with sage and orange
rind.
6. Pour stock into dish and
sprinkle top with demerara sugar.
7. Cook, uncovered, in centre of
oven for 30 minutes, or until
ingredients are cooked through.

CORN AND SAUSAGE CASSEROLE
Serves 4

1lb (½ kilo) pork sausages
1lb (½ kilo) small new
potatoes, boiled
1oz (25gm) butter
1 can (11½oz or 326gm)
sweetcorn with green and red
peppers
4oz (100gm) mushrooms,
washed, trimmed and sliced
¼ pint (125ml) stock or white
wine
1 tablespoon cream or top of
milk

1. Preheat oven to very moderate,
325 deg F or gas 3 (170 deg C).
2. Place sausages and potatoes in
a dry frying pan. Fry very slowly
in the fat that comes from the
sausages until lightly browned.
Drain off the fat.
3. Grease a shallow, ovenproof
dish with butter and arrange
sausages, potatoes, sweetcorn
and mushrooms in alternate
layers in it.
4. Add remaining ingredients.
5. Cover closely with lid or foil
and cook in centre of oven for
about 25 minutes.

SAVOURY SAUSAGE POT
Serves 4–6

2 tablespoons dripping
2 medium onions, peeled and
chopped
1oz (25gm) flour
1 can (1lb 12oz or 800gm)
peeled tomatoes
1 large green pepper, de-seeded
and chopped
1 tablespoon Worcestershire
sauce
1 level teaspoon yeast extract
salt and pepper
sugar
1 bayleaf
1½lb (¾ kilo) skinless pork
sausages
2 tablespoons fresh white
breadcrumbs
1 tablespoon finely grated
Cheddar cheese
1oz (25gm) butter

1. Preheat oven to moderate to
moderately hot, 375 deg F or gas 5
(190 deg C).
2. Melt dripping in a pan and fry
onions gently until light golden
brown.
3. Sprinkle in flour and stir over
gentle heat for 1 minute.
4. Remove pan from heat and
gradually blend in tomatoes and
green pepper.
5. Return to heat and bring to
the boil, stirring.
6. Add Worcestershire sauce and
yeast extract and season to taste
with salt, pepper and sugar. Add
bayleaf and simmer gently for
10–15 minutes.
7. Cut sausages into thick,
slanting slices and add to
prepared sauce. Transfer to a
casserole and sprinkle top with a
mixture of breadcrumbs and
cheese.
8. Dot with butter and cook,
uncovered, just above centre of
oven for about 30 minutes, or
until sausages are cooked.

PATIO CASSEROLE
Serves 4

1lb (½ kilo) pork sausages
1 can (1lb or ½ kilo) butter
beans
1oz (25gm) butter
1 medium onion, peeled and
finely chopped
1 level dessertspoon flour
2 tablespoons tomato ketchup
1 wine glass dry white wine or
cider
squeeze of lemon juice
salt and pepper

1. Preheat oven to moderate, 350
deg F or gas 4 (180 deg C).
2. Place sausages in a dry frying
pan and fry very slowly until
lightly browned all over. Pour
off fat and cut each sausage into
three.
3. Stir in drained butter beans,
then transfer to a casserole.
4. Melt ½oz (12gm) butter in the
frying pan and cook onion for
2–3 minutes, or until tender.
5. Sprinkle in flour and stir
over gentle heat for 1 minute.
6. Remove pan from heat and
gradually blend in ketchup, wine
or cider and lemon juice. Season
with salt and pepper.
7. Return to heat, bring to the
boil, stirring, then pour over
sausages in casserole.
8. Dot with remaining butter
and cook, uncovered, above
centre of oven for about 20
minutes, or until cooked through.

COUNTRY SAUSAGE BAKE
Serves 4

1oz (25gm) cooking fat
1lb (½ kilo) potatoes, peeled and
cut into ¼-inch slices
2 parsnips, peeled and cut into
¼-inch slices
1lb (½ kilo) beef sausages
½ pint (250ml) stock
salt and pepper
chopped parsley

1. Preheat oven to moderate to
moderately hot, 375 deg F or gas 5
(190 deg C).
2. Melt fat in a flameproof
casserole, add vegetables, cover
and fry gently for 10 minutes.
3. Arrange sausages on the
vegetables, add stock and season
to taste with salt and pepper.
4. Cover closely with lid or foil

and cook just above centre of
oven for 45 minutes.
5. Remove lid and cook for a
further 15 minutes, or until
sausages are brown.
6. Sprinkle with parsley before
serving.

SAUSAGE FLAVIUS
Serves 4

1 tablespoon oil
1lb (½ kilo) chipolata
sausages
4 back bacon rashers, trimmed
and cut into small pieces
1 small onion, peeled and
chopped
1 small can (3½oz or 87gm)
pimentos, drained and sliced
¼ pint (125ml) stock
¼ pint (125ml) dry cider
salt
freshly ground black pepper

1. Preheat oven to moderate,
350 deg F or gas 4 (180 deg C).
2. Heat oil in a frying pan and
gently fry sausages until browned
all over. Drain well over pan and
transfer to a casserole.
3. Add bacon to fat remaining in
the pan and cook for 2–3 minutes,
or until lightly browned. Drain
well over pan and scatter over
sausages.
4. Fry onion in fat remaining in
the pan until lightly browned.
Drain off fat.
5. Add pimentos, stock and cider
and season to taste with salt and
pepper. Pour over sausages in
casserole.
6. Cook, uncovered, above centre
of oven for about 25–30 minutes,
or until sausages are cooked
through and sauce is reduced and
slightly thickened.

CUPBOARD LOVE
Serves 4

A lifesaver straight from the kitchen shelf.

1 can (1lb or ½ kilo) cocktail sausages
1 can (15oz or 425gm) minestrone soup
1 small can (8oz or 200gm) curried baked beans
1 can (1lb 4oz or 500gm) potatoes, drained and sliced
½oz (12gm) butter
½oz (12gm) finely grated Parmesan cheese

1. Preheat oven to moderate, 350 deg F or gas 4 (180 deg C).
2. Drain sausages and place in a casserole.
3. Pour minestrone soup over.
4. Stir in curried baked beans.
5. Arrange potatoes neatly over top of casserole, dot with butter and sprinkle with cheese.
6. Cook, uncovered, above centre of oven for about 40–45 minutes, or until heated through and golden brown.

SAUSAGE HOTPOT
Serves 4–6

1lb (½ kilo) pork sausagemeat
1 level teaspoon mixed dried herbs
2lb (1 kilo) potatoes, peeled and thinly sliced
8oz (200gm) onions, peeled and thinly sliced
1 can (14oz or 397gm) peeled tomatoes
½ pint (250ml) beef stock
salt and pepper

1. Preheat oven to moderate to moderately hot, 375 deg F or gas 5 (190 deg C).
2. Mix sausagemeat with herbs and roll into small balls.
3. Fry without any extra fat until golden brown all over. Remove from pan and drain on absorbent paper.
4. Place all the ingredients except stock and seasoning in layers in a casserole, finishing with a neatly arranged layer of potatoes.
5. Pour stock over and season.
6. Cover closely with lid or foil and cook in centre of oven for 30 minutes.
7. Remove cover and cook for a further 30 minutes, or until potatoes are golden brown.

CHELSEA SUPPER
Serves 4–6

1lb (½ kilo) pork sausagemeat
4oz (100gm) onion, peeled and grated
½ level teaspoon dried marjoram or mixed herbs
1 can (10½oz or 298gm) condensed cream of chicken soup
¼ pint (125ml) milk
salt and pepper
6oz (150gm) quick-cooking macaroni, cooked and drained
1 can (11½oz or 326gm) sweetcorn kernels
1oz (25gm) flaked almonds, lightly toasted

1. Preheat oven to moderate, 350 deg F or gas 4 (180 deg C).
2. Mix sausagemeat with onion and herbs and roll into about 24 small balls. Fry without any extra fat until golden brown all over.
3. Empty soup in a casserole, blend in milk and season with salt and pepper. Add macaroni, sweetcorn and prepared sausage balls.
4. Cover closely with lid or foil and cook in centre of oven for about 30 minutes, or until cooked through.
5. Remove lid and scatter top with flaked almonds before serving.

SAUSAGE FANDANGO
Serves 4

1½oz (37gm) butter
1 large onion, peeled and sliced
1 can (4oz or 100gm) pimentos, drained and cut into strips
4 celery sticks, washed, trimmed and chopped
salt and pepper
1lb (½ kilo) pork sausagemeat
½ packet sage and onion stuffing mix

1. Preheat oven to moderate, 350 deg F or gas 4 (180 deg C).
2. Melt 1oz (25gm) butter in a pan and fry onion for 2–3 minutes, or until tender.
3. Add pimentos and celery and continue cooking until soft. Season with salt and pepper.
4. Spread half the sausagemeat in the base of a casserole. Add vegetable mixture, then cover

with remaining sausagemeat.
5. Sprinkle top with dry stuffing mix and dot with remaining butter.
6. Cook, uncovered, above centre of oven for about 45 minutes–1 hour, or until sausagemeat is cooked through and top is golden brown and crisp.

BUDGET BEANO
Serves 6

1lb (½ kilo) butter beans
1oz (25gm) brown sugar
1 tablespoon black treacle
½ level teaspoon ground cloves
2 level teaspoons mild paprika pepper
2 tablespoons tomato purée
8oz (200gm) streaky bacon rashers, trimmed and cut into small pieces
2 garlic cloves, peeled and crushed
1 onion, peeled and chopped
bouquet garni
½ pint (250ml) beef stock
salt and pepper
1lb (½ kilo) leftover cooked sausages, meat or poultry, cut into cubes

1. Soak beans overnight in cold water to cover.
2. Preheat oven to cool, 300 deg F or gas 2 (150 deg C).
3. Drain beans and place in a large pan together with sugar, treacle, ground cloves, paprika pepper and tomato purée.
4. Lightly fry bacon pieces in a frying pan until fat begins to run. Add garlic and onion and continue cooking gently for 2–3 minutes, then add to beans.
5. Add bouquet garni and stock to beans, season to taste with salt and pepper and stir well together.
6. Cover closely with lid or foil and cook in centre of oven for 3–4 hours, then add sausages, meat or poultry and more stock if necessary. Continue cooking for a further 45 minutes–1 hour, or until beans are quite tender.

Offal

Oxtail cooked until it is falling from the bones, liver with sherry sauce and braised sweetbreads are just three of the recipes I have chosen to make the most of these tasty and economical meats.

OXTAIL CASSEROLE WITH ONION DUMPLINGS
Serves 4

1 oxtail (about 2–2½lb or 1–1¼ kilo), cut into joints
1½oz (37gm) flour
salt and pepper
2oz (50gm) dripping or lard
2 streaky bacon rashers, trimmed and cut into small pieces
1 large onion, peeled and chopped
1 carrot, peeled and chopped
2 sticks celery, washed, trimmed and chopped
1¼ pints (approximately ¾ litre) beef stock
bouquet garni
6oz (150gm) self-raising flour
3oz (75gm) shredded suet
1 tablespoon finely chopped onion
water to bind

1. Preheat oven to cool, 300 deg F or gas 2 (150 deg C).
2. Trim away excess fat then toss oxtail pieces in flour seasoned with salt and pepper.
3. Heat dripping or lard in a pan and fry pieces of oxtail and bacon until browned. Transfer with a draining spoon to a casserole.
4. Add onion, carrot and celery to fat remaining in the pan and cook for 2–3 minutes, stirring from time to time.
5. Sprinkle in any remaining flour and stir over gentle heat for 1 minute.
6. Remove pan from heat and gradually blend in stock.
7. Return to heat, bring to the boil and simmer for 2 minutes, stirring continuously. Pour over oxtail in casserole and add bouquet garni.
8. Cover with lid or foil and cook ·in centre of oven for about 3½–4

hours, or until oxtail is quite tender.
9. Meanwhile prepare dumplings. Place remaining dry ingredients in a bowl, season with ½ teaspoon salt and mix well together.
10. Bind to a soft but not sticky dough with water, then shape into 10–12 balls with floured hands.
11. Remove casserole from oven and add dumplings.
12. Increase oven temperature to moderately hot, 400 deg F or gas 6 (200 deg C). Cover casserole and cook towards top of oven for about 15 minutes.
13. Remove cover and cook for a further 5–10 minutes, or until meat is tender and dumplings are lightly browned.

CAERNARVON CASSEROLE
Serves 4

An oxtail casserole with plenty of flavour. For the best results make it a day in advance, then skim off the fat and reheat on top of cooker on the day required.

1 oxtail (about 2–2½lb or 1–1¼ kilo) cut into joints
2–3 tablespoons oil
1 medium onion, peeled and sliced
1 garlic clove, peeled and crushed
8oz (100gm) carrots, peeled and sliced
1 level teaspoon ground ginger
1oz (25gm) flour
1 can (8oz or 100gm) peeled tomatoes
¾ pint (375ml) stock
1lb (½ kilo) leeks, well washed and cut into slices

1. Preheat oven to very moderate, 325 deg F or gas 3 (170 deg C).
2. Trim off excess fat from oxtail.

3. Heat oil in a flameproof casserole and fry pieces of oxtail until brown all over. Remove with a draining spoon and keep on one side.
4. Add onion, garlic and carrots to fat remaining in the casserole and cook gently for 2–3 minutes.
5. Sprinkle in ginger and flour and stir over gentle heat for 1 minute.
6. Remove casserole from heat and gradually blend in tomatoes and stock, stirring well.
7. Return to heat and add oxtail to casserole.
8. Bring to the boil, then cover closely with lid or foil.
9. Cook in centre of oven for about 3 hours, or until meat is tender, adding leeks to the casserole for the last 30 minutes of cooking time.

OLD ENGLISH CASSEROLE
(Illustrated on page 36)
Serves 4

8oz (200gm) butter beans
1oz (25gm) butter
1 large oxtail, cut into joints
2 onions, peeled and chopped
1oz (25gm) flour
¾ pint (375ml) stock
good pinch of marjoram
1 bayleaf
2 carrots, peeled and sliced
2 teaspoons lemon juice
salt and pepper

1. Soak the butter beans overnight in cold water to cover.
2. Preheat oven to moderate to moderately hot, 375 deg F or gas 5 (190 deg C).
3. Melt butter in a frying pan and fry oxtail until golden brown, then transfer to a casserole.
4. Fry onions in fat remaining in the frying pan for 2–3 minutes, then add to meat in the casserole.
5. Sprinkle flour into fat remaining in the pan and stir over gentle heat for 2–3 minutes.
6. Remove pan from heat and gradually blend in stock.
7. Return to heat, bring to the boil, stirring, then pour over the meat.
8. Add well drained butter beans, marjoram, bayleaf, carrots and lemon juice. Season well with salt and pepper.
9. Cover closely with lid or foil and cook in centre of oven for 30 minutes.
10. Reduce oven temperature to cool, 300 deg F or gas 2 (150 deg C) and cook for a further 2½–3 hours, or until meat is tender.

CASSEROLE OF KIDNEYS
Serves 4

8oz (200gm) lamb's kidneys
12oz (300gm) ox kidney
1oz (25gm) dripping or lard
2 large onions, peeled and chopped
1oz (25gm) flour
2 tablespoons onion chutney
1 pint (approximately ½ litre) beef stock
2 large carrots, peeled and sliced
4oz (100gm) mushrooms, washed, trimmed and sliced
salt and pepper

1. Preheat oven to moderate, 350 deg F or gas 4 (180 deg C).
2. Skin, halve and core lamb's kidneys. Trim ox kidney. Cut all kidney into small pieces.
3. Melt dripping or lard in a flameproof casserole and fry onions gently for 2–3 minutes, or until tender.
4. Sprinkle in flour and stir over gentle heat for 1 minute.
5. Remove casserole from heat and gradually blend in chutney and stock.
6. Return to heat, bring to the boil and simmer for 2 minutes, stirring continuously.
7. Add kidneys, carrots and mushrooms, and season with salt and pepper.
8. Cover with lid or foil and cook in centre of oven for about 1 hour, or until meat and vegetables are tender.

KIDNEY AND ONION STEW
(Illustrated on page 36)
Serves 4–6

Just a few herbs transform this homely dish.

2 ox kidneys
2oz (50gm) flour
salt and pepper
2 medium onions, peeled and sliced
1 tablespoon chopped parsley
½ level teaspoon sweet basil
1 pint (approximately ½ litre) beef stock

1. Preheat oven to moderate, 350 deg F or gas 4 (180 deg C).
2. Skin each kidney, cut in half and remove core. Cut into small pieces then toss in flour seasoned with salt and pepper.
3. Arrange kidneys in a casserole together with onions, parsley, basil and stock.
4. Cover closely with lid or foil and cook in centre of oven for 1½–2 hours, or until meat is tender.
5. Serve with jacket baked potatoes and baked tomatoes.

DEVIL'S ROLLS
Serves 4

8oz (200gm) prunes
1lb (½ kilo) lamb's liver, thinly sliced
1oz (25gm) flour
salt and pepper
8 streaky bacon rashers, trimmed
made English mustard
8oz (200gm) onions, peeled and thinly sliced
2 tablespoons tomato ketchup
dash of Tabasco sauce
¾ pint (375ml) stock

1. Soak prunes overnight in cold water to cover.
2. Preheat oven to very moderate, 325 deg F or gas 3 (170 deg C).
3. Toss liver in flour well seasoned with salt and pepper.
4. Stretch bacon on a board with the back of a knife, spread with a little made mustard and cut each rasher in half.
5. Drain and stone prunes, then wrap each one in liver and bacon to form a roll. Secure with cocktail sticks.
6. Scatter half the onion in the base of a casserole, arrange prepared rolls on top and cover with remaining onion.
7. Add tomato ketchup and Tabasco sauce to stock and pour into the casserole.
8. Cover with lid or foil and cook in centre of oven for about 1–1½ hours, or until meat is tender.

Clementine chicken (see page 65)   Coq au vin (see page 66)

Duckling with grapes (see page 73)   Casserole of pheasant (see page 77)

Cottage casserole (see page 80)   Westside herrings (see page 83)

Scottish supper (see page 85)   Bell Inn smokies (see page 88)

FERRY BOAT LIVER
Serves 4

1lb (½ kilo) lamb's or ox liver,
thinly sliced
1oz (25gm) flour
salt and pepper
2 level teaspoons curry powder
1oz (25gm) butter
1 streaky bacon rasher,
trimmed and cut into small
pieces
4oz (100gm) mushrooms,
washed, trimmed and sliced
1 can (15oz or 425gm) red
kidney beans
½ pint (250ml) beef stock

1. Preheat oven to very moderate,
325 deg F or gas 3 (170 deg C).
2. Toss liver in flour seasoned
with salt, pepper and curry
powder.
3. Melt butter in a flameproof
casserole and fry bacon for 2–3
minutes. Add liver and brown on
both sides.
4. Add mushrooms, sprinkle in
any remaining flour and stir over
gentle heat for 1 minute.
5. Remove casserole from heat
and stir in drained beans.
Gradually blend in stock.
6. Return to heat, bring to the
boil and simmer for 2 minutes,
stirring continuously.
7. Adjust seasoning if necessary,
then cover with lid or foil and
cook in centre of oven for about
1½ hours, or until meat is tender.

GROVE CASSEROLE
Serves 4

4 streaky bacon rashers,
trimmed and cut into four
1 medium onion, peeled and
chopped
1lb (½ kilo) lamb's liver, thinly
sliced
1oz (25gm) flour
salt and pepper
oil
2 oranges
½ pint (250ml) chicken stock
good pinch of sugar
1 tablespoon lemon juice
2 tomatoes, peeled and chopped
1 level tablespoon tomato purée
1 tablespoon chopped parsley

1. Preheat oven to moderate,
350 deg F or gas 4 (180 deg C).
2. Fry bacon in a pan until
golden brown, then transfer to a
casserole using a draining spoon.
3. Fry onion in fat from bacon
until transparent, then drain
well over pan and place in
casserole with bacon.
4. Toss liver in flour well
seasoned with salt and pepper.
5. Fry liver in fat remaining in
the pan, adding a little oil if
necessary, until golden brown
on both sides. Transfer to
casserole.
6. Sprinkle any remaining flour
into pan and stir over gentle
heat for 1 minute.
7. Remove pan from heat and
gradually blend in finely grated
rind and juice of 1 orange, stock,
sugar and lemon juice.
8. Return to heat, bring to the
boil and simmer for 2 minutes,
stirring continuously.
9. Add tomatoes and tomato
purée and season if necessary.
Stir sauce into ingredients in
casserole.
10. Cover closely with lid or foil
and cook in centre of oven for
about 30 minutes.
11. Divide remaining orange into
segments, discarding any pith
and pips, and add to casserole.
12. Continue cooking for a
further 15 minutes, or until meat
is tender.
13. Serve sprinkled with parsley.

NEAPOLITAN LIVER
Serves 4

1lb (½ kilo) lamb's liver, thinly
sliced
1oz (25gm) flour
salt and pepper
1 dessertspoon olive oil
½oz (12gm) butter
2 large onions, peeled and
sliced
½ pint (250ml) chicken stock
2 level tablespoons tomato
purée
1 garlic clove, peeled and
crushed
2 level teaspoons oregano or
marjoram
¼ pint (125ml) single cream

1. Preheat oven to moderate,
350 deg F or gas 4 (180 deg C).
2. Toss liver in flour well
seasoned with salt and pepper.
3. Heat oil and butter in a
flameproof casserole and gently
fry onions until tender.
4. Add liver and brown on both
sides.
5. Sprinkle in any remaining
flour.
6. Remove casserole from heat
and gradually blend in stock
and tomato purée.
7. Add garlic and herbs and stir
well together.
8. Return to heat, bring to the
boil and simmer for 2 minutes,
stirring continuously.
9. Cover closely with lid or foil
and cook in centre of oven for
about 45 minutes, or until meat
is tender.
10. Arrange liver on a serving
dish.
11. Stir cream into casserole and
reheat sauce, taking care not to
boil. Pour over liver and serve
with freshly cooked rice or
noodles.

STUFFED LIVER
Serves 4

2oz (50gm) mushrooms,
chopped
1 onion, peeled and chopped
1½oz (37gm) butter or
margarine
1 dessertspoon finely chopped
parsley
2oz (50gm) fresh white
breadcrumbs
salt and pepper
little milk to bind
1lb (½ kilo) lamb's liver, thinly
sliced
1oz (25gm) flour
4 bacon rashers
1 packet (1 pint or
approximately ½ litre) French
onion soup mix
¾ pint (375ml) water

1. Preheat oven to moderately
hot, 400 deg F or gas 6 (200 deg C).
2. Prepare stuffing by mixing
mushrooms and onion with 1oz
(25gm) melted butter or
margarine.
3. Stir in parsley and
breadcrumbs, season well with
salt and pepper, then bind
together with a little milk.
4. Toss liver in flour seasoned
with salt and pepper.
5. Grease a baking tin with
remaining butter, place liver
slices in the base and spread each
piece with stuffing mixture. Cover
with bacon rashers.
6. Cover with lid or foil and cook
in centre of oven for 30 minutes.
7. Meanwhile, make up soup
according to packet directions but
using only ¾ pint (375ml) water.
8. Pour soup around liver and
continue cooking for a further
10–15 minutes, or until meat is
tender and sauce heated through.

PORKERS
Serves 4

A good combination of liver and
belly of pork with the added
interest of capers.

1lb (½ kilo) pig's or lamb's liver
1oz (25gm) flour
salt and pepper
4oz (100gm) belly of pork
2oz (50gm) dripping or lard
2 large onions, peeled and
sliced
½ pint (250ml) stock
2 level tablespoons capers,
drained
3 tablespoons single cream or
top of the milk

1. Preheat oven to very moderate,
325 deg F or gas 3 (170 deg C).
2. Cut liver into strips and toss
in flour well seasoned with salt
and pepper.
3. Trim rind from pork and cut
into neat strips.
4. Melt dripping or lard in a
flameproof casserole and add
liver, pork and onions. Season
well. Fry together, turning as
necessary, until lightly browned
all over.
5. Sprinkle any remaining flour
into casserole and stir over gentle
heat for 1 minute.
6. Remove casserole from heat
and gradually blend in stock.
7. Return to heat, bring to the
boil and simmer for 2 minutes,
stirring continuously.
8. Cover closely with lid or foil
and cook in centre of oven for
about 45 minutes, or until meats
are tender.
9. Stir in drained capers and
cream or milk just before serving.

LIVER IN SHERRY SAUCE
Serves 4

1lb (½ kilo) liver
1oz (25gm) flour
salt and pepper
4 streaky bacon rashers,
trimmed and cut into small
pieces
1oz (25gm) dripping or lard
1 large onion, peeled and
chopped
2 carrots, peeled and sliced
¾ pint (375ml) beef stock
1–2 tablespoons tomato
ketchup
1 teaspoon Worcestershire
sauce
1–2 tablespoons dry sherry

1. Preheat oven to moderate,
350 deg F or gas 4 (180 deg C).
2. Cut liver into small strips and
toss in flour seasoned with salt
and pepper.
3. Fry bacon in a pan until fat
begins to run, then add liver and
fry until browned on both sides.
Use a draining spoon to transfer
to a casserole.
4. Add dripping or lard to pan if
necessary and fry onion for 3–4
minutes, or until tender.
5. Add carrots and continue
cooking for 1 minute.
6. Sprinkle in any remaining
flour and stir over gentle heat for
1 minute.
7. Remove pan from heat and
gradually blend in stock, tomato
ketchup, Worcestershire sauce
and sherry.
8. Return to heat, bring to the
boil and simmer for 2 minutes,
stirring continuously.
9. Check seasoning and pour
over liver in casserole.
10. Cover with lid or foil and
cook in centre of oven for about
45 minutes–1 hour, or until meat
is tender.

LIVER WITH SAVOURY DUMPLINGS
Serves 4

1lb ($\frac{1}{2}$ kilo) lamb's liver, thinly sliced
1oz (25gm) flour
salt and pepper
2 tablespoons oil
8oz (200gm) onions, peeled and sliced
4 streaky bacon rashers, trimmed and cut into small pieces
4oz (100gm) button mushrooms
little soy sauce
$\frac{3}{4}$ pint (375ml) chicken stock
4oz (100gm) self-raising flour
1 level teaspoon dry mustard
1 tablespoon finely chopped parsley
2oz (50gm) shredded suet
4 tablespoons water

1. Preheat oven to moderate, 350 deg F or gas 4 (180 deg C).
2. Wash liver, pat dry on kitchen paper then cut into chunks.
3. Toss liver in flour seasoned with salt and pepper.
4. Heat oil in a flameproof casserole and gently fry onions until tender. Add bacon and continue cooking for 2–3 minutes.
5. Add liver, mushrooms and soy sauce and stir over gentle heat for 3–4 minutes.
6. Sprinkle in any remaining flour and stir over gentle heat for 1 minute.
7. Remove casserole from heat and gradually blend in stock.
8. Return to heat, bring to the boil and simmer for 2 minutes, stirring continuously.
9. Cover closely with lid or foil and cook in centre of oven for 25 minutes.
10. Meanwhile prepare dumplings. Mix self-raising flour, salt and dry mustard together in a bowl. Stir in parsley and suet and mix to a soft but not sticky dough with water.
11. Knead lightly on a floured board, then divide into eight pieces and form into small balls.
12. Remove cover from casserole, adjust seasoning if necessary and add dumplings. Continue cooking for a further 30 minutes, or until meat is tender and dumplings cooked through.

FAMILY CASSEROLE
(Illustrated on page 36)
Serves 4

1lb ($\frac{1}{2}$ kilo) lamb's liver
2oz (50gm) butter
4 back bacon rashers, trimmed and cut into small pieces
1 onion, peeled and sliced
2oz (50gm) flour
salt
freshly ground black pepper
1 pint (approximately $\frac{1}{2}$ litre) beef stock
2 tomatoes, peeled and chopped
4oz (100gm) button mushrooms, washed, trimmed and chopped
3 sticks celery, washed and chopped

1. Preheat oven to moderate, 350 deg F or gas 4 (180 deg C).
2. Cut liver into 1-inch strips.
3. Melt butter in a frying pan and fry bacon and onion for 4–5 minutes, or until lightly browned. Remove from pan with a draining spoon and transfer to a casserole.
4. Toss liver in flour seasoned with salt and pepper, then fry in fat remaining in the pan until browned on both sides. Transfer to casserole.
5. Sprinkle in any remaining flour and stir over gentle heat for 1 minute.
6. Remove pan from heat and gradually blend in stock.
7. Return to heat, bring to the boil and simmer for 2 minutes, stirring continuously. Add contents of pan to the casserole.
8. Add tomatoes, mushrooms and celery and more seasoning if necessary.
9. Cover closely with lid or foil and cook in centre of oven for about 45 minutes, or until meat is tender.

SPEEDY SUPPER
Serves 4–6

1 can (1lb or $\frac{1}{2}$ kilo) ox tongue
1 can (10$\frac{1}{2}$oz or 298gm) condensed tomato soup
dash of Worcestershire sauce
2 teaspoons capers, drained
1 level tablespoon creamed horseradish

1. Preheat oven to moderate, 350 deg F or gas 4 (180 deg C).
2. Cut the tongue into 4–6 slices and arrange in a shallow casserole.
3. Blend together undiluted soup, Worcestershire sauce, capers and creamed horseradish and pour over the tongue.
4. Cover with lid or foil and cook in centre of oven for about 30 minutes, or until heated through.
5. Serve with freshly cooked vegetables.

DEVILLED TONGUE
Serves 4–6

1lb ($\frac{1}{2}$ kilo) cooked ox tongue, thickly sliced
1 level tablespoon flour
1 tablespoon vinegar
2 tablespoons tomato ketchup
few drops Worcestershire sauce
$\frac{1}{2}$ level teaspoon dry mustard
$\frac{1}{4}$ level teaspoon ground ginger
$\frac{1}{2}$ pint (250ml) stock

1. Preheat oven to moderate, 350 deg F or gas 4 (180 deg C).
2. Cut the tongue into small strips and place in a shallow casserole.
3. Blend flour with vinegar, tomato ketchup, Worcestershire sauce, mustard and ground ginger, then gradually add stock.
4. Pour sauce over tongue.
5. Cover closely with lid or foil and cook in centre of oven for about 30 minutes, or until heated through.
6. Serve with creamed potatoes and sprigs of watercress.

BRAISED SWEETBREADS
Serves 4

1lb (½ kilo) sweetbreads
juice of half a lemon
1oz (25gm) butter
2 onions, peeled and sliced
2 carrots, peeled and sliced
1 small turnip, peeled and
sliced
3 sticks celery, washed and
chopped
1 bouquet garni
½oz (12gm) flour
salt and pepper
½ pint (250ml) chicken stock

1. Wash sweetbreads, soak in
ice-cold water for 1 hour, then
drain and cook for 15 minutes in
a pan of slightly salted water,
together with lemon juice. Drain
sweetbreads and transfer to ice-
cold water.
2. Remove any sinews and
membrane from sweetbreads, then
place between two plates and put
a heavy weight on top.
3. Preheat oven to moderately
hot, 400 deg F or gas 6 (200 deg C).
4. Melt butter in a flameproof
casserole and fry onions, carrots,
turnip and celery together for
3–4 minutes. Add bouquet garni.
5. Sprinkle flattened sweetbreads
with flour seasoned with salt and
pepper and arrange on top of
vegetables.
6. Pour in stock.
7. Cook, uncovered, in centre of
oven for 40–45 minutes, or until
cooked through and browned on
top.

SWEETBREADS COUNTRY STYLE
Serves 4

Tender sweetbreads in a tasty
tomato sauce.

1lb (½ kilo) calf's or lamb's
sweetbreads
few drops lemon juice
1 medium onion, peeled and
thinly sliced
8oz (100gm) carrots, peeled
and thinly sliced
2 sticks celery, scrubbed and
chopped
8oz (100gm) tomatoes, skinned
and sliced
salt and pepper
½–¾ pint (250–375ml) chicken
stock
2 level tablespoons cornflour
1 tablespoon chopped parsley

1. Soak sweetbreads for at least
1 hour in cold water to cover.
2. Preheat oven to moderate,
350 deg F or gas 4 (180 deg C).
3. Drain sweetbreads and place
in a saucepan with a little lemon
juice and cold water to cover.
4. Bring very slowly to the boil
and simmer calf's sweetbreads for
5 minutes or lamb's sweetbreads
for 10 minutes.
5. Drain well, plunge into cold
water and remove any gristle and
skin.
6. Place the prepared onion,
carrots, celery and tomatoes in
an ovenproof dish and sprinkle
with salt and pepper.
7. Pour sufficient stock into the
dish to just cover the vegetables.
8. Place sweetbreads on top of
vegetables.
9. Cover closely with lid or foil
and cook in centre of oven for
about 45 minutes, or until
sweetbreads are tender.
10. Lift out sweetbreads and
arrange on a hot serving dish.
Keep warm.
11. Drain liquid from vegetables.
Arrange vegetables on serving
dish with sweetbreads.
12. Pour liquid into a small
saucepan and stir in cornflour
blended to a smooth paste with a
little water.
13. Add parsley, bring to the boil
and simmer gently for 1 minute,
stirring continuously. Season
well, then pour over sweetbreads
before serving.

SAVOURY HEARTS
Serves 4

4 calf's or sheep's hearts
2oz (50gm) butter
4oz (100gm) onions, peeled and
chopped
4oz (100gm) celery, washed,
trimmed and chopped
4oz (100gm) fresh white
breadcrumbs
2 oranges
1 egg, beaten
salt
cayenne pepper
¾ pint (375ml) beef stock
watercress to garnish

1. Preheat oven to moderate,
350 deg F or gas 4 (180 deg C).
2. Prepare hearts by cutting away
veins and arteries and washing
well in cold water.
3. Melt butter in a pan, then add
onions, celery, breadcrumbs and
finely grated rind of 1 orange.
4. Remove pan from heat and stir
in juice of 2 oranges and sufficient
egg to bind together. Season with
salt and pepper.
5. Fill the hearts with the
prepared mixture and sew them
up with a needle and thread.
6. Arrange hearts in a casserole
and pour in the stock.
7. Cover with lid or foil and cook
in centre of oven for about 1½–2
hours, or until hearts are tender,
basting occasionally during
cooking.
8. Arrange hearts on a hot
serving dish and garnish with
watercress. Serve gravy
separately.

TRIPE LYONNAISE
Serves 6

1½–2lb (1 kilo) dressed tripe
2oz (50gm) butter
1oz (25gm) flour
½ pint (250ml) stock or water
2 level teaspoons tomato purée
salt and pepper
good pinch of sugar
2 large onions, peeled and
chopped
1–2 tablespoons wine vinegar

1. Preheat oven to very moderate,
325 deg F or gas 3 (170 deg C).
2. Cut tripe into neat pieces.
3. Melt butter in a pan and fry
tripe until golden brown all over.
4. Sprinkle in the flour and stir
over gentle heat for 1 minute.
5. Remove pan from heat and
blend in stock or water and
tomato purée, and season well
with salt, pepper and sugar.
6. Return to heat, bring to the
boil and simmer for 2 minutes,
stirring continuously.
7. Place onions in the base of a
casserole and pour tripe mixture
over top.
8. Cover closely with lid or foil
and cook in centre of oven for
about 1½–2 hours, or until tripe is
tender.
9. Stir in vinegar just before
serving.

LANCASHIRE CASSEROLE
Serves 4

1lb (½ kilo) dressed tripe
1oz (25gm) lard
1oz (25gm) flour
¾ pint (375ml) beef stock
¼ level teaspoon ground ginger
¼ level teaspoon ground nutmeg
celery salt
pepper
2 medium onions, peeled and
thinly sliced
2 carrots, peeled and thinly
sliced
1 turnip, peeled and sliced
2oz (50gm) Lancashire cheese,
finely grated

1. Preheat oven to cool, 300 deg F
or gas 2 (150 deg C).
2. Wash tripe thoroughly and cut
into 2-inch pieces.
3. Melt lard in a pan, sprinkle in
flour and stir over gentle heat for
1 minute.
4. Remove pan from heat and
gradually blend in stock.
5. Return to heat, bring to the
boil and simmer gently for
2 minutes, stirring continuously.
6. Stir in spices and season well
with celery salt and pepper.
7. Add prepared vegetables and
simmer for 3–4 minutes, then add
tripe and transfer to a casserole.
8. Cover closely with lid or foil
and cook in centre of oven for
2–3 hours, or until tripe is tender.
9. Sprinkle top with grated
cheese before serving.

SCALLOPED TRIPE
Serves 4

1lb (½ kilo) dressed tripe
4 tablespoons oil
4 tablespoons vinegar
2½oz (62gm) butter
1 large onion, peeled and
finely chopped
8oz (200gm) button mushrooms,
washed, trimmed and sliced
1oz (25gm) flour
1 pint (approximately ½ litre)
tomato juice
1 level teaspoon dried
marjoram
4 tablespoons fresh white
breadcrumbs

1. Place tripe in cold water to
cover and simmer gently until
tender. Drain well and cut into
thin strips.
2. Mix oil and vinegar together,
pour over prepared tripe and
leave to stand for about 1 hour.
3. Preheat oven to moderate to
moderately hot, 375 deg F or gas 5
(190 deg C).
4. Melt 1oz (25gm) butter in a
pan and lightly fry onion for
2–3 minutes. Add mushrooms and
continue cooking gently for 7–8
minutes.
5. Sprinkle in the flour and
stir over gentle heat for 1 minute.
6. Remove pan from heat and
gradually blend in tomato juice
and marjoram.
7. Return pan to heat, bring to
the boil and simmer gently for
2 minutes, stirring continuously.
8. Grease a casserole with ½oz
(12gm) butter and arrange
alternate layers of drained tripe
and prepared sauce in it.
9. Sprinkle top with breadcrumbs
and dot with remaining butter.
10. Cook, uncovered, in centre of
oven for about 20 minutes, or
until heated through and golden
on top.

Chicken

I have chosen a selection of recipes suitable for the family and for entertaining. If you are using a frozen bird, do make sure it is completely thawed before starting the preparation.

DAWLISH CHICKEN
Serves 4

1oz (25gm) butter
1 tablespoon oil
1 dressed chicken (about
3lb or 1¼ kilo) cut into 4 joints
1 onion, peeled and finely
chopped
1 stick celery, washed,
trimmed and chopped
2 streaky bacon rashers,
trimmed and cut into small
pieces
1oz (25gm) flour
salt and pepper
1 level teaspoon dry mustard
¾ pint (375ml) chicken stock
3 tomatoes, peeled and cut into
quarters

1. Preheat oven to very moderate,
325 deg F or gas 3 (170 deg C).
2. Heat butter and oil in a large
frying pan and fry chicken joints
until golden brown all over.
Drain well over pan and transfer
to a casserole.
3. Add onion, celery and bacon to
fat remaining in pan and cook
gently for 2–3 minutes.
4. Mix flour with salt, pepper and
mustard. Sprinkle over the fried
vegetables and stir over gentle
heat for 1 minute.
5. Remove pan from heat and
gradually blend in stock.
6. Return to heat, bring to the
boil and simmer for 2 minutes,
stirring continuously.
7. Add tomatoes to prepared
sauce, season to taste and pour
over the chicken in casserole.
8. Cover closely with lid or foil
and cook in the centre of oven for
about 1½ hours, or until chicken
is tender.

BRAISED CHICKEN
Serves 4–6

1 dressed chicken (about 3lb or
1½ kilo)
1 tablespoon flour
salt and pepper
2oz (50gm) butter
1 tablespoon oil
1 large leek, washed, trimmed
and cut into slices
1lb (½ kilo) carrots, peeled and
sliced
2 sticks celery, washed,
trimmed and cut into small
pieces
¼ level teaspoon powdered
mace
¼ pint (125ml) chicken stock
¼ pint (125ml) dry white wine or
cider

1. Preheat oven to moderate,
350 deg F or gas 4 (180 deg C).
2. Coat chicken in flour seasoned
with salt and pepper.
3. Heat butter and oil in a deep,
flameproof casserole and fry
chicken until golden brown all
over. Drain well over casserole
and keep on one side.
4. Add leek, carrots and celery
to fat remaining in the casserole
and fry gently for 3–4 minutes, or
until tender.
5. Stir in mace and any
remaining flour and stir over
gentle heat for 1 minute.
6. Remove casserole from heat
and gradually blend in stock and
wine or cider.
7. Replace chicken in casserole
and cover closely with lid or foil.
8. Cook in centre of oven for
1–1½ hours, or until chicken is
tender.

MANOR HOUSE CHICKEN
Serves 4

2oz (50gm) butter or
margarine
1 dressed chicken (about 2lb
or 1 kilo), cut into 4 joints
2 level tablespoons flour
salt and pepper
1 level tablespoon chopped
parsley
1 level tablespoon chopped
chives
¼ level teaspoon dried thyme
¼ level teaspoon dried sage
¾ pint (375ml) milk

1. Preheat oven to moderate to
moderately hot, 375 deg F or gas 5
(190 deg C).
2. Melt butter or margarine in a
frying pan and fry chicken joints
until golden brown all over.
Drain well over pan and transfer
to an ovenproof dish.
3. Add flour, salt, pepper and
herbs to fat remaining in the
pan and stir over gentle heat for
1 minute.
4. Remove pan from heat and
gradually blend in milk.
5. Return to heat, bring to the
boil and simmer for 2 minutes,
stirring continuously.
6. Pour sauce over chicken and
cook, uncovered, in centre of oven
for about 45 minutes, or until
chicken is tender.

CHICKEN GOULASH
Serves 4–6

1 dressed chicken (about 3lb or
1¼ kilo) cut into 4–6 joints
1½oz (37gm) flour
salt
freshly ground black pepper
2oz (50gm) butter
2 large onions, peeled and
sliced
1 green pepper, de-seeded and
cut into slices
1–2 level tablespoons mild
paprika pepper
1 can (14oz or 397gm) peeled
tomatoes
½ pint (250ml) chicken stock
1 bayleaf
1 carton soured cream

1. Preheat oven to very moderate,
325 deg F or gas 3 (170 deg C).
2. Toss chicken joints in flour
seasoned with salt and pepper.
3. Melt butter in a flameproof
casserole and fry chicken joints
until golden brown all over.
Drain well over casserole and
keep on one side.
4. Add onions and green pepper
to fat remaining in casserole and
cook gently for 3–4 minutes
without browning.
5. Sprinkle in any remaining
flour, add paprika pepper and stir
over gentle heat for 1 minute.
6. Remove casserole from heat
and gradually blend in tomatoes
and stock.
7. Return to heat, bring to the
boil and simmer for 2 minutes
stirring continuously.
8. Return chicken to pan, add
bayleaf and cover closely with lid
or foil.
9. Cook in centre of oven for
1¼–1½ hours, or until chicken is
tender.
10. Remove bayleaf and stir in
soured cream just before serving.
11. Serve with freshly cooked
rice or buttered noodles.

KENTISH CASSEROLE
Serves 4–6

2oz (50gm) butter
1 dressed chicken (about 3lb or
1¼ kilo) cut into 6 joints
1 large onion, peeled and
chopped
6oz (150gm) button mushrooms,
washed and trimmed
1oz (25gm) flour
1 level teaspoon dry mustard
½ pint (250ml) unsweetened
apple juice
¼ pint (125ml) chicken stock
salt
freshly ground black pepper
2–3 tablespoons cream
1 tablespoon finely chopped
parsley

1. Preheat oven to moderate,
350 deg F or gas 4 (180 deg C).
2. Melt butter in a frying pan
and fry chicken joints until
golden brown all over. Drain
well over pan and transfer to a
casserole.
3. Fry onion in fat remaining in
the pan until transparent, then
add mushrooms and continue
cooking for 3–4 minutes.
4. Sprinkle in flour and mustard
and stir over gentle heat for
1 minute.
5. Remove pan from heat and
gradually blend in apple juice
and stock.
6. Return to heat, bring to the
boil and simmer for 2 minutes,
stirring continuously. Season
to taste with salt and pepper.
7. Pour prepared sauce over
chicken joints.
8. Cover closely with lid or foil
and cook in centre of oven for
about 1 hour, or until chicken is
tender.
9. Stir in cream and parsley
before serving.

BLENHEIM CASSEROLE
Serves 4–6

1 dressed chicken (about 3lb or
1½ kilo) cut into 4–6 joints
1oz (25gm) flour
salt
freshly ground black pepper
1oz (25gm) butter
1 tablespoon oil
1 large leek, washed, trimmed
and sliced
1 can (11½oz or 326gm)
sweetcorn kernels, drained
2 tablespoons sweet chutney,
finely chopped
1 tablespoon dry sherry
¾ pint (375ml) chicken stock

1. Preheat oven to moderate,
350 deg F or gas 4 (180 deg C).
2. Toss chicken joints in flour
seasoned with salt and pepper.
3. Heat butter and oil in a large
frying pan and fry chicken joints
until golden brown all over.
Drain well over pan and transfer
to a casserole.
4. Add leek to fat remaining in
the pan and cook gently for 3–4
minutes, or until tender. Sprinkle
in any remaining flour and stir
over gentle heat for 1 minute.
5. Remove pan from heat and stir
in sweetcorn, chutney and sherry
and mix well together.
6. Gradually blend in stock and
stir well.
7. Return to heat, bring to the
boil and simmer for 2 minutes,
stirring continuously.
8. Pour prepared sauce over
chicken in casserole and cover
closely with lid or foil.
9. Cook in centre of oven for
about 1 hour, or until chicken is
tender.
10. Serve with buttered noodles
and freshly cooked peas.

SUTTON CASSEROLE
Serves 4

4 chicken joints
1oz (25gm) flour
2oz (50gm) butter
1 medium onion, peeled and
thinly sliced
1 medium carrot, peeled and
thinly sliced
4oz (100gm) mushrooms,
peeled and sliced
1 can (10½oz or 298gm)
condensed tomato soup
1 level teaspoon basil or mixed
herbs
4 tablespoons water

1. Preheat oven to moderate,
350 deg F or gas 4 (180 deg C).
2. Toss chicken joints in flour.
3. Melt butter in a flameproof
casserole, fry the chicken till
lightly browned all over. Drain
well over casserole and keep on
one side.
4. Add onion and carrot to fat
remaining in the pan and fry
till tender.
5. Mix in the mushrooms,
tomato soup, herbs and water
and place the chicken joints on
top.
6. Cover and cook in centre of
oven for 1 hour, or until chicken
is tender. Season if necessary.
7. Serve with freshly boiled rice.

HOLIDAY CHICKEN
Serves 4–6

1 dressed chicken (about 3lb
or 1½ kilo) cut into 4–6 joints
½oz (12gm) flour
2oz (50gm) butter
1 can (15oz or 425gm) cream of
asparagus soup
¼ level teaspoon dried chives

1. Preheat oven to moderate,
350 deg F or gas 4 (180 deg C).
2. Toss chicken joints in flour.
3. Melt butter in a flameproof
casserole and fry chicken joints
until golden brown all over.
4. Drain off any excess fat then
pour asparagus soup over
chicken.
5. Stir in chives.
6. Cover closely with lid or foil
and cook in centre of oven for
about 45 minutes–1 hour, or until
chicken is tender.
7. Adjust seasoning if necessary
before serving.

CHICKEN WITH WALNUTS
Serves 4–6

1 dressed chicken (about 3lb
or 1½ kilo) cut into 4–6 joints
salt and pepper
2oz (50gm) butter
6oz (150gm) mushrooms,
washed, trimmed and cut into
quarters
1 tablespoon dry sherry
1oz (25gm) flour
¾ pint (375ml) chicken stock
2 sticks celery, washed,
trimmed and cut into small
pieces
1 tablespoon oil
4oz (100gm) walnuts, halved
paprika pepper

1. Preheat oven to moderate,
350 deg F or gas 4 (180 deg C).
2. Sprinkle chicken joints with
salt and pepper.
3. Melt butter in a large frying
pan and fry chicken joints until
golden brown all over. Drain well
over pan and transfer to a
casserole.
4. Add mushrooms to fat
remaining in the pan and cook
gently for 2–3 minutes. Stir in
sherry.
5. Sprinkle in flour and stir over
gentle heat for 1 minute.
6. Remove pan from heat and
gradually blend in stock.
7. Return to heat, bring to the
boil and simmer for 2 minutes,
stirring continuously.
8. Pour sauce over chicken in
casserole and cover closely with
lid or foil.
9. Cook in centre of oven for
about 50 minutes, then add
celery and continue cooking for
15 minutes, or until chicken
is tender.
10. Heat oil in a pan and toss
walnuts in it until browned, then
drain well on absorbent kitchen
paper and scatter over top of
prepared chicken.
11. Sprinkle with paprika pepper
before serving.

TARRAGON CHICKEN WITH ORANGE
Serves 4

1oz (25gm) butter
2 tablespoons oil
1 dressed chicken (about 3lb or
1½ kilo), cut into 4 joints
1 large onion, peeled and finely
chopped
1 can frozen concentrated
orange juice, thawed
¼ pint (125ml) stock
1 level tablespoon dried
tarragon
1oz (25gm) cornflour blended
with 1 tablespoon water
finely chopped parsley

1. Preheat oven to moderate, 350
deg F or gas 4 (180 deg C).
2. Melt butter and oil in a
flameproof casserole and fry
chicken joints until golden brown
all over. Drain well over pan and
keep on one side.
3. Fry onion gently in fat
remaining in the casserole for
2–3 minutes.
4. Stir in orange juice, stock and
tarragon, bring to the boil and
add chicken.
5. Cover with lid or foil and cook
in centre of oven for about 1 hour,
or until chicken is tender, basting
occasionally with the orange
sauce.
6. Remove chicken and arrange
on a serving dish.
7. Skim excess fat from sauce and
add blended cornflour. Bring to
the boil for 2–3 minutes on the top
of the stove, stirring continuously.
8. Pour over chicken and garnish
with parsley.

CHICKEN WITH PINEAPPLE
Serves 4–6

1 dressed chicken (about 3lb or
1½ kilo), cut into 4–6 joints
1oz (25gm) flour
salt and pepper
2oz (50gm) butter
1 onion, peeled and chopped
1 level dessertspoon ground
ginger
2 tablespoons clear honey
1 can (13oz or 376gm) crushed
pineapple
¾ pint (375ml) chicken stock
juice of half a lemon
3 tablespoons brandy
finely chopped parsley

1. Preheat oven to very moderate,
325 deg F or gas 3 (170 deg C).
2. Toss chicken joints in flour
well seasoned with salt and
pepper.
3. Melt butter in a large frying
pan and fry chicken joints until
golden brown all over. Drain well
over pan and transfer to a
casserole.
4. Fry onion in fat remaining in
the pan for 2–3 minutes, then
sprinkle in any remaining flour
and stir over gentle heat for 1
minute.
5. Remove pan from heat and stir
in ground ginger, honey,
pineapple and stock.
6. Return to heat, bring to the
boil and simmer gently for 2–3
minutes, stirring continuously.
Add lemon juice.
7. Pour prepared sauce over
chicken in casserole.
8. Cover closely with lid or foil
and cook in centre of oven for
about 1½ hours, or until chicken
is tender.
9. Skim any fat from surface of
casserole. Gently heat brandy in a
small pan, flame and pour into
casserole. Stir well.
10. Serve sprinkled with parsley.

CHICKEN AMALFI
Serves 4–6

1 dressed chicken (about 3lb or
1½ kilo)
salt
1 medium onion, peeled
1 large lemon
1 stick celery, washed and
chopped
4 carrots, washed, peeled and
cut into quarters
1 small bayleaf
1oz (25gm) butter
1oz (25gm) flour
1 egg
1 tablespoon finely chopped
parsley

1. Preheat oven to moderate, 350
deg F or gas 4 (180 deg C).
2. Sprinkle the inside of chicken
with a little salt, and insert
onion.
3. Place chicken in a large
casserole and add water to the
depth of 1 inch.
4. Add a thin strip of lemon rind,
celery, carrots, bayleaf and
washed giblets, except for the
liver.
5. Cover closely with lid or foil
and cook in centre of oven for
about 1 hour, or until chicken is
tender.
6. Drain well, reserving the
stock, and discard celery, bayleaf
and giblets.
7. Carve chicken into serving
portions, arrange on a serving
dish together with carrots, and
keep hot.
8. Melt butter in a pan, sprinkle
in flour and cook over gentle heat
for 1 minute.
9. Remove pan from heat and
gradually blend in ¾ pint (375ml)
strained stock from the chicken.
10. Return to heat, bring to the
boil and simmer for 2 minutes,
stirring continuously. Remove
from heat and leave to cool
slightly.
11. Whisk lemon juice and egg
together, then gradually beat into
prepared sauce. Stir over gentle
heat for 2 minutes, taking care
not to allow it to boil.
12. Stir in chopped parsley and
adjust seasoning if necessary.
13. Pour over prepared chicken
and serve at once.

KENTUCKY CASSEROLE
Serves 4

1 dressed chicken (about 3lb or
1½ kilo), cut into 4 joints
1½oz (37gm) flour
salt and pepper
2oz (50gm) butter
1 medium onion, peeled and
chopped
1 can (8oz or 200gm) tomato
juice
¾ pint (375ml) chicken stock
1 bayleaf
½ level teaspoon mixed dried
herbs
salt and pepper
1 can (8oz or 200gm) sweetcorn
kernels
4 small firm tomatoes, peeled
finely chopped parsley

1. Preheat oven to moderate, 350
deg F or gas 4 (180 deg C).
2. Toss chicken joints in flour
well seasoned with salt and
pepper.
3. Melt butter in a pan and fry
chicken joints until golden brown
all over. Drain well over pan and
transfer to a casserole.
4. Fry onion in fat remaining in
the pan until tender, then
sprinkle in any remaining flour
and stir over gentle heat for
1 minute.
5. Remove pan from heat and
gradually blend in tomato juice
and stock.
6. Return to heat, bring to the
boil and simmer for 2–3 minutes,
stirring continuously.
7. Add bayleaf and herbs and
season well to taste with salt and
pepper.
8. Pour prepared sauce over
chicken.
9. Cover closely with lid or foil
and cook in centre of oven for
about 1 hour.
10. Add drained sweetcorn and
tomatoes and cook for a further
30 minutes, or until chicken is
tender.
11. Remove bayleaf and serve
sprinkled with chopped parsley.

PENNSYLVANIA CASEROLE
Serves 4

4 chicken joints
1oz (25gm) flour
salt and pepper
4 back bacon rashers, trimmed
2oz (50gm) butter or margarine
2 small onions, peeled and
chopped
3 carrots, peeled and sliced
2 sticks celery, washed and
chopped
pinch of oregano or mixed
herbs
1 can (10½oz or 298gm)
condensed celery soup
¼ pint (125ml) water
¼ pint (125ml) milk

1. Preheat oven to moderate to moderately hot, 375 deg F or gas 5 (190 deg C).
2. Toss chicken joints in flour seasoned with salt and pepper.
3. Cut each bacon rasher into four pieces.
4. Melt butter or margarine in a large frying pan and fry bacon, onions, carrots and celery for 3–4 minutes.
5. Remove with a draining spoon and place in an ovenproof casserole.
6. Add oregano or mixed herbs to celery soup, blend to a smooth consistency with water and milk and pour into casserole.
7. Cover closely with lid or foil and cook in centre of oven for about 1 hour, or until chicken is tender.
8. Serve with freshly boiled rice.

YANKEE CHICKEN
Serves 4–6

Tender chicken in a peanut butter sauce.

1 dressed chicken (about 3lb or
1½ kilo), cut into 4–6 joints
salt and pepper
1oz (25gm) butter
1 tablespoon oil
2 medium onions, peeled and
chopped
2 large tomatoes, peeled and
chopped
1 large green pepper, de-seeded
and cut into small strips
½ pint (250ml) chicken stock
4oz (100gm) smooth peanut
butter

1. Preheat oven to very moderate, 325 deg F or gas 3 (170 deg C).
2. Sprinkle chicken joints with salt and pepper.
3. Melt butter in a large frying pan and fry joints until golden brown all over. Drain well over pan and transfer to a casserole.
4. Add oil to pan if necessary and fry onions for 3–4 minutes, or until soft.
5. Add tomatoes and green pepper and continue cooking for 2–3 minutes. Season to taste with salt and pepper and add to chicken in caserole.
6. Blend stock and peanut butter together and stir into the casserole.
7. Cover closely with lid or foil and cook in centre of oven for 1–1½ hours, or until chicken is tender.

CHICKEN JOSEPHINE
Serves 4–6

2oz (50gm) butter or margarine
1 dressed chicken (about 3lb or
1½ kilo), cut into 4–6 joints
1 large onion, peeled and sliced
1oz (25gm) flour
3 level teaspoons ground ginger
2 level teaspoons French
mustard
¾ pint (375ml) chicken stock
1 tablespoon sherry
4oz (100gm) mushrooms,
washed, trimmed and sliced
1 tablespoon finely chopped
parsley

1. Preheat oven to very moderate, 325 deg F or gas 3 (170 deg C).
2. Melt butter or margarine in a large frying pan and fry chicken until golden brown all over. Drain well over pan and transfer to a casserole.
3. Add onion to fat remaining in the pan and fry for 3–4 minutes, or until tender.
4. Sprinkle in flour and stir over gentle heat for 1 minute.
5. Remove pan from heat, stir in ginger and French mustard, then gradually blend in chicken stock and sherry.
6. Return to heat, bring to the boil and simmer for 2 minutes, stirring continuously.
7. Check seasoning, stir in mushrooms and parsley and pour over chicken in casserole.
8. Cook in centre of oven for about 1¼ hours, or until chicken is tender.

POULET BASQUE
(Illustrated on page 36)
Serves 4

1 dressed chicken (about 3lb or
1½ kilo)
salt and pepper
3 tablespoons olive oil
2 large green peppers,
de-seeded and cut into strips
4 tomatoes, skinned and
quartered
4oz (100gm) button mushrooms,
washed
2oz (50gm) lean bacon, cut in
small dice
¼ pint (125ml) dry white wine

1. Preheat oven to moderate, 350 deg F or gas 4 (180 deg C).
2. Sprinkle chicken with salt and pepper.
3. Heat oil in a large pan and fry chicken until golden brown all over.
4. Transfer chicken to a casserole, draining well.
5. Add green peppers, tomatoes, mushrooms and bacon to pan in which chicken was cooked and fry lightly for 2–3 minutes.
6. Add wine, stir well to remove any sediment around the pan, then pour around chicken in casserole.
7. Cover closely with lid or foil and cook in centre of oven for 30 minutes.
8. Remove cover and continue cooking for a further 30–45 minutes, or until chicken is golden brown and tender.
9. Serve with boiled rice and crisp green salad.

CHICKEN VERMOUTH
Serves 4–6

1 dressed chicken (about 3lb or
1½ kilo), cut into 4–6 joints
salt
freshly ground black pepper
1oz (25gm) butter
1 tablespoon oil
1 large onion, peeled and sliced
2 rounded tablespoons flour
1 pint (approximately ½ litre)
chicken stock
1 bayleaf
4 tablespoons sweet white
vermouth
4oz (100gm) green grapes,
halved and de-seeded

1. Preheat oven to moderate, 350
deg F or gas 4 (180 deg C).
2. Sprinkle chicken joints with
salt and pepper.
3. Heat butter and oil in a large
frying pan and fry chicken joints
until golden brown all over. Drain
well over pan and transfer to a
casserole.
4. Add onion to fat remaining in
the pan and cook gently for 2–3
minutes, or until transparent.
5. Sprinkle in flour and stir over
gentle heat for 1 minute.
6. Remove pan from heat and
gradually blend in stock. Add
bayleaf and stir in vermouth.
7. Return to heat, bring to the
boil and simmer for 2 minutes,
stirring continuously. Season to
taste with salt and pepper.
8. Pour prepared sauce over
chicken in casserole.
9. Cover closely with lid or foil
and cook in centre of oven for
about 50 minutes.
10. Remove bayleaf, stir in grapes
and return to oven for a further
10–15 minutes, or until chicken is
tender.

CASSEROLE CAPRICE
Serves 4–6

1 dressed chicken (about 3lb or
1½ kilo), cut into 4–6 joints
salt and pepper
1oz (25gm) butter
1 tablespoon oil
2 leeks, washed, trimmed and
chopped
1½oz (37gm) flour
2 level tablespoons mild
paprika pepper
1 pint (approximately ½ litre)
chicken stock
1 bayleaf
1 level tablespoon chopped
parsley
1 cooking apple
1 firm banana

1. Preheat oven to very moderate,
325 deg F or gas 3 (170 deg C).
2. Sprinkle chicken joints with
salt and pepper.
3. Melt butter and oil in a large
frying pan and fry chicken joints
until golden brown all over. Drain
well over pan and transfer to a
casserole.
4. Add leeks to fat remaining in
the pan and cook for 3–4 minutes,
or until tender.
5. Sprinkle in flour and paprika
pepper and stir over gentle heat
for 1 minute.
6. Remove pan from heat and
gradually blend in stock.
7. Return to heat, bring to the
boil and simmer gently for 2
minutes, stirring continuously.
8. Add bayleaf and pour sauce
over chicken in casserole.
9. Cover closely with lid or foil
and cook in centre of oven for
about 1 hour.
10. Add parsley, peeled, cored and
grated apple and peeled and
sliced banana. Continue cooking
for 10–15 minutes, or until
chicken is tender.

CLEMENTINE CHICKEN
(Illustrated on page 53)
Serves 6

Chicken flavoured with the
tanginess of oranges and lemons.

6 chicken joints
salt and pepper
1 tablespoon oil
1oz (25gm) butter
1 onion, peeled and sliced
1oz (25gm) flour
¾ pint (375ml) chicken stock
1 thin-skinned lemon, cut into
slices
1 small, thin-skinned orange,
cut into slices
2 bayleaves
1 level teaspoon sugar
sprig of watercress

1. Preheat oven to moderate to
moderately hot, 375 deg F or gas 5
(190 deg C).
2. Sprinkle chicken joints with
salt and pepper.
3. Heat oil and butter in a frying
pan and fry joints quickly till
golden brown. Drain well over
pan and transfer to a casserole.
4. Add onion to fat remaining in
the pan and cook gently for about
5 minutes, or until tender.
5. Sprinkle in flour and stir over
gentle heat for 1 minute.
6. Remove pan from heat and
gradually blend in stock.
7. Return to heat, bring to the
boil and simmer for 2 minutes,
stirring continuously.
8. Add lemon and orange slices
and bayleaves. Season with salt,
pepper and sugar and pour over
chicken.
9. Cover closely with lid or foil
and cook in centre of oven for
about 45 minutes, or until
chicken is tender, removing the
lid 15 minutes before end of
cooking time to allow top to
brown.
10. Serve garnished with
watercress.

CHICKEN BONNE FEMME
Serves 4–6

A classic French casserole of chicken.

1 dressed chicken (about 3lb or 1½ kilo), cut into 4–6 joints
salt and pepper
1oz (25gm) butter
3oz (75gm) streaky bacon in the piece, trimmed and cut into small strips
12 button onions
2oz (50gm) mushrooms, washed, trimmed and cut into quarters
1oz (25gm) flour
¾ pint (375ml) chicken stock
bouquet garni
10–12 small new potatoes, scraped or 2–3 medium potatoes, peeled and cut into small pieces
1 tablespoon finely chopped parsley

1. Preheat oven to moderate, 350 deg F or gas 4 (180 deg C).
2. Sprinkle chicken joints with salt and pepper.
3. Melt butter in a large frying pan and fry joints until golden brown all over. Drain well over pan and transfer to a casserole.
4. Place bacon and onions in a pan of cold water, bring to the boil and drain well.
5. Add bacon and onions to fat remaining in the pan and fry for 3–4 minutes, or until lightly browned.
6. Add mushrooms, sprinkle in flour and stir over gentle heat for 1 minute.
7. Remove pan from heat and gradually blend in stock.
8. Return to heat, bring to the boil and simmer for 2 minutes, stirring continuously.
9. Add bouquet garni to chicken in casserole and pour prepared sauce over.
10. Cover closely with lid or foil and cook in centre of oven for about 25 minutes.
11. Add potatoes and continue cooking for a further 40 minutes, or until chicken and potatoes are tender.
12. Remove bouquet garni and sprinkle with chopped parsley before serving.

POULET EN COCOTTE
Serves 4–6

1 dressed chicken (about 4lb or 2 kilo)
salt
freshly ground black pepper
2oz (50gm) butter
1 tablespoon oil
4 streaky bacon rashers, trimmed and cut into small pieces
4 shallots or small onions, peeled and roughly chopped
2 carrots, peeled and roughly chopped
2 tablespoons Cognac
4 tomatoes, peeled, de-seeded and roughly chopped
1 level teaspoon sugar
bouquet garni
¼ pint (125ml) chicken stock
¼ pint (125ml) red wine

1. Preheat oven to very moderate, 325 deg F or gas 3 (170 deg C).
2. Sprinkle chicken with salt and pepper.
3. Heat butter and oil in a deep, flameproof casserole and fry chicken until golden brown all over. Drain well over casserole and keep on one side.
4. Add bacon to fat remaining in the pan and cook gently for 2–3 minutes. Add shallots and carrots and continue cooking for 3–4 minutes.
5. Add Cognac and flame.
6. Stir in tomatoes, sugar, bouquet garni, stock and wine.
7. Replace chicken in casserole and cover closely with lid or foil.
8. Cook in centre of oven for about 1–1½ hours, or until chicken is tender.

COQ AU VIN
(Illustrated on page 53)
Serves 4

A classic from Burgundy.

3oz (75gm) butter
2 tablespoons oil
4oz (100gm) streaky bacon, trimmed and cut into small pieces
12 button onions, peeled
2 garlic cloves, peeled and crushed
4 chicken joints
3 tablespoons Cognac
1 bayleaf
6 peppercorns
few stalks parsley
½ pint (250ml) chicken stock
½ pint (250ml) red wine
1 level teaspoon sugar
4oz (100gm) button mushrooms, washed
few sprigs of watercress

1. Preheat oven to very moderate, 325 deg F or gas 3 (170 deg C).
2. Heat half the butter and the oil in a large frying pan and fry bacon, onions and garlic for 8–10 minutes, or until lightly browned. Remove from the pan with a draining spoon and keep on one side.
3. Add remaining butter to pan and cook chicken joints for 10 minutes, or until golden brown all over.
4. Remove pan from heat, pour Cognac over and set alight with a match. When flames have died down, transfer chicken and juices in pan to a casserole.
5. Add prepared bacon and onion mixture, bayleaf, peppercorns and parsley to casserole.
6. Pour stock and red wine over and add sugar.
7. Cover closely with lid or foil and cook in centre of oven for about 1 hour.
8. Remove lid, add mushrooms and return to oven for a further 15–20 minutes, or until chicken is tender.
9. Thicken, if liked, with a little cornflour blended with water.
10. Serve garnished with sprigs of watercress.

CHICKEN AMERICANO
Serves 4–6

1 dressed chicken (about 3lb or
1½ kilo), cut into 4–6 joints
2 level tablespoons flour
salt and pepper
2–3 tablespoons oil
12 small onions, peeled
2 carrots, peeled and sliced
2 sticks celery, washed and
chopped
2 level tablespoons tomato
purée
½ pint (250ml) chicken stock
2 level teaspoons capers,
drained
2–3 cocktail gherkins, drained
and chopped

1. Preheat oven to very moderate,
325 deg F or gas 3 (170 deg C).
2. Toss chicken joints in flour
seasoned with salt and pepper.
3. Heat oil in a pan and fry
chicken joints until golden brown
all over. Transfer to a casserole.
4. Add onions, carrots, celery and
tomato purée blended with
chicken stock to casserole.
5. Cover closely with lid or foil
and cook in centre of oven for
1½–2 hours, or until chicken is
tender.
6. Stir in capers and gherkins
before serving.

CARMEN CASSEROLE
Serves 4–6

1 dressed chicken (about 3lb or
1½ kilo), cut into 4–6 joints
salt and pepper
1oz (25gm) butter
1 tablespoon oil
1 garlic clove, peeled and
crushed
2 tomatoes, peeled and roughly
chopped
1 can (3½oz or 87gm) pimentos,
drained and cut into small
strips
12 stuffed olives, drained and
halved
2 level tablespoons capers,
drained
4 tablespoons tomato ketchup
juice of half a lemon
dash of Tabasco sauce

1. Preheat oven to very moderate,
325 deg F or gas 3 (170 deg C).
2. Sprinkle chicken joints with
salt and pepper.
3. Heat butter and oil in a large
frying pan and fry chicken joints
and garlic until golden brown all
over.
4. Add tomatoes, pimentos,
olives, capers, tomato ketchup,
lemon juice and Tabasco sauce.
Season to taste with salt and
pepper.
5. Transfer to a casserole and
cover closely with lid or foil.
6. Cook in centre of oven for
1¼–1½ hours, or until chicken is
tender.
7. Serve with freshly boiled rice.

SPANISH CHICKEN
Serves 4

3–4 tablespoons oil
1 dressed chicken (about 3lb or
1½ kilo)
1lb (½ kilo) tomatoes, peeled
and sliced
2 onions, peeled and sliced
2 bayleaves
1 medium glass brandy
¼ pint (125ml) chicken stock
1 level teaspoon sugar
pinch of nutmeg
salt and pepper

1. Preheat oven to very moderate,
325 deg F or gas 3 (170 deg C).
2. Heat oil in a flameproof
casserole and fry chicken until
golden.
3. Add tomatoes, onions,
bayleaves, brandy, stock, sugar
and nutmeg and season well with
salt and pepper.
4. Cover closely with lid or foil
and cook in centre of oven for 1¼
hours, or until chicken is tender.
5. Remove bayleaves before
serving.

CHICKEN CACCIATORE
Serves 4–6

Chicken in a tasty tomato sauce.

1 dressed chicken (about 3lb or
1½ kilo), cut into 4–6 joints
1oz (25gm) cornflour
salt
freshly ground black pepper
1oz (25gm) butter
1 tablespoon oil
8oz (200gm) tomatoes, peeled
and quartered
pinch of dried basil
1 teaspoon chopped parsley
1 large onion, peeled and sliced
1 garlic clove, peeled and
crushed
1 can (2oz or 50gm) tomato
purée
¾ pint (375ml) chicken stock
2 tablespoons red wine
(optional)
pinch of sugar

1. Preheat oven to moderate, 350
deg F or gas 4 (180 deg C).
2. Toss chicken joints in
cornflour seasoned with salt and
pepper.
3. Heat butter and oil in a large
frying pan and fry chicken joints
until golden brown all over. Drain
well over pan and transfer to a
casserole.
4. Place tomatoes in casserole on
top of chicken and sprinkle with
basil and parsley.
5. Add onion and garlic to fat
remaining in the pan and cook
gently for 2–3 minutes.
6. Sprinkle in remaining
cornflour and stir over gentle
heat for 1 minute.
7. Remove pan from heat and
gradually blend in tomato purée,
stock and red wine, if used.
Add sugar and check seasoning.
8. Return to heat, bring to the
boil and simmer for 2 minutes,
stirring continuously.
9. Pour prepared sauce over
chicken in casserole and cover
closely with lid or foil.
10. Cook in centre of oven for
about 1 hour, or until chicken is
tender.

CHICKEN MONTEMARE
Serves 4–6

The surprising mixture of chicken and prawns is most successful.

1 dressed chicken (about 4lb or 2 kilo), cut into 4–6 joints
1oz (25gm) flour
salt
freshly ground black pepper
2oz (50gm) butter
1 large onion, peeled and chopped
2 streaky bacon rashers, trimmed and cut into small pieces
4 tomatoes, peeled and chopped
¾ pint (375ml) chicken stock
1 small packet frozen peas
2oz (50gm) peeled prawns
1 tablespoon chopped parsley

1. Preheat oven to moderate, 350 deg F or gas 4 (180 deg C).
2. Toss chicken joints in flour seasoned with salt and pepper.
3. Melt butter in a large frying pan and fry chicken until golden brown all over. Drain well over pan and transfer to a casserole.
4. Add onion and bacon to fat remaining in the pan and fry gently for 3–4 minutes, or until lightly browned.
5. Stir in tomatoes, sprinkle in any remaining flour and stir over gentle heat for 1 minute.
6. Remove pan from heat and gradually blend in stock.
7. Return to heat, bring to the boil and simmer for 2 minutes, stirring continuously.
8. Pour prepared sauce over chicken in casserole.
9. Cover closely with lid or foil and cook in centre of oven for about 45 minutes.
10. Add peas and cook for a further 15–20 minutes, or until peas are cooked and chicken is tender. Skim fat from surface.
11. Stir in prawns and parsley and check seasoning before serving.

CHICKEN VALENCIA
Serves 6

4 tablespoons olive oil
6 chicken joints
1 garlic clove, peeled and crushed
½ level teaspoon turmeric powder
1 tablespoon water
4oz (100gm) stoned green olives
1 lemon, sliced and pips removed
3 tablespoons sugar
¾ pint (375ml) chicken stock
salt and pepper

1. Preheat oven to very moderate, 325 deg F or gas 3 (170 deg C).
2. Heat oil in a flameproof casserole and fry chicken joints with garlic until golden brown all over.
3. Blend turmeric with water and stir into casserole.
4. Add olives, lemon slices and sugar.
5. Pour stock into casserole, season to taste and stir well.
6. Cover closely with lid or foil and cook in centre of oven for about 1¼ hours, or until chicken is tender.
7. Skim fat from surface and serve. Alternatively, thicken sauce after cooking with a little flour or cornflour blended with water.

CHICKEN CICERO
Serves 4–6

1 dressed chicken (about 3lb or 1½ kilo), cut into 4–6 joints
salt
freshly ground black pepper
1oz (25gm) butter
1 tablespoon oil
1 large onion, peeled and sliced
1oz (25gm) flour
¾–1 pint (375ml – approximately ½ litre) chicken stock
1 level teaspoon dried marjoram
8oz (200gm) courgettes, trimmed and sliced
2 tablespoons peanuts

1. Preheat oven to moderate, 350 deg F or gas 4 (180 deg C).
2. Sprinkle chicken with salt and pepper.
3. Heat butter and oil in a large frying pan and fry joints until golden brown all over. Drain well

over pan and transfer to a casserole.
4. Add onion to fat remaining in the pan and cook for 2–3 minutes, or until transparent.
5. Sprinkle in flour and stir over gentle heat for 1 minute.
6. Remove pan from heat and gradually blend in stock.
7. Return to heat, bring to the boil and simmer for 2 minutes, stirring continuously.
8. Stir in marjoram and pour over chicken in casserole.
9. Cover with lid or foil and cook in centre of oven for about 45 minutes.
10. Stir in courgettes and continue cooking for about 20 minutes, or until chicken is tender.
11. Add peanuts and stir in well just before serving.

AZTEC CHICKEN
Serves 4–6

1 dressed chicken (about 3lb or 1½ kilo), cut into 4–6 joints
salt and pepper
1oz (25gm) butter
1 tablespoon oil
1 medium onion, peeled and chopped
¼ level teaspoon dried thyme
1 level teaspoon dried chives
1 level tablespoon finely chopped parsley
¼ pint (125ml) tomato ketchup
3 level tablespoons smooth peanut butter
1 pint (approximately ½ litre) chicken stock

1. Preheat oven to very moderate, 325 deg F or gas 3 (170 deg C).
2. Sprinkle chicken joints with salt and pepper.
3. Melt butter and oil in a large frying pan and fry joints until golden brown all over. Drain well over pan and transfer to a casserole.
4. Add onion, thyme, chives and parsley to fat remaining in the pan and mix well together. Transfer to casserole.
5. Blend tomato ketchup with peanut butter and add to the stock. Pour over chicken in casserole and stir well together.
6. Cover closely with lid or foil and cook in centre of oven for about 1–1½ hours, or until chicken is tender.
7. Serve with freshly boiled rice.

SPICED CHICKEN AND APRICOTS
Serves 4–6

1oz (25gm) butter
1 dressed chicken (about 3lb or
1½ kilo), cut into 4–6 joints
1 can (15oz or 425gm) apricot
halves
1 green pepper, de-seeded and
sliced
1 pint (approximately ½ litre)
chicken stock
3 tablespoons Fruity sauce
1 level teaspoon flaked onions
salt
1 level tablespoon cornflour
1 tablespoon water
sprigs of watercress to garnish

1. Preheat oven to moderate, 350
deg F or gas 4 (180 deg C).
2. Melt butter in a flameproof
casserole and fry chicken joints
until golden brown all over.
3. Add apricots together with
their syrup, green pepper, stock,
Fruity sauce and onions and
season to taste with salt.
4. Cover closely with lid or foil
and cook in centre of oven for
about 1 hour, or until chicken is
tender.
5. Remove chicken and keep on
one side. Blend cornflour with
water, then stir into hot liquor in
casserole.
6. Bring to the boil on top of
cooker and simmer for 2 minutes,
stirring continuously.
7. Check seasoning, then return
chicken to casserole and garnish
with watercress.

CHICKEN SAMANTHA
Serves 4–6

Chicken topped with a creamy
curried onion sauce.

1 dressed chicken (about 3lb or
1½ kilo)
salt and pepper
2 large onions, peeled and
sliced
2oz (50gm) butter
1 glass white wine
3 tablespoons double cream
2 level teaspoons curry powder
1 tablespoon flaked almonds,
lightly toasted
1 tablespoon finely chopped
parsley

1. Preheat oven to moderate, 350
deg F or gas 4 (180 deg C).
2. Sprinkle chicken with salt and
pepper.
3. Place onions in the base of a
shallow casserole.
4. Spread chicken with softened
butter and arrange on top of
onions. Pour in wine.
5. Cover with lid or foil and cook
in centre of oven for about 1 hour.
6. Remove lid and continue
cooking until chicken is tender
and lightly browned.
7. Transfer chicken to a serving
dish and keep hot.
8. Sieve the onions together with
the liquid and pour into a
saucepan. Bring to the boil and
simmer till liquid is slightly
reduced.
9. Stir in cream and curry powder
and check seasoning. Reheat
gently if necessary, then pour
around prepared chicken.
10. Sprinkle with toasted almonds
and chopped parsley before
serving.

PEPPERY CHICKEN
Serves 4

3 tablespoons oil
4 chicken joints
8 very small onions, peeled
1 small green pepper, de-seeded
and sliced
4 streaky bacon rashers,
trimmed and chopped
1½oz (37gm) flour
¾ pint (375ml) chicken stock
1 teaspoon Tabasco sauce
salt
4oz (100gm) small mushrooms,
washed and trimmed

1. Preheat oven to moderate, 350
deg F or gas 4 (180 deg C).
2. Heat oil in a frying pan and
fry chicken joints until golden
brown all over.
3. Drain chicken well over pan
and transfer to a casserole.
4. Add onions, green pepper and
bacon to oil remaining in the pan
and fry for a few minutes.
Transfer to casserole using a
draining spoon.
5. Sprinkle flour into pan and stir
over gentle heat for 1 minute.
6. Remove pan from heat and
gradually blend in stock.
7. Return to heat, bring to the
boil and simmer for 2 minutes,
stirring continuously.
8. Add Tabasco sauce and salt,
and stir in mushrooms. Pour into
casserole.
9. Cover closely with lid or foil
and cook in centre of oven for
about 1 hour, or until chicken is
tender.
10. Serve with freshly boiled rice.

CHICKEN ANTIGUA
Serves 4–6

1 dressed chicken (about 3lb or
1½ kilo), cut into 4–6 joints
salt
freshly ground black pepper
2oz (50gm) butter
1 tablespoon oil
1 onion, peeled and chopped
1oz (25gm) flour
2 level teaspoons curry powder
2 level teaspoons tomato purée
¾ pint (375ml) chicken stock
2 large, very firm bananas
1oz (25gm) flaked almonds,
lightly toasted

1. Preheat oven to very moderate,
325 deg F or gas 3 (170 deg C).
2. Sprinkle chicken joints with
salt and pepper.
3. Heat butter and oil in a large
frying pan and fry joints until
golden brown all over. Drain well
over pan and transfer to a
casserole.
4. Add onion to fat remaining in
the pan and fry gently for 3–4
minutes.
5. Sprinkle in flour and curry
powder and stir over gentle heat
for 1 minute.
6. Remove pan from heat and
gradually blend in tomato purée
and stock.
7. Return to heat, bring to the
boil and simmer for 2 minutes,
stirring continuously.
8. Pour prepared sauce over
chicken.
9. Cover closely with lid or foil
and cook in centre of oven for
about 1–1½ hours, or until chicken
is tender, adding peeled and sliced
bananas 10–15 minutes before the
end of cooking time.
10. Serve sprinkled with flaked
almonds.

CALYPSO CURRY
Serves 4–6

1 dressed chicken (about 3lb or
1½ kilo), cut into 4–6 joints
1oz (25gm) flour
salt and pepper
1 level tablespoon curry powder
1oz (25gm) butter
1 tablespoon oil
1 onion, peeled and chopped
1 can (1lb 14oz or 850gm) fruit
cocktail
2 level tablespoons desiccated
coconut, soaked in 3
tablespoons boiling water
½ pint (250ml) chicken stock

1. Preheat oven to very moderate,
325 deg F or gas 3 (170 deg C).
2. Toss chicken joints in flour
seasoned with salt, pepper and
curry powder.
3. Heat butter and oil in a large
frying pan and fry chicken joints
until golden brown all over. Drain
well over pan and transfer to a
casserole.
4. Fry onion in fat remaining in
the pan for 2–3 minutes or until
transparent.
5. Drain fruit cocktail, reserving
the syrup, and stir fruit into the
onions.
6. Sprinkle in any remaining
seasoned flour and stir over
gentle heat for 1 minute.
7. Remove pan from heat and
gradually blend in strained
coconut liquor and stock made up
to ¾ pint (375ml) with the
reserved fruit syrup.
8. Return to heat, bring to the
boil and simmer for 2 minutes,
stirring continuously. Check
seasoning.
9. Pour prepared sauce over
chicken in casserole and cover
closely with lid or foil.
10. Cook in centre of oven for
about 1¼ hours, or until chicken is
tender.
11. Serve with freshly boiled rice
and cucumber and tomato salad.

CURRIED CHICKEN
Serves 6

1oz (25gm) butter or margarine
1 tablespoon oil
1 dressed chicken (about 4lb or
2 kilo), cut into 6 joints
1 medium onion, peeled and
finely chopped
2–3 level tablespoons curry
powder
1 rounded teaspoon curry paste
1oz (25gm) flour
½ pint (250ml) chicken stock
1 dessert apple, peeled, cored
and chopped
1 tablespoon mango chutney
2oz (50gm) sultanas
1 level dessertspoon soft brown
sugar
salt and pepper
1 carton soured cream
strained juice of half a lemon

1. Preheat oven to moderate, 350
deg F or gas 4 (180 deg C).
2. Heat butter or margarine and
oil in a large frying pan and fry
chicken joints until golden brown
all over. Drain well over pan and
keep on one side.
3. Fry onion gently in fat
remaining in the pan for 5
minutes, or until tender.
4. Sprinkle in curry powder and
continue cooking very gently for
3–4 minutes, stirring occasionally.
5. Stir in curry paste. Sprinkle
in flour and stir over gentle heat
for 1 minute.
6. Remove pan from heat and
gradually blend in stock.
7. Add apple, chutney, sultanas
and sugar.
8. Return to heat, stir well
together and season to taste.
9. Return chicken to sauce, bring
to the boil, then transfer to a
casserole.
10. Cover closely with lid or foil
and cook in centre of oven for
1–1½ hours, or until chicken is
tender.
11. Stir in soured cream and
lemon juice and return to oven
for a further 10 minutes, or until
heated through.
12. Serve with freshly boiled rice.

Lombardy casserole (see page 93) Aubergines à la provençale (see page 93)

Banana togo (see page 94) Gardeners' casserole (see page 97)

Stuffed peaches (see page 99)   Spiked apples (see page 99)
West Country prunes (see page 100)   Buttered fruits (see page 101)

Duckling

In most of these recipes the duckling is divided into joints first to save last-minute carving. Frozen duckling is ideal, as it tends to be less fatty than fresh.

DUCKLING WITH PEACHES
Serves 4

1 oven-ready duckling (about
4lb or 2 kilo), cut into 4 joints
salt and pepper
1oz (25gm) butter
1 tablespoon oil
½ pint (250ml) dry white wine
pinch of dried sage
1 can (15oz or 425gm) peach
slices
1 tablespoon brandy
2 level teaspoons arrowroot

1. Preheat oven to very moderate, 325 deg F or gas 3 (170 deg C).
2. Sprinkle duckling joints with salt and pepper.
3. Heat butter and oil in a flameproof casserole and fry duckling joints until golden brown all over.
4. Drain off fat thoroughly, then add wine, sage, the syrup drained from peach slices and half the fruit.
5. Cover closely with lid or foil and cook in centre of oven for about 1½ hours, or until duckling is tender.
6. Carefully lift out duckling portions and drain well over pan. Transfer to a serving dish and keep hot.
7. Skim fat from juices in casserole.
8. Pour brandy into a small pan, warm gently, then set alight. When flames have disappeared, stir into casserole. Place over gentle heat on top of cooker until bubbling.
9. Blend arrowroot with a little water, stir into casserole and bring to the boil.
10. Add remaining peach slices and heat through gently, then pour over duckling.
11. Sprinkle with a little chopped parsley before serving.

DUCKLING WITH GRAPES
(Illustrated on page 53)
Serves 4

This recipe comes from Madeira.

1 oven-ready duckling (about
4lb or 2 kilo)
salt and pepper
1lb (½ kilo) green grapes
(seedless if possible)
½ bottle Madeira wine
2oz (50gm) butter
sprigs of watercress
lettuce leaves
1 orange, peeled and cut into
skinless segments
few glacé cherries, halved
few slices cucumber

1. Sprinkle duckling with salt and pepper. Prick skin with a fork.
2. Keep seedless grapes whole or cut large grapes in half and remove pips.
3. Place duckling and grapes in a bowl, pour Madeira wine over and leave to marinate overnight.
4. Preheat oven to moderate, 350 deg F or gas 4 (180 deg C).
5. Stuff about half the grapes inside the duckling together with the butter, then place in a casserole.
6. Pour half the wine into the casserole and keep remaining wine and grapes on one side.
7. Cook, uncovered, in centre of oven for 1½ hours.
8. Drain off fat from dish and add remaining wine. Return to oven for a further 30 minutes, or until duckling is tender.
9. Place duckling on a serving dish and garnish with remaining grapes and sprigs of watercress.
10. Surround with lettuce leaves, orange segments, halved glacé cherries and cucumber slices. Serve the sauce separately.

LODGE DUCKLING
Serves 4

1oz (25gm) butter
1 oven-ready duckling (about
4lb or 2 kilo), cut into 4 joints
2 medium onions, peeled and
sliced
1oz (25gm) flour
½ pint (250ml) stock made from
giblets
¼ pint (125ml) lager or light ale
bouquet garni
salt and pepper
sprigs of watercress

1. Preheat oven to moderate, 350 deg F or gas 4 (180 deg C).
2. Melt butter in a flameproof casserole and fry duckling portions until golden brown.
3. Drain well over pan and keep on one side.
4. Fry onions in fat remaining in the casserole for 2–3 minutes, or until tender.
5. Sprinkle in flour and stir over gentle heat for 1 minute.
6. Remove casserole from heat and gradually blend in stock and lager or light ale.
7. Return to heat, bring to the boil and simmer for 2 minutes, stirring continuously.
8. Return duckling portions to casserole, add bouquet garni and season to taste with salt and pepper.
9. Cover closely with lid or foil and cook in centre of oven for about 1½ hours, or until duckling is tender.
10. Transfer duckling to a serving dish and garnish with watercress.
11. Remove bouquet garni and skim fat from sauce in casserole. Check seasoning and pour sauce into a sauceboat to serve with the duckling.

LINCOLNSHIRE DUCKLING
Serves 4

1 oven-ready duckling (about
4lb or 2 kilo), cut into 4 joints
salt
freshly ground black pepper
1 large onion, peeled and
chopped
1 bayleaf
½ pint (250ml) red wine
4 streaky bacon rashers,
trimmed and cut into small
pieces
¼ pint (125ml) stock made from
giblets
2 carrots, peeled and chopped
2 sticks celery, washed and
chopped
4oz (100gm) button mushrooms
grated rind of 1 lemon
finely chopped parsley

1. Sprinkle duckling joints with
salt and pepper.
2. Place in a bowl together with
onion and bayleaf. Pour red wine
over and leave to stand in a
cool place for 2 hours.
3. Preheat oven to moderate,
350 deg F or gas 4 (180 deg C).
4. Remove duckling joints with a
draining spoon and dry on
absorbent kitchen paper.
Reserve the marinade.
5. Cook bacon gently in a frying
pan until fat begins to run, then
add duckling and cook with
bacon until browned all over.
Drain well, then transfer to a
casserole.
6. Cook, uncovered, in centre of
oven for 15 minutes.
7. Remove casserole from oven
and pour marinade and stock
over. Add carrots, celery and
mushrooms and cover closely
with lid or foil.
8. Reduce oven temperature to
cool, 300 deg F or gas 2 (150 deg
C), replace casserole and
continue cooking for a further
1½–2 hours, or until duckling is
tender.
9. Skim fat from surface and
remove bayleaf. Thicken, if liked,
with a little cornflour blended
with water, then serve sprinkled
with lemon rind and parsley.

BUCKINGHAM BRAISE
Serves 4

1 oven-ready duckling (about
4lb or 2 kilo)
1½lb (¾ kilo) cooking apples,
peeled, cored and sliced
juice of 1 orange
1lb (½ kilo) leeks, washed,
trimmed and sliced
salt
freshly ground black pepper
½ pint (250ml) stock made from
giblets

1. Preheat oven to moderate,
350 deg F or gas 4 (180 deg C).
2. Prick skin of duckling all
over with a fork.
3. Cover the base of a roasting
tin or casserole with apples.
Sprinkle with orange juice.
4. Scatter leeks over top and
season well with salt and pepper.
5. Pour in stock.
6. Place duckling on top and
season with salt and pepper.
7. Cover closely with lid or foil
and cook in centre of oven for
1 hour.
8. Remove cover and continue
cooking for about a further hour,
or until apples and leeks are
cooked and duckling is golden
brown and tender.
9. Remove duckling to a serving
dish and keep hot.
10. Strain apples and leeks,
reserving liquid, and arrange
them around duckling.
11. Skim fat from reserved liquid,
then serve separately as a sauce
with the duckling.

DUCKLING WITH SWEET
AND SOUR CHERRIES
Serves 4

Select red cherries if available
and prepare them, according to
the recipe, one or two days
before making the casserole.

Sweet and Sour Cherries

1lb (½ kilo) red cherries
6oz (150gm) granulated sugar
¼ pint (125ml) wine vinegar
4 whole cloves
pinch of cinnamon

1. Select cherries in perfect
condition. Rinse in cold water,
pat dry on kitchen paper and
place in a bowl.
2. Place sugar, vinegar, cloves

and cinnamon in a pan. Stir over
gentle heat until sugar has
dissolved, then bring to the boil.
3. Pour over cherries, so that
they are completely covered.
Allow to cool.
4. Cover closely and leave to
stand for 2–3 days.

Duckling

1 oven-ready duckling (about
4lb or 2 kilo), cut into 4 joints
1oz (25gm) flour
salt and pepper
1oz (25gm) butter
1 medium onion, peeled and
chopped
1 pint (approximately ½ litre)
stock made from giblets
2 teaspoons soy sauce
¼ level teaspoon ground
cinnamon

1. Preheat oven to very moderate,
325 deg F or gas 3 (170 deg C).
2. Toss duckling joints in flour
seasoned with salt and pepper.
3. Melt butter in a large frying
pan and fry duckling joints until
golden brown all over. Drain
well over pan and transfer to a
casserole.
4. Add onion to fat remaining in
the pan and cook gently for 2–3
minutes, or until tender.
5. Sprinkle in any remaining
flour and stir over gentle heat for
1 minute.
6. Remove pan from heat and
gradually blend in stock and soy
sauce. Add cinnamon.
7. Return to heat, bring to the
boil and simmer for 2 minutes,
stirring continuously. Pour over
duckling in casserole.
8. Cover closely with lid or foil
and cook in centre of oven for
1½–2 hours, or until duckling is
tender.
9. Skim fat from surface then stir
in prepared cherries and return
to oven. Cook, uncovered, for a
further 10 minutes, or until
heated through.

DUCKLING MONTE CRISTO
Serves 4

1 oven-ready duckling (about
4lb or 2 kilo), cut into 4 joints
1oz (25gm) flour
salt
freshly ground black pepper
½oz (12gm) butter
1 tablespoon oil
4 bacon rashers, trimmed and
chopped
1 large onion, peeled and
chopped
4oz (100gm) mushrooms,
washed, trimmed and chopped
¼ pint (125ml) dry white wine
¼ pint (125ml) stock made from
giblets
1 small can (5oz or 125gm)
orange juice
bouquet garni
1 can (3½oz or 87gm)
pimentos, drained and cut
into strips
1 tablespoon finely chopped
parsley

1. Preheat oven to moderate,
350 deg F or gas 4 (180 deg C).
2. Toss duckling joints in flour
seasoned with salt and pepper.
3. Heat butter and oil in a
flameproof casserole and fry
duckling joints until golden
brown all over. Drain well over
casserole and keep on one side.
4. Add bacon and onion to fat
remaining in the casserole and
fry gently together for 3–4
minutes. Stir in mushrooms and
continue cooking for 2 minutes.
5. Return duckling to casserole,
sprinkle in any remaining
flour and stir over gentle heat for
1 minute.
6. Remove casserole from heat,
gradually stir in wine, stock and
orange juice, and add bouquet
garni and pimentos.
7. Return to heat, bring to the
boil and simmer for 2 minutes,
stirring continuously.
8. Cover closely with lid or foil
and cook in centre of oven for
about 1½ hours, or until duckling
is tender.
9. Transfer duckling to a serving
dish. Skim fat from sauce,
remove bouquet garni, then pour
sauce over duckling.
10. Sprinkle with parsley before
serving.

SICILIAN CASSEROLE
Serves 4

Green olives stuffed with
pimento add their flavour to this
dish.

1oz (25gm) butter
1 oven-ready duckling (about
4lb or 2 kilo), cut into 4 joints
1 onion, peeled and sliced
1 glass Marsala wine
1 teaspoon mild paprika
pepper
½ pint (250ml) stock made from
giblets
bouquet garni
salt and pepper
12 olives stuffed with pimento
1 level tablespoon flour
2 tomatoes, peeled, cut into
strips and de-seeded

1. Preheat oven to moderate,
350 deg F or gas 4 (180 deg C).
2. Melt butter in a flameproof
casserole and fry duckling
portions until golden brown all
over.
3. Drain off fat, add onion to
duckling, cover casserole and
cook gently until onion is soft.
4. Remove cover, pour in
Marsala wine and heat gently
until reduced by half.
5. Stir in paprika pepper and
cook for 2–3 minutes.
6. Add stock, bouquet garni and
salt and pepper.
7. Cover closely with lid or foil
and cook in centre of oven for
1½ hours, or until duckling is
tender.
8. Blanch olives in boiling water
for 5 minutes, drain well, then
leave in cold water.
9. Transfer duckling to a serving
dish and keep hot. Remove
bouquet garni.
10. Skim fat from liquid in the
casserole. Blend flour with
1 tablespoon of the liquid.
Return this to the casserole and
stir over gentle heat on top of
cooker until it comes to the boil.
Simmer for 3–4 minutes.
11. Add tomatoes and drained
olives, reheat and adjust
seasoning.
12. Spoon sauce over duckling
on the serving dish.

NORMANDY DUCKLING
Serves 4

1 oven-ready duckling (about
4lb or 2 kilo), cut into 4 joints
1 onion, peeled
1 carrot, peeled
6 peppercorns
bouquet garni
salt and pepper
1oz (25gm) butter
1 tablespoon oil
1lb (½ kilo) cooking apples,
peeled, cored and sliced
1 tablespoon brandy
2–3 tablespoons double cream

1. Rinse duckling giblets, then
place in a pan with cold water to
cover. Add onion, carrot,
peppercorns, bouquet garni, salt
and pepper. Simmer gently for
1 hour. Strain and reserve stock.
2. Preheat oven to moderate, 350
deg F or gas 4 (180 deg C).
3. Heat butter and oil in a large
frying pan and fry duckling
joints until golden brown all
over. Drain well over pan and
transfer to a casserole.
4. Add apples to fat remaining
in the pan and fry lightly for
3–4 minutes. Drain off fat, then
add to casserole.
5. Add ½ pint (250ml) prepared
stock to the casserole.
6. Cover closely with lid or foil
and cook in centre of oven for
about 1½ hours, or until duckling
is tender.
7. Transfer duckling portions to a
serving dish and keep warm.
8. Skim fat from liquor in
casserole.
9. Warm the brandy in a pan over
gentle heat, flame, then add to
juices in the casserole,
together with the cream.
10. Stir well together, heat gently
but do not boil, then pour over
the duckling.

Game

Casseroling is an excellent way of cooking game, as it brings out the fullest flavour. If you use older birds many of these recipes can be quite economical.

HIGHLAND PHEASANT
Serves 4

1 pheasant, plucked and drawn
1oz (25gm) flour
salt and pepper
2oz (50gm) butter
2 small onions, peeled and
finely chopped
1 garlic clove, peeled and
crushed
2 large cooking apples, peeled,
cored and sliced
2 sticks celery, washed,
trimmed and chopped
¾ pint (375ml) chicken stock
1 dessertspoon whisky
1 bayleaf
2–3 tablespoons cream

1. Preheat oven to moderate,
350 deg F or gas 5 (190 deg C).
2. Sprinkle pheasant with flour
seasoned with salt and pepper.
3. Melt butter in a flameproof
casserole and fry pheasant until
golden brown all over. Drain well
and keep on one side.
4. Add onions and garlic to fat
remaining in the casserole and
cook gently for 2–3 minutes.
5. Add apples and celery and
continue cooking for 3–4 minutes.
6. Sprinkle in any remaining
flour and stir over gentle heat
for 1 minute.
7. Remove casserole from heat
and gradually blend in stock and
whisky.
8. Return to heat, bring to the
boil and simmer for 2 minutes,
stirring continuously. Season to
taste with salt and pepper.
9. Return pheasant to casserole
and add bayleaf.
10. Cover closely with lid or foil
and cook in centre of oven for
about 1–1¼ hours, or until
pheasant is tender.
11. Stir in cream and check
seasoning just before serving.

DALESIDE PHEASANT
Serves 4

Pheasant with celery and a rich
cream sauce.

1oz (25gm) butter
1 tablespoon oil
1 pheasant, plucked and drawn
2 bacon rashers, cut into small
pieces
½ pint (250ml) stock
1 dessertspoon finely chopped
parsley
pinch of thyme
1 bayleaf
1 small glass of port
salt and pepper
1 head celery, cleaned and cut
into 1-inch pieces
1 egg yolk
½ pint (250ml) cream
watercress and potato crisps
to garnish

1. Preheat oven to moderate,
350 deg F or gas 4 (180 deg C).
2. Heat butter and oil in a
flameproof casserole and fry
pheasant until golden brown.
3. Add bacon, stock, parsley,
thyme, bayleaf and port. Season
well with salt and pepper.
4. Cover closely with lid or foil
and cook in centre of oven for
30 minutes.
5. Add celery and continue
cooking for a further 35–40
minutes, or until pheasant is
tender.
6. Transfer pheasant and celery
to a serving dish, draining well
over pan, and keep hot.
7. Beat egg yolk with cream and
very gradually blend it into the
hot stock in the casserole. Heat
gently, taking care not to let it
boil. Remove bayleaf.
8. Pour sauce over the prepared
pheasant and garnish with
watercress and potato crisps.

PHEASANT WITH CHESTNUTS
Serves 4

1oz (25gm) butter
1 tablespoon oil
1 pheasant, plucked, drawn
and jointed
6oz (150gm) chestnuts, weighed
when peeled
2 medium onions, peeled and
sliced
3 level tablespoons flour
½ pint (250ml) chicken stock
¼ pint (125ml) orange juice
¼ pint (125ml) dry white wine
bouquet garni
salt and pepper
chopped parsley
watercress
few slices fresh orange

1. Preheat oven to moderate,
350 deg F or gas 4 (180 deg C).
2. Heat butter and oil in a pan
and fry pheasant joints until
golden brown all over. Drain over
pan and transfer to a casserole.
3. Add chestnuts and onions
to fat remaining in the pan and
fry gently until lightly browned.
Transfer to casserole.
4. Sprinkle flour into fat
remaining in the pan and stir
over gentle heat for 1 minute.
5. Remove pan from heat and
gradually blend in stock, orange
juice and white wine.
6. Return to heat, bring to the
boil and simmer gently for
2 minutes, stirring continuously.
7. Add bouquet garni, season well
with salt and pepper and pour
over pheasant in casserole.
8. Cover closely with lid or foil
and cook in centre of oven for
about 1 hour, or until pheasant is
tender.
9. Serve sprinkled with parsley
and garnished with watercress
and orange slices.

CASSEROLE OF PHEASANT
(Illustrated on page 53)
Serves 4

Pheasant cooked in red wine
sauce with mushrooms.

1oz (25gm) butter
1 tablespoon oil
1 pheasant, plucked, drawn
and jointed
6oz (150gm) button onions,
peeled
3 level tablespoons flour
¾ pint (375ml) chicken stock
1 wine glass red wine
bouquet garni
finely grated rind and juice of
half an orange
salt and pepper
4oz (100gm) button mushrooms,
washed and sliced
1 dessertspoon redcurrant jelly
small triangles of fried bread
to garnish
chopped parsley

1. Preheat oven to moderate,
350 deg F or gas 4 (180 deg C).
2. Heat butter and oil in a frying
pan and fry pheasant joints until
golden brown all over. Drain well
over pan and transfer to a
casserole.
3. Place onions in fat remaining
in the pan and fry until lightly
browned, then transfer with a
draining spoon to casserole.
4. Sprinkle flour into fat
remaining in the pan and stir
over gentle heat for 1 minute.
5. Remove pan from heat and
gradually blend in stock and wine.
6. Return to heat, bring to the
boil and simmer for 2 minutes,
stirring continuously.
7. Add bouquet garni, orange
rind and juice and season well
with salt and pepper. Pour into
casserole.
8. Cover closely with lid or foil
and cook in centre of oven for
about 1 hour.
9. Stir in mushrooms and
redcurrant jelly and continue
cooking for a further 30 minutes,
or until pheasant is tender.
10. Garnish with triangles of
fried bread and sprinkle with
parsley.
11. Serve with redcurrant jelly,
if liked.

PARTRIDGE WITH CABBAGE
Serves 4

This is a classic style of cooking
partridge and an ideal way of
using older birds.

1 hard green cabbage (about
2lb or 1 kilo), washed and
trimmed
salt
freshly ground black pepper
4 streaky bacon rashers,
trimmed
1oz (25gm) bacon fat or
dripping
2 partridges, plucked, drawn
and trussed
2 carrots, peeled and chopped
1 onion, peeled and stuck with
2 cloves
bouquet garni
1 pint (approximately ½ litre)
chicken stock

1. Preheat oven to very moderate,
325 deg F or gas 3 (170 deg C).
2. Cut cabbage in four and cut
away hard stalk.
3. Cook in boiling salted water
for 5 minutes, then drain well
and season with salt and pepper.
4. Line the base of a casserole
with bacon rashers, then arrange
about a third of the cooked
cabbage on top.
5. Melt bacon fat or dripping
in a pan and fry partridges until
golden brown all over.
6. Drain well and arrange on
top of cabbage in casserole. Add
carrots, onion and bouquet garni.
7. Arrange remaining cabbage on
top and cover with stock.
8. Cover closely with lid or foil
and cook in centre of oven for
1–1½ hours, or until partridges
are tender.
9. Remove partridges from
casserole and cut into neat
joints. Drain cabbage and reserve
liquor. Remove and discard onion
and bouquet garni.
10. Chop cabbage and place on a
warm serving dish and arrange
partridges on top. If liked, the
strained juices may be thickened
with 1 dessertspoon arrowroot
blended with 1 tablespoon stock
and served as sauce.

TYROLEAN CASSEROLE
Serves 4

2 partridges, plucked, drawn
and trussed
salt and pepper
juice of half a lemon
2oz (50gm) butter
1 small red cabbage
1 onion, peeled and sliced
½ pint (250ml) cider
1 teaspoon sugar
1 dessertspoon vinegar
2 streaky bacon rashers

1. Preheat oven to moderate,
350 deg F or gas 4 (180 deg C).
2. Season partridges inside with
salt and pepper and sprinkle
with lemon juice.
3. Melt butter in a flameproof
casserole and fry partridges
until golden brown all over.
4. Drain well over casserole and
keep on one side.
5. Discard outer leaves and hard
stalk of cabbage, shred remainder
finely, then place in casserole.
6. Add onion, cider, sugar and
vinegar and season well with
salt and pepper.
7. Cover closely with lid or foil
and cook in centre of oven for
30 minutes.
8. Wrap each partridge in a
bacon rasher and place on top of
prepared cabbage. Return to
oven and cook, covered, for a
further 1–1½ hours, or until
partridges are tender.

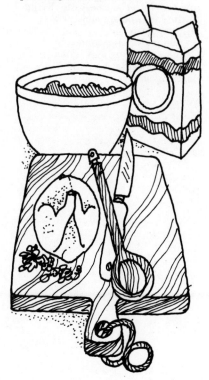

PARTRIDGES ALGARVE
Serves 4

2 tablespoons oil
2 partridges, plucked, drawn
and trussed
1 glass dry white wine
¼ pint (125ml) chicken stock
1 garlic clove, peeled
bouquet garni
salt
freshly ground black pepper
1 teaspoon arrowroot
1 tablespoon water
½ ripe melon, peeled, de-seeded
and cut into cubes
2 tomatoes, peeled, de-seeded
and cut into small pieces

1. Preheat oven to moderate,
350 deg F or gas 4 (180 deg C).
2. Heat oil in a flameproof
casserole and fry partridges
until golden brown all over.
3. Add wine and allow to boil
until reduced by half.
4. Add stock, garlic and bouquet
garni. Season well with salt and
pepper.
5. Cover closely with lid or foil
and cook in centre of oven for
about 1–1¼ hours, or until
partridges are tender.
6. Remove partridges from pan,
cut in half and trim back bones.
Arrange on a serving dish and
keep hot.
7. Discard garlic clove and
bouquet garni.
8. Blend arrowroot with water
and stir into the casserole. Bring
to the boil and simmer for 2
minutes, stirring.
9. Add melon and tomatoes.
Check seasoning and reheat if
necessary before pouring over
partridges.

LAIRD'S CASSEROLE
Serves 4

2 grouse, plucked and drawn
½ pint (250ml) red wine
2 tablespoons olive oil
1 onion, peeled and chopped
6 juniper berries, crushed
bouquet garni
1oz (25gm) butter
1lb (½ kilo) mixed vegetables
(onions, carrots, celery,
peeled and sliced)
1oz (25gm) flour
¼ pint (125ml) stock
1 tablespoon tomato purée
salt and pepper
3–4 glacé cherries
few sprigs of parsley

1. Place grouse in a bowl.
2. Pour wine into a pan and add
the oil, onion, juniper berries and
bouquet garni. Bring to the boil,
then remove from heat and allow
to cool.
3. Pour over the grouse and leave
to stand in a cool place for 2–3
hours.
4. Preheat oven to cool, 275 deg F
or gas 1 (140 deg C).
5. Drain grouse well, reserving
marinade.
6. Melt butter in a frying pan
and fry the birds, one at a time,
until golden brown all over.
Drain well over pan and transfer
to a casserole.
7. Add vegetables to butter
remaining in the pan and fry
gently for 4–5 minutes.
8. Sprinkle in the flour and stir
over gentle heat for 1 minute.
9. Remove pan from heat and
gradually blend in strained
marinade, stock and tomato
purée.
10. Return to heat, bring to the
boil and simmer for 2 minutes,
stirring continuously. Season to
taste with salt and pepper and
pour into the casserole.
11. Cover closely with lid or foil
and cook in centre of oven for
3–4 hours, or until grouse are
tender.
12. Transfer to a serving dish
and decorate with halved glacé
cherries and sprigs of parsley.

PIGEON IN A POT
Serves 4

2 pigeons, halved
1oz (25gm) flour
salt and pepper
½oz (12gm) butter
1 small onion, peeled and sliced
1 small apple, peeled, cored and
sliced
½ pint (250ml) chicken stock
½ pint (250ml) cider
bouquet garni
finely chopped parsley
2 bacon rashers, crisply fried
and crumbled

1. Preheat oven to very moderate,
325 deg F or gas 3 (170 deg C).
2. Toss pigeon joints in flour
seasoned with salt and pepper.
3. Melt butter in a frying pan
and fry pigeon joints until golden
brown all over. Drain well over
pan and transfer to a casserole.
4. Add onion and apple to fat
remaining in the pan and cook
gently for 2–3 minutes, or until
lightly browned.
5. Sprinkle in any remaining
flour and stir over gentle heat for
1 minute.
6. Remove pan from heat and
gradually blend in stock and
cider.
7. Return to heat, bring to the
boil and simmer gently for 2–3
minutes, stirring continuously.
8. Add bouquet garni to casserole
and pour prepared sauce over.
9. Cover closely with lid or foil
and cook in centre of oven for
about 2 hours, or until pigeons
are tender.
10. Serve sprinkled with parsley
and crumbled bacon rashers.

PIGEONS IN RED WINE
Serves 4

6oz (150gm) belly of pork
2oz (50gm) butter
4 pigeons, preferably larded
1 large carrot, peeled and
chopped
1 large onion, peeled and
chopped
1 stick celery, washed and
chopped
1 garlic clove, peeled and
crushed
1oz (25gm) flour
½ pint (250ml) red wine
½ pint (250ml) chicken stock
salt and pepper
pinch of powdered ginger
pinch of powdered mace
8oz (200gm) button mushrooms
3 lumps sugar
1 tablespoon wine vinegar

1. Preheat oven to moderate,
350 deg F or gas 4 (180 deg C).
2. Discard skin and bones
from pork, then cut meat into
small strips, about ¼ inch wide.
3. Melt butter in a pan and fry
pigeons until golden brown all
over. Drain well over pan and
transfer to a casserole, breast side
down.
4. Add pork, carrot, onion,
celery and garlic to fat
remaining in the pan and cook
very gently for about 5 minutes.
Transfer with a draining spoon
to casserole.
5. Sprinkle flour into fat
remaining in pan and stir over
gentle heat for 1 minute.
6. Remove pan from heat and
gradually blend in red wine and
stock.
7. Return to heat, bring to the
boil and simmer for 2 minutes,
stirring continuously.
8. Season with salt and pepper,
stir in ginger and mace, then pour
over ingredients in casserole.
9. Cover closely with lid or foil
and cook in centre of oven for
about 45 minutes.
10. Add mushrooms, sugar and
vinegar and continue cooking
for a further 50 minutes, or until
pigeons are tender.

PIGEONS WITH CHERRIES
Serves 4

1½oz (37gm) margarine
2 pigeons, plucked and drawn
2 small onions, peeled and
sliced
1oz (25gm) flour
1¼ pints (¾ litre) chicken stock
bouquet garni
1 tablespoon soured cream
1 can (15oz or 425gm) stoneless,
red cherries, drained

1. Preheat oven to very moderate,
325 deg F or gas 3 (170 deg C).
2. Melt 1oz (25gm) margarine in
a flameproof casserole and fry
pigeons until brown all over.
Drain well over casserole and
keep on one side.
3. Fry onions in fat remaining
in the casserole for 3–4 minutes,
or until tender.
4. Split pigeons in half and trim
back bone. Return them to the
casserole, sprinkle with flour
and cook over gentle heat for
1 minute.
5. Remove casserole from heat
and gradually blend in stock.
6. Return to heat, bring to the
boil and simmer for 2 minutes,
stirring continuously. Add
bouquet garni.
7. Cover with lid or foil and cook
in centre of oven for about 2
hours, or until pigeons are
tender.
8. Remove pigeons and keep
warm.
9. Reduce sauce to a syrupy
consistency by boiling. Strain,
blend in soured cream, replace
pigeons in sauce and reheat.
10. Melt remaining margarine
in a small saucepan and fry
cherries until heated through.
11. Place pigeons on a serving
dish, pour sauce over and scatter
hot cherries over the top.

COUNTRY DUMPLING CASSEROLE
Serves 4

A simple casserole of rabbit
topped with herby dumplings.

1 rabbit (about 2lb or 1 kilo),
cut into joints
1oz (25gm) flour
salt and pepper
1oz (25gm) dripping or lard
8oz (200gm) parsnips, peeled
and diced
8oz (200gm) carrots, peeled and
diced
1 medium onion, peeled and
chopped
1 pint (approximately ½ litre)
chicken stock
4oz (100gm) self-raising flour
1½oz (37gm) shredded suet
½ level teaspoon mixed dried
herbs

1. Preheat oven to moderate,
350 deg F or gas 4 (180 deg C).
2. Toss rabbit joints in flour
seasoned with salt and pepper.
3. Melt dripping or lard in a pan
and fry rabbit joints until brown
all over. Drain well over pan and
transfer to a casserole.
4. Add vegetables to casserole
together with stock.
5. Cover closely with lid or foil
and cook in centre of oven for
about 1–1¼ hours.
6. Meanwhile, prepare dumplings.
Mix remaining ingredients in a
bowl, season with ½ teaspoon
salt and bind to a soft but not
sticky dough with water.
7. Knead dough on a lightly
floured board and divide into
eight pieces. Form into small
balls with floured hands.
8. Remove cover from casserole,
adjust seasoning if necessary and
add dumplings.
9. Replace cover and continue
cooking for a further 20–30
minutes, or until dumplings are
well risen and cooked through.
Remove cover, if liked, for the
last 10 minutes to brown
dumplings.

COTTAGE CASSEROLE
(Illustrated on page 54)
Serves 4–6

1 rabbit (about 3lb or 1½ kilo),
cut into joints
1½oz (37gm) flour
salt
freshly ground black pepper
2oz (50gm) dripping
1 large leek, washed and sliced
2 teaspoons yeast extract
1 pint (approximately ½ litre)
chicken stock or water
2 carrots, peeled and sliced
1 stick celery, cleaned and
chopped
1 bayleaf
2 tablespoons tomato ketchup
dash of Worcestershire sauce
chopped parsley to garnish

1. Preheat oven to moderate,
350 deg F or gas 4 (180 deg C).
2. Toss rabbit joints in flour
seasoned with salt and pepper.
3. Melt dripping in a pan and
fry rabbit joints until golden
brown all over. Transfer to a
casserole using a draining spoon.
4. Add leek to fat remaining in
the pan and fry gently for 2–3
minutes.
5. Sprinkle in any remaining flour
and stir over gentle heat for 1
minute.
6. Remove pan from heat. Stir in
yeast extract, then gradually
blend in stock or water.
7. Return to heat, bring to the
boil and simmer for 2 minutes,
stirring continuously.
8. Add carrots, celery, bayleaf,
tomato ketchup and
Worcestershire sauce. Stir well
together, then pour over rabbit
in casserole.
9. Cover closely with lid or foil
and cook in centre of oven for
about 2 hours, or until rabbit is
tender.
10. Remove bayleaf and sprinkle
with parsley before serving.

NORFOLK RABBIT
Serves 4–6

An unusual combination of
cheese sauce and rabbit.

1 rabbit (about 3lb or 1½ kilo),
cut into joints
1lb (½ kilo) carrots, peeled and
sliced
1lb (½ kilo) onions, peeled and
sliced
2 pints (approximately 1 litre)
water
salt and pepper
1½oz (37gm) butter or
margarine
1½oz (37gm) flour
½ pint (250ml) stock from the
cooked rabbit (see method)
¼ pint (125ml) milk
½ level teaspoon made mustard
4oz (100gm) Cheddar cheese,
grated

1. Preheat oven to very moderate,
325 deg F or gas 3 (170 deg C).
2. Place rabbit joints in a
flameproof casserole with carrots,
onions and water. Season well
with salt and pepper and bring
to the boil.
3. Cover closely with lid or foil
and cook in centre of oven for
about 1½ hours, or until rabbit is
tender. Strain rabbit well,
reserving stock.
4. Increase oven temperature to
moderate to moderately hot,
375 deg F or gas 5 (190 deg C).
5. Melt butter or margarine in a
pan, sprinkle in flour and stir
over gentle heat for 1 minute.
6. Remove pan from heat and
gradually blend in ½ pint (250ml)
rabbit stock and the milk.
7. Return to heat, bring to the
boil and simmer for 3 minutes,
stirring continuously.
8. Remove pan from heat and beat
in mustard, cheese and salt and
pepper to taste.
9. Return to heat, bring to the
boil and simmer gently until
cheese melts.
10. Pour this sauce over rabbit
in the casserole and cook,
uncovered, in centre of oven for
20–30 minutes, or until top is
golden brown.

HUNTERS' RABBIT
Serves 6

Wine and mushrooms add interest
to this French country recipe.

1oz (25gm) butter
2 tablespoons oil
1 rabbit (about 3lb or 1½ kilo),
cut into joints
2–3 shallots, peeled and
chopped
1½oz (37gm) flour
½ pint (250ml) dry white wine
¼ pint (125ml) chicken stock
¼ pint (125ml) tomato juice
salt and pepper
1 bayleaf
4oz (100gm) button mushrooms

1. Preheat oven to moderate,
350 deg F or gas 4 (180 deg C).
2. Heat butter and oil in a
flameproof casserole and fry
rabbit joints until browned all
over.
3. Add shallots and fry gently
for 2–3 minutes, or until tender.
4. Sprinkle in flour and stir over
gentle heat for 1 minute.
5. Remove casserole from heat
and blend in wine and stock.
Stir in tomato juice and season
to taste with salt and pepper.
Add bayleaf.
6. Return to heat, bring to the
boil and simmer for 2 minutes,
stirring continuously.
7. Cover closely with lid or foil
and cook in centre of oven for
1½–2 hours, or until rabbit is
tender, adding mushrooms 30
minutes before the end of cooking
time.

RABBIT IN TARRAGON MUSTARD SAUCE
Serves 4–6

1 rabbit (about 3lb or 1½ kilo),
cut into joints
2 pints (approximately 1 litre)
water
1 dessertspoon vinegar
3 tablespoons French mustard
1oz (25gm) flour
3 tablespoons oil
1 large onion, peeled and
chopped
1 garlic clove, peeled and
crushed
1 pint (approximately ½ litre)
chicken stock
¼–½ level teaspoon dried
tarragon
2 tablespoons cream or top of
the milk

1. Soak rabbit joints overnight
in water and vinegar. Discard
liquid and wash and dry rabbit.
2. Preheat oven to moderate,
350 deg F or gas 4 (180 deg C).
3. Spread rabbit joints with
mustard and coat in flour.
4. Heat oil in a large pan and fry
rabbit until golden brown all
over. Drain well over pan and
transfer to a casserole.
5. Fry onion and garlic in fat
remaining in pan for 2–3 minutes.
6. Sprinkle in any remaining
flour and stir over gentle heat
for 1 minute.
7. Remove pan from heat and
gradually blend in stock.
8. Return to heat, bring to the
boil and simmer for 2 minutes,
stirring continuously.
9. Stir in tarragon, season with
salt and pepper to taste and pour
into casserole.
10. Cover closely with lid or foil
and cook in centre of oven for
about 1½ hours, or until rabbit is
tender.
11. Stir in cream or top of the
milk before serving.

TUCKER BAG CASSEROLE
Serves 4–6

1 packet (8oz or 200gm) mixed
dried fruit (apples, prunes,
apricots, etc.)
1 rabbit (about 3lb or 1½ kilo),
cut into joints
1 large onion, peeled and sliced
1 bayleaf
½ pint (250ml) dry cider
½ pint (250ml) chicken stock
2 tablespoons redcurrant jelly
salt
freshly ground black pepper
1oz (25gm) cornflour
2 tablespoons cider vinegar
1 tablespoon finely chopped
parsley

1. Soak dried fruit overnight in
cold water to cover.
2. Place rabbit joints in a bowl
and add onion, bayleaf and cider.
Leave to soak overnight.
3. Preheat oven to very moderate,
325 deg F or gas 3 (170 deg C).
4. Discard onion and place
rabbit joints, bayleaf and cider
in a flameproof casserole,
together with stock and
redcurrant jelly. Season with
salt and pepper and bring to the
boil.
5. Drain dried fruits. Leave
prunes whole, cut remainder into
small pieces and add to casserole.
6. Cover with lid or foil and cook
in centre of oven for about 1½
hours, or until rabbit is tender.
7. Transfer rabbit with a draining
spoon to a serving dish and keep
hot.
8. Blend cornflour with vinegar
and a little of the hot stock, then
stir into casserole on top of
cooker. Bring to the boil and
simmer for 2 minutes, stirring
continuously.
9. Pour prepared sauce over
rabbit and serve sprinkled with
chopped parsley.

CURRIED RABBIT
Serves 4

1 rabbit (about 2lb or 1 kilo),
cut into joints
2oz (50gm) flour
salt and pepper
2oz (50gm) butter or margarine
1 large onion, peeled and
chopped
1 cooking apple, peeled, cored
and chopped
2 level tablespoons curry
powder
1 teaspoon curry paste
1½ pints (approximately ¾ litre)
chicken stock
1 tablespoon redcurrant jelly
1 tablespoon mango chutney,
chopped
2oz (50gm) sultanas
juice of half a lemon
1 bayleaf

1. Preheat oven to very moderate,
325 deg F or gas 3 (170 deg C).
2. Toss rabbit joints in flour
seasoned with salt and pepper.
3. Melt butter or margarine in a
flameproof casserole and fry
rabbit joints until golden
brown all over. Drain well over
pan and keep on one side.
4. Add onion and apple to fat
remaining in the casserole and
cook for 4–5 minutes, or until
tender.
5. Sprinkle in any remaining
flour and add curry powder and
curry paste. Stir over gentle heat
for 1 minute.
6. Remove casserole from heat
and gradually blend in stock.
7. Return to heat, bring to the
boil and simmer for 2 minutes,
stirring continuously.
8. Stir in redcurrant jelly,
chutney, sultanas and lemon
juice and season to taste with
salt and pepper.
9. Return rabbit to casserole and
add bayleaf.
10. Cover with lid or foil and
cook in centre of oven for about
1½ hours, or until rabbit is tender.
Remove bayleaf.
11. Serve with freshly boiled rice
and separate dishes of desiccated
coconut, sliced tomatoes, mango
chutney and thinly sliced
cucumber.

MINSTER CASSEROLE
Serves 4

1 hare, jointed
1oz (25gm) flour
salt and pepper
2oz (50gm) butter
2 medium onions, peeled and
sliced
4oz (100gm) ham, diced
4oz (100gm) mushrooms,
washed, trimmed and cut into
quarters
1 garlic clove, peeled and
crushed
2 sticks celery, washed,
trimmed and sliced
2 carrots, peeled and sliced
½ level teaspoon dried thyme
1 bayleaf
1 pint (approximately ½ litre)
chicken stock
1 tablespoon finely chopped
parsley

1. Preheat oven to very moderate,
325 deg F or gas 3 (170 deg C).
2. Toss hare joints in flour
seasoned with salt and pepper.
3. Melt butter in a flameproof
casserole and fry hare gently with
onions until lightly browned.
4. Add all remaining ingredients
except parsley, and stir well
together.
5. Cover closely with lid or foil
and cook in centre of oven for
2½–3 hours, or until hare is
tender.
6. Add more seasoning if
necessary and serve sprinkled
with finely chopped parsley.

FLEMISH CASSEROLE
Serves 4–6

1 hare, jointed
½ pint (250ml) light ale
1 garlic clove, peeled and
crushed
1 bouquet garni
3 large onions, peeled and
sliced
¼ level teaspoon grated nutmeg
1oz (25gm) flour
salt and pepper
1oz (25gm) dripping or lard
½ pint (250ml) chicken stock
1 level tablespoon made
mustard
1 teaspoon wine vinegar
1 carrot, peeled and coarsely
grated
4 potatoes, boiled and sliced
a little extra dripping

1. Place hare in a large bowl
and add light ale, garlic, bouquet
garni, onions and nutmeg. Cover
and leave in refrigerator or cool
place overnight.
2. Preheat oven to very moderate,
325 deg F or gas 3 (170 deg C).
3. Remove hare joints from bowl,
reserving marinade, and wipe
dry on absorbent kitchen paper.
4. Toss in flour seasoned with
salt and pepper.
5. Heat dripping or lard in a
flameproof casserole and fry
hare gently until lightly browned.
6. Remove casserole from heat
and gradually pour in stock,
mustard, vinegar and reserved
marinade.
7. Remove bouquet garni. Return
casserole to heat, bring to the
boil and simmer for 2 minutes,
stirring continuously.
8. Stir in grated carrot.
9. Cover closely with lid or foil
and cook in centre of oven for
about 2 hours.
10. Cover with slices of potato,
dot with dripping and continue
cooking, uncovered, for a further
30 minutes, or until potatoes are
browned.

JUGGED HARE
Serves 6

It is difficult to better this
traditional method of cooking
hare.

1oz (25gm) dripping
1 hare (ask the butcher to skin
and joint the hare, reserving
the blood)
1 bacon rasher, cut into small
pieces
1½ pints (approximately ¾ litre)
stock
1½oz (37gm) flour
1 onion, peeled and stuck with
2 cloves
salt and pepper
bouquet garni
6 peppercorns
small blade of mace
juice of half a lemon
1 tablespoon redcurrant jelly
1 glass port

1. Preheat oven to very moderate,
325 deg F or gas 3 (170 deg C).
2. Melt dripping in a flameproof
casserole and fry hare joints
together with bacon until lightly
browned.
3. Add stock and stir in flour
blended to a cream with a little
water.
4. Add onion, salt, pepper,
bouquet garni, peppercorns,
mace and lemon juice.
5. Cover closely with lid or foil
and cook in centre of oven for
about 3 hours, or until hare is
tender.
6. Remove onion and bouquet
garni and stir in strained blood,
redcurrant jelly and port. Reheat
without boiling and serve.

Fish

For a delicious meal in a hurry a fish casserole is often the answer, as it is fairly quick to prepare and does not require long, slow cooking.

SOUSED HERRINGS
Serves 4

4 herrings
salt
freshly ground black pepper
¼ pint (125ml) cider vinegar
¼ pint (125ml) water
½ teaspoon pickling spice
2 bayleaves
1 small onion, peeled and sliced

1. Preheat oven to moderate, 350 deg F or gas 4 (180 deg C).
2. Remove herring heads with scissors and discard.
3. Scrape each herring from tail to head with back of knife to remove scales. Slit fish along underside to tail and remove roe and blood vessels.
4. Open each fish out and place cut side down on board. Press firmly along centre backbone to flatten fish.
5. Turn over and remove backbone.
6. Trim tails and fins with scissors, then rinse and pat dry on kitchen paper.
7. Season with salt and pepper.
8. Roll each herring up from tail to head and place close together in a shallow casserole.
9. Pour vinegar and water over and sprinkle with pickling spice. Add bayleaves and onion.
10. Cover closely with lid or foil and cook in centre of oven for about 45 minutes, or until fish is cooked through.
11. Allow to cool in liquid in dish before serving.

WESTSIDE HERRINGS
(Illustrated on page 54)
Serves 4

4 large herrings
1 tablespoon made mustard
1 tablespoon tomato purée
good pinch of marjoram
salt
freshly ground black pepper
2 tablespoons cream
1 level teaspoon sugar
2 teaspoons finely grated onion
a little melted butter
¼ pint (125ml) cider
¼ pint (125ml) water
paprika pepper

1. Preheat oven to moderate, 350 deg F or gas 4 (180 deg C).
2. Scale, clean and bone herrings as for soused herrings (see previous recipe).
3. Blend together mustard, tomato purée, marjoram, salt, pepper, cream, sugar and onion.
4. Spread prepared mixture over herrings, roll up neatly and arrange in a shallow casserole.
5. Brush tops with butter.
6. Pour mixture of cider and water into dish.
7. Cover closely with lid or foil and cook in centre of oven for about 40 minutes, or until fish is cooked through.
8. Allow to cool in dish then drain well, sprinkle with a little paprika pepper and serve with salad.

HERRING HOTPOT
Serves 4

4 large herrings
salt and pepper
2½oz (62gm) butter
4 tomatoes, skinned and sliced
2 large Spanish onions, peeled and sliced
4 medium potatoes, peeled and thinly sliced
¼ teaspoon dried chervil or fennel

1. Preheat oven to hot, 425 deg F or gas 7 (220 deg C).
2. Scale, clean and bone herrings as for soused herrings (see this page). Season well with salt and pepper.
3. Grease a shallow casserole with ½oz (12gm) butter, then place herrings in the base.
4. Cover with a layer of tomatoes, then a layer of onions and then a layer of potatoes.
5. Season with salt and pepper, sprinkle with chervil or fennel and dot with 1oz (25gm) butter.
6. Cover with another layer of tomatoes, onions, and finally a layer of overlapping potatoes.
7. Season, sprinkle with chervil or fennel, and dot with remaining butter.
8. Cover closely with lid or foil and cook in centre of oven for 30–40 minutes.
9. Remove cover and cook for a further 10 minutes, or until fish is cooked through and potato topping is browned.

SOZZLED HERRINGS
Serves 4

Herrings cooked in brown ale.

4 large herrings
1 large onion, peeled and sliced
1 small can brown ale
2 bayleaves
2 level teaspoons sugar
½ level teaspoon salt

1. Preheat oven to cool, 300 deg F or gas 2 (150 deg C).
2. Scale, clean and bone herrings as for soused herrings (see previous page).
3. Roll up each herring neatly and arrange in a shallow casserole. Scatter onion over top.
4. Pour brown ale over, add bayleaves and sprinkle with sugar and salt.
5. Cover closely with lid or foil and cook in centre of oven for about 1 hour, or until fish is cooked through.
6. Cool, then drain off liquid.
7. Serve with mixed salad.

HERRINGS MARGARETA
Serves 4

4 large herrings
½oz (12gm) butter
salt and pepper
3 teaspoons made mustard
3 teaspoons tomato purée
4 tablespoons single cream

1. Preheat oven to moderate, 350 deg F or gas 4 (180 deg C).
2. Clean and fillet herrings.
3. Cut each fillet into two. Cut butter into eight. Place a dot of butter on each fillet and roll up with skin side outside.
4. Pack prepared herrings upright, closely together, in a shallow casserole. Season with salt and pepper.
5. Mix mustard, tomato purée and cream to a smooth sauce and pour over the fish.
6. Cover closely with lid or foil and cook in centre of oven for 30 minutes, or until fish is cooked through.

HERRING AND TOMATO CASSEROLE
Serves 4

4 herrings
salt and pepper
1 onion, peeled and finely chopped
1 bayleaf
1 large can (14oz or 397gm) peeled tomatoes
½oz (12gm) butter

1. Preheat oven to moderate to moderately hot, 375 deg F or gas 5 (190 deg C).
2. Scale, clean and bone herrings as for soused herrings (see previous page).
3. Sprinkle fish with salt and pepper, roll up neatly and arrange in a shallow casserole.
4. Scatter onion over fish, add bayleaf and pour tomatoes over. Dot top with butter.
5. Cook in centre of oven for about 30 minutes, or until fish is cooked through.
6. Serve with creamed potatoes and peas.

MACKEREL IN CIDER
Serves 4

A good way of ensuring moist and flavoursome mackerel.

4 whole mackerel
salt and pepper
1 small onion, peeled and sliced
½ pint (250ml) dry cider
1 bayleaf
1 lemon, cut into slices
2oz (50gm) butter
few sprigs of parsley

1. Preheat oven to moderate, 350 deg F or gas 4 (180 deg C).
2. Clean and wipe mackerel, leaving heads on. Trim tails and fins.
3. Lay fish in a shallow, ovenproof dish and season with salt and pepper.
4. Scatter onion over top of fish. Add cider, bayleaf and half the lemon slices. Dot top with butter.
5. Cover closely with lid or foil and cook in centre of oven for 35–45 minutes, or until fish is cooked through.
6. Remove bayleaf and lemon slices and carefully transfer fish to a serving dish. Garnish with remaining fresh lemon slices and parsley.

MACKEREL IN BARBECUE SAUCE
Serves 4

Herrings can also be cooked in this way.

2oz (50gm) butter
4 large mackerel
salt and pepper
1 onion, peeled and finely chopped
1 level teaspoon black treacle
2 level teaspoons made mustard
1 level teaspoon salt
1 level teaspoon paprika pepper
1 level teaspoon sugar
1 can (2¼oz or 56gm) tomato purée
¼ pint (250ml) water
1 tablespoon vinegar

1. Preheat oven to moderate, 350 deg F or gas 4 (180 deg C).
2. Grease a shallow casserole with ½oz (12gm) butter.
3. Remove heads, scale and clean mackerel, then arrange them in buttered casserole. Dot with ½oz (12gm) butter and season well with salt and pepper.
4. Cook in centre of oven for 15 minutes.
5. Melt remaining butter in a pan and lightly fry onion. Stir in remaining ingredients, blend well and bring to the boil.
6. Pour sauce over mackerel and return to oven and cook for a further 15 minutes, or until fish is cooked through.

SCOTTISH SUPPER
(Illustrated on page 54)
Serves 2–3

A quickly prepared supper dish –
add poached eggs for a more
substantial meal.

1 can (14oz or 397gm)
sweetcorn kernels
1lb (½ kilo) smoked, boneless
cod fillet
1oz (25gm) butter
salt and pepper
¼ pint (125ml) single cream
paprika pepper

1. Preheat oven to moderate,
350 deg F or gas 4 (180 deg C).
2. Drain sweetcorn. Skin fish if
necessary and cut into strips.
3. Arrange layers of sweetcorn
and fish in a casserole, dotting
with a little butter and
seasoning with salt and pepper
between each layer.
4. Pour cream over top.
5. Cook, uncovered, in centre of
oven for about 25–30 minutes, or
until fish is cooked through.
6. Sprinkle with paprika pepper
before serving.

JUNIOR HOTPOT
Serves 4

A recipe using fish and baked
beans to tempt the children.

1lb (½ kilo) cod fillet
salt and pepper
1½lb (¾ kilo) potatoes, peeled
1oz (25gm) butter
1 can (1lb or ½ kilo) baked beans
in tomato sauce
4oz (100gm) Cheddar cheese,
finely grated

1. Poach cod gently in water
seasoned with salt and pepper for
10–12 minutes, or until cooked.
2. Cook potatoes in boiling,
salted water until tender. Drain
thoroughly.
3. Preheat oven to moderate to
moderately hot, 400 deg F or gas 6
(200 deg C).
4. Flake drained, cooked fish,
discarding any skin and bones
and arrange in the base of a
shallow casserole. Season with a
little pepper and dot with ½oz
(12gm) butter.
5. Arrange baked beans over fish

and sprinkle with 2oz (50gm)
cheese.
6. Cut potatoes into slices and
arrange neatly to completely
cover top of casserole. Sprinkle
with remaining cheese and dot
with remaining butter.
7. Cook, uncovered, above centre
of oven for about 30 minutes,
or until heated through and
golden brown on top.

COD CREME GRATIN
Serves 4

1½lb (¾ kilo) cod
1 glass white wine
salt
3–4 black peppercorns
1oz (25gm) butter
1oz (25gm) flour
1½oz (37gm) Gruyère cheese,
finely grated
1 tablespoon cream
2oz (50gm) peeled prawns
1–2 teaspoons Tabasco sauce
2 tablespoons fresh white
breadcrumbs
2 tomatoes, thinly sliced

1. Poach cod gently for 10–12
minutes, or until cooked, in water
and wine seasoned with salt and
black peppercorns. Strain fish,
reserving liquor.
2. Preheat oven to hot, 425 deg F
or gas 7 (220 deg C).
3. Melt butter in a pan, sprinkle
in flour and stir over gentle heat
for 1 minute.
4. Remove pan from heat and
gradually blend in ½ pint (250ml)
liquor from cooked fish.
5. Return to heat, bring to the
boil and simmer for 2 minutes,
stirring continuously.
6. Remove from heat, beat in
cheese until it has melted into
the sauce, then add cream,
prawns and Tabasco sauce.
7. Divide fish into neat pieces
and arrange in a shallow
casserole.
8. Pour prepared sauce over,
sprinkle with breadcrumbs and
arrange slices of tomato around
edge.
9. Cook, uncovered, above centre
of oven for 10–15 minutes or until
top is browned.

COD PROVENÇAL
Serves 4

Black olives are traditional
to this dish and give a good
colour contrast but green ones
can be used if liked.

1½lb (¾ kilo) cod fillet
1oz (25gm) butter
2 tablespoons olive oil
2 onions, peeled and sliced
1 garlic clove, peeled, and
crushed
1 can (14oz or 397gm) peeled
tomatoes
1 bayleaf
salt and pepper
2oz (50gm) black olives
juice of half a lemon
chopped parsley

1. Preheat oven to moderate,
350 deg F or gas 4 (180 deg C).
2. Skin fish and cut into chunky
pieces.
3. Heat butter and oil in a pan
and fry onions and garlic for
2–3 minutes.
4. Add drained tomatoes, bayleaf
and salt and pepper to taste.
Cook gently for 5 minutes.
5. Place half the tomato mixture
in the base of a shallow casserole,
arrange fish on top and pour
remaining tomato mixture over.
6. Cover closely with lid or foil
and cook in centre of oven for
about 25 minutes, or until fish
is cooked through.
7. Stir in black olives and lemon
juice and sprinkle with parsley.

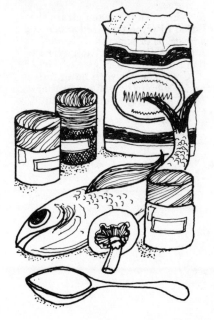

COD PANAMA
Serves 3–4

2oz (50gm) butter
1lb (½ kilo) cod fillet
salt and pepper
juice of 1 lemon
1oz (25gm) flour
¾ pint (375ml) milk and water mixed
2 cloves
pinch of mixed spice
few drops Tabasco sauce
4 tomatoes, peeled and chopped
little chopped parsley
1 can (4oz or 100gm) pimento, drained and cut into strips

1. Preheat oven to moderate, 350 deg F or gas 4 (180 deg C).
2. Grease a casserole with ½oz (12gm) butter. Arrange fish in the base, season with salt and pepper and sprinkle with lemon juice.
3. Dot with ½oz (12gm) butter, cover loosely with foil and cook in centre of oven for about 30 minutes.
4. Melt remaining butter in a pan, sprinkle in flour and stir over gentle heat for 1 minute.
5. Remove pan from heat and gradually blend in milk and water. Add cloves, mixed spice and Tabasco sauce.
6. Return to heat, bring to the boil and simmer for 2 minutes, sitrring continuously.
7. Add tomatoes and parsley and simmer gently for about 10 minutes.
8. When fish is cooked, drain the liquid into the prepared sauce and add strips of pimento. Mix well together, then pour back over the fish.
9. Cover closely with lid or foil and return to oven for a further 10–15 minutes, or until heated through.

COD PORTUGUESE
Serves 4

2oz (50gm) butter
8oz (200gm) boiled potatoes, cut into slices
1 onion, peeled and chopped
8oz (200gm) tomatoes, cut into slices
good pinch of lemon thyme
4 cod steaks, ½ inch thick
juice of half a lemon
salt and pepper
4 tablespoons cider
a little chopped parsley

1. Preheat oven to moderately hot, 400 deg F or gas 6 (200 deg C).
2. Grease a shallow, ovenproof dish with ½oz (12gm) butter.
3. Cover base of dish with sliced potatoes. Scatter chopped onion over top, then cover with sliced tomatoes. Sprinkle with lemon thyme.
4. Place cod on top of vegetables, sprinkle with lemon juice and season well with salt and pepper.
5. Pour cider over and dot top with remaining butter.
6. Cover closely with lid or foil and cook in centre of oven for 45–50 minutes, or until fish is cooked through.
7. Serve sprinkled with parsley.

FISH ANTONIO
Serves 4–6

1½–2lb (¾–1 kilo) cod or haddock in one piece
3 tablespoons oil
salt and pepper
1oz (25gm) butter
1 tablespoon finely chopped parsley
2 ripe bananas
2 tomatoes, peeled and chopped
1 tablespoon grated onion
1 level teaspoon sugar
12 pimento-stuffed olives, drained and sliced
1–2oz (25–50gm) cheese, finely grated
¼ pint (125ml) tomato juice
squeeze of lemon juice
dash of Worcestershire sauce

1. Preheat oven to moderate, 350 deg F or gas 4 (180 deg C).
2. Brush fish with oil and season with salt and pepper.
3. Grease a shallow casserole with ½oz (25gm) butter and place fish in the base. Sprinkle with chopped parsley and dot with remaining butter.
4. Cover closely with lid or foil and cook in centre of oven for 20 minutes.
5. Meanwhile, heat a little oil in a pan and fry bananas until lightly browned. Stir in tomatoes, onion, sugar and olives.
6. Spread prepared mixture over fish in casserole and sprinkle with grated cheese.
7. Season tomato juice with salt and pepper, add lemon juice and Worcestershire sauce and pour around fish.
8. Return casserole to oven for about a further 15 minutes, or until fish is cooked through and top is golden brown.

BAKED FISH MARTINIQUE
Serves 4

A tasty way of serving cod or haddock, Caribbean style.

1½oz (37gm) butter
4 cod or haddock steaks
1 tablespoon grated onion
6oz (150gm) fresh white breadcrumbs
pinch of dried thyme
pinch of dried sage
2 tablespoons peeled and chopped cucumber
1 tablespoon chopped green pepper
1 dessertspoon finely chopped parsley
finely grated rind and juice of half a lemon
salt and pepper
8 streaky bacon rashers

1. Preheat oven to moderate to moderately hot, 375 deg F or gas 5 (190 deg C).
2. Grease an ovenproof dish with ½oz (12gm) butter and place fish in the base.
3. Melt remaining butter in a pan and fry onion for 2 minutes, or until tender. Stir in breadcrumbs, thyme, sage, cucumber, green pepper, parsley, lemon rind and juice.
4. Blend well together, then season with salt and pepper.
5. Top fish with prepared mixture, then cover with bacon rashers.
6. Cook, uncovered, in centre of oven for about 30–35 minutes, or until fish is cooked through and top is brown.

SWEET FISH CURRY
Serves 4

2oz (50gm) butter
2 medium onions, peeled and
chopped
1 garlic clove, peeled and
crushed
2oz (50gm) mushrooms,
washed, trimmed and sliced
1 level tablespoon Madras
curry powder
½ pint (250ml) water
finely grated rind and juice of
half a lemon
3 tablespoons mango chutney,
chopped
1 cooking apple, peeled and
grated
1 carrot, peeled and grated
1½lb (¾ kilo) white fish, skinned,
boned and cut into small
pieces
salt and pepper

1. Preheat oven to moderate, 350
deg F or gas 4 (180 deg C).
2. Melt butter in a flameproof
casserole and gently fry onions
and garlic for 2–3 minutes, or
until tender.
3. Add mushrooms and continue
cooking for 1 minute.
4. Stir in curry powder and
gradually blend in water. Bring to
the boil, then stir in lemon rind
and juice, chutney, apple and
carrot. Add more seasoning if
necessary.
5. Stir in fish.
6. Cover closely with lid or foil
and cook in centre of oven for
about 35–40 minutes, or until fish
is cooked through.
7. Serve with freshly boiled rice.

SUNSET BAKE
Serves 4

1½lb (¾ kilo) tomatoes
1lb (½ kilo) haddock or cod
fillets
1oz (25gm) butter
2oz (50gm) onions, peeled and
finely chopped
1 level tablespoon chopped
parsley
2 level teaspoons anchovy
essence
1 lemon
1½oz (37gm) Cheddar cheese,
finely grated
1 tablespoon melted butter

1. Preheat oven to moderate, 350
deg F or gas 4 (180 deg C).
2. Peel and slice tomatoes fairly
thickly. Put a layer of tomato
slices in a shallow casserole.
3. Skin fish and arrange it in
pieces down the centre of the dish.
4. Mix butter with onion, parsley
and anchovy essence and heap
this on to the fish.
5. Put layers of tomato slices
down both sides of the fish,
finishing with slices of tomato
alternating with slices of lemon.
6. Sprinkle cheese over the fish
and brush the top layer of tomato
and lemon with melted butter.
7. Cook, uncovered, just above
centre of oven for 45 minutes, or
until fish is cooked through.

VIKING CASSEROLE
Serves 4

1lb (½ kilo) haddock or cod
fillets
1 onion, peeled and finely
chopped
3 tablespoons white wine
1oz (25gm) butter
1½lb (¾ kilo) potatoes, peeled
and sliced
8oz (200gm) tomatoes, peeled
and sliced
1 teaspoon flour
1 teaspoon paprika pepper
1 teaspoon salt
3 bacon rashers, trimmed and
chopped
1 small carton soured cream
¼ level teaspoon dried chervil

1. Skin fish and cut into cubes.
2. Put fish and onion in a bowl,
add wine and leave to marinate
for 1 hour.
3. Preheat oven to moderate, 350

deg F or gas 4 (180 deg C).
4. Grease a casserole with ½oz
(12gm) butter. Arrange potatoes
in the base, dot with remaining
butter and cover with tomatoes.
5. Mix flour, paprika pepper and
salt together and sprinkle over
the tomatoes.
6. Cook, covered, in centre of
oven for about 1 hour.
7. Remove from oven and
increase oven temperature to hot,
425 deg F or gas 7 (220 deg C).
8. Place fish and bacon in the
dish, pour marinade over and
return to hot oven for 15 minutes.
9. Remove from oven and reduce
heat to very moderate, 325 deg F
or gas 3 (170 deg C).
10. Spoon soured cream and
chervil over fish and cook for
about a further 45 minutes, or
until fish and bacon are cooked
through.

INNSBRUCK CASSEROLE
Serves 4

1½lb (¾ kilo) haddock
1½oz (37gm) butter or
margarine
2 onions, peeled and chopped
1 carton soured cream
1 rounded tablespoon capers,
drained
finely grated rind and juice of 1
small lemon
1 tablespoon finely chopped
parsley
salt
freshly ground black pepper
paprika pepper

1. Preheat oven to moderate to
moderately hot, 375 deg F or gas 5
(190 deg C).
2. Skin and fillet fish and cut into
small pieces.
3. Melt 1oz (25gm) butter or
margarine in a pan and fry
onions until tender but not
browned.
4. Stir in soured cream, capers,
lemon rind and juice and parsley.
Season well with salt and pepper.
5. Grease a shallow casserole
with remaining butter and
arrange fish in the base. Pour
prepared sauce over.
6. Cook, uncovered, above centre
of oven for about 25 minutes, or
until fish is cooked through.
7. Serve sprinkled with paprika
pepper.

SUMMER FISH CASSEROLE
Serves 2

8oz (200gm) haddock
1 can (11½oz or 326gm)
sweetcorn kernels
2 hard-boiled eggs, chopped
salt and pepper
1 packet (½ pint or 250ml)
parsley sauce mix
½ pint (250ml) milk
1 tablespoon fresh white
breadcrumbs
½oz (12gm) butter
paprika pepper
chopped parsley

1. Preheat oven to moderately hot, 400 deg F or gas 6 (200 deg C).
2. Poach haddock in water for 15 minutes, or until cooked through, then strain. Remove skin and bones and flake fish.
3. Heat sweetcorn, drain well and arrange in layers in a casserole, together with eggs and fish, seasoning well between layers with salt and pepper.
4. Make up parsley sauce according to packet directions, using milk.
5. Pour sauce over mixture in casserole and sprinkle with breadcrumbs. Dot with butter.
6. Cook, uncovered, in centre of oven for about 20 minutes, or until heated through and golden brown on top.
7. Sprinkle with paprika pepper and chopped parsley before serving.

NORWEGIAN CASSEROLE
Serves 4–6

1½lb (¾ kilo) haddock fillet
salt
freshly ground black pepper
4oz (100gm) peeled prawns
1 can (10½oz or 298gm)
condensed tomato soup
2–3 tablespoons single cream or
top of the milk
lemon wedges and sprigs of
parsley to garnish

1. Preheat oven to moderate, 350 deg F or gas 4 (180 deg C).
2. Cut haddock into four to six pieces and sprinkle with salt and pepper. Place in a shallow casserole.
3. Mix prawns with tomato soup and cream or top of the milk and pour over fish.
4. Cover closely with lid or foil and cook in centre of oven for about 30 minutes, or until fish is cooked through.
5. Serve garnished with lemon wedges and sprigs of parsley.

HADDOCK IN CHEESE SAUCE
Serves 6

1½lb (¾ kilo) haddock fillet
2½oz (62gm) butter
salt and pepper
pinch of dried marjoram
approximately ½ pint (250ml)
milk
1oz (25gm) flour
½ level teaspoon made mustard
3–4oz (75–100gm) cheese,
grated

1. Preheat oven to moderate to moderately hot, 375 deg F or gas 5 (190 deg C).
2. Skin fish and cut into even-sized pieces.
3. Grease an ovenproof dish with ½oz (12gm) butter and place fish in the base. Sprinkle with salt, pepper and marjoram.
4. Add 4 tablespoons milk and dot with 1oz (25gm) butter.
5. Cover closely with lid or foil and cook in centre of oven for 25–30 minutes, or until fish is cooked through.
6. Drain and reserve liquid from fish and keep fish warm.
7. Melt remaining butter in a pan, sprinkle in flour and stir over gentle heat for 1 minute.
8. Remove pan from heat and gradually blend in fish liquor made up to ½ pint (250ml) with milk.
9. Return to heat, bring to the boil and simmer for 2 minutes, stirring continuously.
10. Season to taste with salt and pepper, add mustard and two-thirds of the cheese. Stir over gentle heat until cheese melts.
11. Pour sauce over fish, sprinkle with remaining cheese and brown under a hot grill.

BELL INN SMOKIES
(Illustrated on page 54)
Serves 4

A recipe from the famous Bell Inn at Aston Clinton in Buckinghamshire.

4 smokies or baby haddock
fillets
4 tomatoes
1oz (25gm) butter
just under ½ pint (250ml) single
cream
freshly ground black pepper
2oz (50gm) Parmesan or
Gruyère cheese, finely grated

1. Preheat oven to moderate, 350 deg F or gas 4 (180 deg C).
2. Trim tails and fins from fish, then strip off skin and remove bones and flake fish.
3. Skin tomatoes, cut in half and scoop out seeds with a teaspoon. Chop flesh roughly.
4. Grease four individual soufflé dishes 3½ inches (9cm) in diameter, with butter.
5. Pour 1 tablespoon cream into each dish, then add flaked fish and chopped tomatoes.
6. Sprinkle with pepper and pour remaining cream over. Cover with grated cheese.
7. Place dishes on a baking sheet and cook, uncovered, in centre of oven for about 20 minutes, or until cooked through.
8. Place under a hot grill to brown tops and serve immediately.

LOUISIANA BAKE
Serves 3–4

1lb (½ kilo) smoked haddock
¼ pint (125ml) milk
¼ pint (125ml) water
1 can (7oz or 198gm) sweetcorn
kernels
1oz (25gm) margarine
1oz (25gm) flour
salt and pepper
4oz (100gm) Cheddar cheese,
finely grated

1. Preheat oven to hot, 425 deg F or gas 7 (220 deg C).
2. Poach haddock in milk and water for 15 minutes, or until cooked through.
3. Strain fish liquid into a measure with liquid from sweetcorn and make up to ½ pint (250ml) with water. Remove skin and bones from fish.
4. Place fish and sweetcorn in a

casserole.
5. Melt margarine in a pan. Sprinkle in flour and stir over gentle heat for 1 minute.
6. Remove pan from heat and gradually blend in liquid.
7. Return to heat, bring to the boil and simmer for 2 minutes, stirring continuously.
8. Season well and pour over fish and sweetcorn in casserole. Sprinkle with cheese.
9. Cook, uncovered, in centre of oven for 20–30 minutes, or until heated through and top is golden brown.

PEDRO'S FANCY
Serves 4

1lb ($\frac{1}{2}$ kilo) white fish
4oz (100gm) mushrooms, washed, trimmed and sliced
1 packet ($\frac{1}{2}$ pint or 250ml) parsley sauce mix
$\frac{1}{2}$ pint (250ml) milk
2 tomatoes, peeled and sliced
2oz (50gm) Cheddar cheese, finely grated
$\frac{1}{2}$oz (12gm) butter

1. Preheat oven to moderate to moderately hot, 375 deg F or gas 5 (190 deg C).
2. Remove skin from fish.
3. Arrange fish in a shallow casserole and scatter prepared mushrooms over top.
4. Make up parsley sauce with the milk, according to packet directions.
5. Pour prepared sauce over the fish, arrange sliced tomatoes on top and sprinkle evenly with grated cheese. Dot with butter.
6. Cook in centre of oven for about 20–25 minutes, or until fish is cooked through and top is golden brown.

HALIBUT WITH TARRAGON CREAM SAUCE
Serves 4

A rich and very special way of serving fish.

1oz (25gm) butter
4 halibut steaks
$\frac{1}{4}$ pint (125ml) white wine
$\frac{1}{4}$ pint (125ml) water
salt and pepper
2 teaspoons finely chopped fresh tarragon
2 egg yolks
$\frac{1}{4}$ pint (125ml) double cream
few lemon slices and tiny sprigs of tarragon to garnish

1. Preheat oven to moderately hot, 400 deg F or gas 6 (200 deg C).
2. Grease an ovenproof dish with $\frac{1}{2}$oz (12gm) butter and arrange halibut steaks in the base. Dot with remaining butter.
3. Pour in white wine and water, season well with salt and pepper and sprinkle with fresh tarragon.
4. Cover closely with lid or foil and cook in centre of oven for about 25 minutes, or until fish is cooked through.
5. Carefully transfer fish to a serving dish and keep hot.
6. Pour cooking liquor into a saucepan and boil until reduced by half. Remove pan from heat.
7. Beat together egg yolks and cream and blend into liquor in the pan.
8. Return pan to heat, stirring well until lightly thickened, taking care not to boil.
9. Pour sauce over fish and garnish with lemon slices and sprigs of tarragon.

DEVILLED HALIBUT
Serves 4

4 halibut steaks
3oz (75gm) butter
2oz (50gm) fresh white breadcrumbs
$\frac{1}{4}$oz (6gm) flour
$\frac{1}{4}$ pint (125ml) milk
salt and pepper
$\frac{1}{2}$ teaspoon anchovy essence
2 level teaspoons made mustard
2 dessertspoons mustard pickle, finely chopped
cayenne pepper

1. Preheat oven to moderate to moderately hot, 375 deg F or gas 5 (190 deg C).
2. Place halibut steaks in base of grill pan, dot with 2oz (50gm) butter and cook under medium heat for about 10 minutes.
3. Transfer fish carefully to a casserole and pour over any juices from the pan.
4. Place breadcrumbs on a baking sheet and cook in centre of oven for about 5 minutes, or until pale golden brown.
5. Melt $\frac{1}{4}$oz (6gm) butter in a pan, sprinkle in flour and stir over gentle heat for 2 minutes.
6. Remove pan from heat and gradually beat in milk.
7. Return to heat, bring to the boil and simmer for 2 minutes, stirring continuously. Season to taste with salt and pepper.
8. Add anchovy essence, mustard and mustard pickle and season if necessary with cayenne pepper.
9. Spread prepared sauce over fish and sprinkle with browned breadcrumbs.
10. Dot with remaining butter.
11. Cook, uncovered, in centre of oven for 15 minutes, or until heated through.
12. Serve with creamed potatoes and buttered carrots.

PLAICE LANCELOT
Serves 4

Plaice in a devilled cream sauce.

1oz (25gm) butter
8 small plaice fillets, skinned
2 teaspoons mild made
mustard
salt and pepper
4oz (100gm) button mushrooms,
washed, trimmed and sliced
3 level dessertspoons cornflour
3 level teaspoons dry mustard
½ pint (250ml) cider
¼ pint (125ml) water
2 blades of mace
2–3 tablespoons cream
watercress to garnish

1. Preheat oven to moderate, 350 deg F or gas 4 (180 deg C).
2. Grease a shallow casserole with ½oz (12gm) butter.
3. Spread plaice fillets with a little made mustard and roll up, starting from the tail. Stand fish upright in the casserole. Season well with salt and pepper.
4. Add mushrooms to casserole and dot with remaining butter.
5. Cover closely with lid or foil and cook in centre of oven for 20–30 minutes, or until fish is cooked through.
6. Drain fish, reserving liquid and mushrooms, transfer to a serving dish and keep hot.
7. Meanwhile, prepare sauce. Blend cornflour, dry mustard and 3 tablespoons cider together in a basin.
8. Place remaining cider, water and mace in a small saucepan, season with salt and pepper and simmer gently for 7–8 minutes.
9. Remove mace, then pour some of this hot liquid on to the blended cornflour, stirring briskly.
10. Add blended mixture to remaining liquid in pan, then add juices from the fish and mushrooms.
11. Bring to the boil and simmer for 2–3 minutes, stirring continuously.
12. Remove pan from heat, stir in cream and check seasoning.
13. Pour prepared sauce over fish and garnish with watercress.

PLAICE FLAMINGO
Serves 4

Serve this dish with creamy potatoes to complement the sauce, and sweetcorn to add a contrast of texture.

1½lb (¾ kilo) plaice fillets
½ teaspoon salt
pinch of pepper
1 level teaspoon paprika pepper
2 tablespoons lemon juice
1 teaspoon grated onion
2oz (50gm) butter, melted
1 dessertspoon finely chopped
parsley

1. Preheat oven to moderate, 350 deg F or gas 4 (180 deg C).
2. Arrange fish in a shallow casserole, skin side down.
3. Mix salt, pepper, paprika pepper, lemon juice, onion and butter together and pour over fish.
4. Cover closely with lid or foil and cook in centre of oven for about 30 minutes, or until fish is cooked through.
5. Serve sprinkled with chopped parsley.

TROUT WITH MINT
Serves 4

4 rainbow trout
salt and pepper
4 sprigs of fresh mint
2oz (50gm) butter
2 lemons
2–3 teaspoons finely chopped
fresh mint

1. Preheat oven to moderate to moderately hot, 375 deg F or gas 5 (190 deg C).
2. Trim tail and remove fins from trout. Season the inside of each fish with salt and pepper and insert a sprig of mint.
3. Arrange trout in a shallow casserole, dot with butter and sprinkle with juice of 1 lemon.
4. Cover closely with lid or foil and cook in centre of oven for 20–30 minutes, or until fish is cooked through.
5. Sprinkle with freshly chopped mint and garnish with slices of lemon.

QUICKY TUNA
Serves 6

4oz (100gm) boiled long-grain
rice (raw weight)
1 can (7oz or 198gm) tuna
1 small onion, finely chopped
3 sticks celery, washed and
chopped
1 can (10½oz or 298gm)
mushroom soup
salt and pepper
1 dessertspoon made mustard
3oz (75gm) cheese, finely
grated

1. Preheat oven to moderately hot, 400 deg F or gas 6 (200 deg C).
2. Mix together rice, tuna, onion, celery, mushroom soup, salt, pepper and mustard. Add 2oz (50gm) cheese and mix thoroughly.
3. Turn into a casserole and sprinkle with remaining cheese.
4. Cook, uncovered, in centre of oven for about 20 minutes, or until heated through and golden on top. Serve with baked tomatoes.

Vegetables

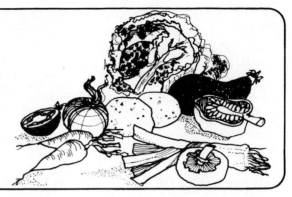

Here is a wide selection of vegetable dishes to accompany the main course. All of them make the most of the oven while it is already in use.

CABBAGE GRATIN
Serves 4–6

1 cabbage, washed, trimmed and finely shredded
2½oz (62gm) butter
4 large tomatoes, peeled and chopped
salt and pepper
nutmeg
3oz (75gm) fresh white breadcrumbs
3oz (75gm) Cheddar cheese, finely grated

1. Preheat oven to moderate, 350 deg F or gas 4 (180 deg C).
2. Cook cabbage in a little boiling, lightly salted water for 5 minutes. Drain well.
3. Grease a deep casserole with ½oz (12gm) butter.
4. Arrange half the cabbage in the base of casserole and cover with half the tomatoes. Season with salt, pepper and a little nutmeg.
5. Sprinkle in half the breadcrumbs and half the cheese, then continue with further layers of cabbage and tomatoes, seasoning as before.
6. Sprinkle remaining breadcrumbs and cheese over top and moisten with remaining butter, melted.
7. Cover closely with lid or foil and cook in centre of oven for 25–30 minutes, or until cabbage is soft and tender.

BAVARIAN RED CABBAGE
Serves 6

A sweet and sour recipe that is particularly good served with sausages, rabbit or pork.

1 small red cabbage (about 2lb or 1 kilo)
1 large onion, peeled and sliced
2 cooking apples, peeled, cored and sliced
salt and pepper
2 tablespoons sugar
5 tablespoons wine vinegar
1 bayleaf
2 large tablespoons redcurrant jelly

1. Preheat oven to cool, 300 deg F or gas 2 (150 deg C).
2. Finely shred the washed and drained red cabbage, discarding stalk and coarse outer leaves.
3. Arrange cabbage in layers in a deep casserole with onion and apples, seasoning well between layers with salt, pepper and sugar.
4. Pour in wine vinegar and tuck bayleaf down side of the casserole.
5. Cover closely with lid or foil and cook in centre of oven for 2–2½ hours, or until cabbage is soft and tender.
6. Adjust seasoning if necessary, stir in redcurrant jelly and return to oven for a further 5–10 minutes, or until heated through.

GRATIN DU JABRON
Serves 4

This recipe comes from London's excellent Capital Hotel in Knightsbridge.

Potatoes served in this way are ideal to prepare in advance for a dinner party.

1lb (½ kilo) potatoes
1oz (25gm) butter
1 small garlic clove, peeled and crushed
salt and pepper
¼ pint (125ml) cream
1oz (25gm) Parmesan cheese, finely grated

1. Scrub potatoes and boil in their skins until cooked through but still quite firm.
2. Allow to cool, then peel off skins and cut potatoes into slices.
3. Melt butter in a frying pan and fry potatoes together with garlic.
4. Preheat oven to moderate to moderately hot, 375 deg F or gas 5 (190 deg C).
5. Arrange potatoes in layers in a shallow, ovenproof dish, seasoning well with salt and pepper.
6. Pour cream over top and sprinkle with grated cheese.
7. Cook, uncovered, in centre of oven for about 15 minutes, or until heated through and golden brown on top.

POTATOES GRUYERE
Serves 4

1½lb (¾ kilo) small new potatoes
1½oz (37gm) butter
4 streaky bacon rashers,
trimmed
2 tablespoons very finely grated
Gruyère cheese
2 tablespoons fine white
breadcrumbs
1 tablespoon finely chopped
parsley

1. Scrape potatoes and boil in
salted water until just tender but
still quite firm. Drain well and
arrange in a shallow casserole.
2. Preheat oven to moderate, 350
deg F or gas 4 (180 deg C).
3. Melt 1oz (25gm) butter in a
small pan and pour over potatoes
in casserole.
4. Grill or fry bacon until cooked,
then cut into small pieces and
scatter over potatoes.
5. Mix together cheese,
breadcrumbs and parsley and
sprinkle over top of casserole.
6. Dot with remaining butter and
cook in centre of oven for about
30 minutes, or until potatoes are
tender and top is golden brown.

MONDAY POTATOES
Serves 4

1 tablespoon oil
1 large onion, peeled and sliced
1lb (½ kilo) cooked potatoes,
sliced
pinch of dried mixed herbs
½ pint (250ml) gravy
1 level teaspoon made mustard

1. Preheat oven to moderate, 350
deg F or gas 4 (180 deg C).
2. Heat oil in a frying pan and fry
onion for 3–4 minutes, or until
tender.
3. Arrange potatoes in a casserole
and scatter fried onions over.
Sprinkle with herbs.
4. Blend gravy with mustard and
pour into the casserole.
5. Cover with lid or foil and cook
in centre of oven for about 20–30
minutes, or until heated through.

SCALLOPED POTATOES MATHILDA
Serves 4–6

½oz (12gm) butter
6 medium potatoes, peeled
and thinly sliced
freshly ground black pepper
1 can (10½oz or 298gm)
condensed cream of mushroom
soup
1 soup can water

1. Preheat oven to moderate, 350
deg F or gas 4 (180 deg C).
2. Grease a deep casserole with
butter.
3. Arrange potatoes in casserole,
seasoning between layers with
pepper.
4. Blend soup with the water and
pour over the potatoes.
5. Cover closely with lid or foil
and cook in centre of oven for 45
minutes.
6. Remove cover and continue
cooking for a further 30–45
minutes, or until potatoes are
tender.

GINGERED CARROTS
Serves 4

Serve with roast beef or pork.

2oz (50gm) butter
8 medium carrots, peeled and
cut into ¼-inch slices
salt
freshly ground black pepper
1 level teaspoon ground ginger
2 teaspoons lemon juice
3 tablespoons water

1. Preheat oven to moderate, 350
deg F or gas 4 (180 deg C).
2. Grease a casserole with ½oz
(12gm) butter.
3. Arrange carrots in casserole
and sprinkle with salt and pepper.
4. Mix ginger with lemon juice
and water and sprinkle over top.
Dot with remaining butter.
5. Cover closely with lid or foil
and cook in centre of oven for
about 1 hour, or until carrots
are tender.

BRAISED CELERY
Serves 4

4 small heads celery, washed
and trimmed
1oz (25gm) butter
salt
freshly ground black pepper
dash of Worcestershire sauce
½ pint (250ml) chicken stock
finely chopped parsley

1. Preheat oven to very moderate,
325 deg F or gas 3 (170 deg C).
2. Discard any bruised or very
coarse outer pieces of celery,
then split each head into two
lengthways.
3. Grease a shallow casserole
with ½oz (12gm) butter.
4. Arrange celery in casserole and
season with salt and pepper.
5. Add Worcestershire sauce to
the stock and pour into casserole.
Dot with remaining butter.
6. Cover with lid or foil and cook
in centre of oven for about 1–1½
hours, or until quite tender.
7. If liked, reserve the cooking
liquid, boil it until well reduced,
then pour it over the cooked
celery. Sprinkle with finely
chopped parsley to serve.

BRAISED CHICORY
Serves 4

4 heads chicory
1oz (25gm) butter
¼ pint (125ml) chicken stock
juice of half a lemon
¼ level teaspoon meat or
vegetable extract

1. Preheat oven to cool, 300 deg F
or gas 2 (150 deg C).
2. Wash chicory and make a
cross cut in the bottom of each
head.
3. Blanch the whole heads in
boiling, salted water for 5
minutes.
4. Grease a shallow casserole
with ½oz (12gm) butter.
5. Drain chicory well and arrange
in casserole. Dot with remaining
butter.
6. Blend stock with lemon juice
and meat or vegetable extract and
pour over the chicory.
7. Cover with buttered foil and
cook in centre of oven for 1–1½
hours, or until chicory is tender.
8. Lift out carefully and serve
with a little liquor from the
casserole.

LOMBARDY CASSEROLE
(Illustrated on page 71)
Serves 4–6

Macaroni and aubergines
together make a tasty supper dish
or a good accompaniment to pork
or chicken dishes.

2 medium aubergines
salt
2–3 tablespoons olive oil
8oz (200gm) quick-cooking
macaroni
½oz (12gm) butter
1 can (9oz or 265gm) Napolitan
or tomato sauce
2oz (50gm) Cheddar cheese,
finely grated

1. Wash aubergines, trim off both
ends and cut into slices. Place in
a colander and sprinkle with salt.
Press down with a plate and leave
to stand for 1 hour, so that the
excess moisture drains off.
2. Wash in cold water and dry on
kitchen paper.
3. Preheat oven to moderate, 350
deg F or gas 4 (180 deg C).
4. Heat oil in a frying pan and
fry aubergine slices until golden
brown on both sides.
5. Cook macaroni in boiling,
salted water according to packet
directions, until just tender.
Drain well.
6. Grease a casserole with butter,
then fill with layers of fried
aubergines, macaroni and tomato
sauce, finishing off with a layer of
aubergines.
7. Sprinkle top with cheese, then
cook, uncovered, above centre of
oven for 15–20 minutes, or until
heated through.

AUBERGINES A LA PROVENÇALE
(Illustrated on page 71)
Serves 4–6

3 medium aubergines
salt
4–5 tablespoons olive oil
1lb (¼ kilo) tomatoes, peeled
and chopped
freshly ground black pepper
1 garlic clove, peeled and
crushed
4 tablespoons fresh white
breadcrumbs
1 tablespoon chopped parsley
1oz (25gm) butter

1. Wash aubergines, trim off both
ends and cut into slices. Place in
a colander and sprinkle with salt.
Press down with a plate and leave
to stand for 1 hour so that the
excess moisture drains off.
2. Wash in cold water and dry on
kitchen paper.
3. Preheat oven to moderate, 350
deg F or gas 4 (180 deg C).
4. Heat oil in a frying pan and
fry aubergine slices until golden
brown on both sides.
5. Transfer to a shallow casserole.
6. Fry tomatoes in oil remaining
in the pan, or add a little more if
necessary, and season well with
salt and pepper. Add garlic.
7. Spread tomatoes over
aubergines in casserole.
8. Mix breadcrumbs with parsley
and sprinkle over top of dish. Dot
with butter.
9. Cook, uncovered, in centre of
oven for about 30 minutes, or
until top is crisp and brown.

STUFFED AUBERGINES
Serves 4

The meaty filling makes this
dish a main meal.

4 aubergines
4 tablespoons oil
1 medium onion, peeled and
sliced
1 garlic clove, peeled and
crushed
1 green pepper, de-seeded and
chopped
1lb (¼ kilo) minced beef
salt and pepper
1 level teaspoon mixed dried
herbs
2oz (50gm) fresh white
breadcrumbs
4oz (100gm) Cheddar cheese,
finely grated
1 can (8oz or 200gm) Napolitan
or tomato sauce

1. Preheat oven to moderate,
350 deg F or gas 4 (180 deg C).
2. Wash aubergines, remove
stalks and cut in half, lengthways.
Scoop out seeds and discard,
then remove some of the flesh
and chop finely.
3. Heat oil in a pan, add onion,
garlic and green pepper and cook
gently for 3–4 minutes.
4. Add minced beef and stir until
browned all over.
5. Add salt and pepper to taste,
mixed herbs, chopped aubergine
flesh and breadcrumbs.
6. Divide the mixture between
aubergine halves and sprinkle
with cheese.
7. Pour tomato sauce into a
shallow casserole and arrange
prepared aubergines in the base.
8. Cover closely with lid or foil
and cook in centre of oven for
30 minutes. Remove cover and
continue cooking for a further
15 minutes, or until aubergines
are tender and tops are lightly
browned.

BANANA TOGO
(Illustrated on page 71)
Serves 4–6

Savoury bananas cooked this way make a delicious accompaniment to gammon or sausages.

1oz (25gm) butter
6 bananas, peeled and sliced
1 onion, peeled and finely chopped
2 tomatoes, peeled and chopped
pinch of turmeric powder

1. Preheat oven to moderate, 350 deg F or gas 4 (180 deg C).
2. Melt butter in a flameproof casserole and add prepared ingredients. Stir over gentle heat for 1 minute.
3. Cover closely with lid or foil and cook in centre of oven for about 30 minutes, or until bananas are cooked through.

BANANA SINGAPORE
Serves 4–6

Curried bananas to serve with pork or fish.

2oz (50gm) butter
1 onion, peeled and chopped
1½oz (37gm) flour
2 level teaspoons curry powder
¾ pint (375ml) chicken stock
2 tablespoons mango chutney, chopped
2 tablespoons sultanas
salt and pepper
6 slightly under-ripe bananas

1. Preheat oven to moderate, 350 deg F or gas 4 (180 deg C).
2. Melt butter in a saucepan and fry onion gently until tender.
3. Sprinkle in flour and curry powder and stir over gentle heat for 1–2 minutes.
4. Remove pan from heat and gradually blend in stock.
5. Return to heat, bring to the boil and simmer gently for 2 minutes, stirring continuously.
6. Stir in mango chutney, sultanas and season to taste.
7. Peel bananas, cut in half lengthways and arrange in a shallow casserole.
8. Pour curry sauce into dish to completely cover bananas.
9. Cover closely with lid or foil and cook in centre of oven for about 20 minutes, or until bananas are tender.

COURGETTES WITH HERBS
Serves 3–4

1lb (½ kilo) courgettes
2oz (50gm) butter
juice of half lemon
few drops of Worcestershire sauce
freshly ground black pepper
1 level teaspoon chopped parsley
½ level teaspoon fresh or dried basil

1. Preheat oven to very moderate, 325 deg F or gas 3 (170 deg C).
2. Cut a slice from each end of washed courgettes, leave whole and cook in boiling, salted water for 2–3 minutes. Drain well and arrange in a shallow casserole.
3. Melt butter in a small saucepan, add lemon juice and Worcestershire sauce and pour over the courgettes, turning them until well coated.
4. Sprinkle with black pepper and scatter herbs over top.
5. Cover closely with lid or foil and cook in centre of oven for about 20–30 minutes, or until courgettes are tender.

TOMATO AND COURGETTE RICE
Serves 6

2oz (50gm) long-grain rice
1lb (½ kilo) courgettes
6 large tomatoes, peeled
1oz (25gm) butter
¼ pint (125ml) chicken stock
salt and pepper

1. Preheat oven to moderate, 350 deg F or gas 4 (180 deg C).
2. Sprinkle rice into a shallow, ovenproof dish.
3. Wash courgettes and arrange them whole and unpeeled on the rice.
4. Arrange tomatoes among the courgettes and dot with the butter.
5. Pour stock over and sprinkle with salt and pepper.
6. Cover closely with lid or foil and cook in centre of oven for about 1–1¼ hours, or until courgettes are tender and rice cooked but moist.

GRATIN AUX COURGETTES
Serves 4

1lb (½ kilo) courgettes
½oz (12gm) butter
2oz (50gm) Gruyère cheese, finely grated
1 egg
¼ pint (125ml) single cream
salt
fresh ground black pepper
ground mace

1. Top and tail courgettes and cut on the slant into ¼-inch slices. Blanch in boiling, salted water until just tender, then drain and transfer to cold water.
2. Preheat oven to moderate to moderately hot, 375 deg F or gas 5 (190 deg C).
3. Grease a shallow casserole or gratin dish with butter.
4. Drain prepared courgettes and arrange in casserole or gratin dish.
5. Beat 1½oz (37gm) cheese together with egg, stir in cream, season with salt, pepper and mace and pour over courgettes.
6. Sprinkle remaining cheese over and dot with remaining butter.
7. Place dish in a roasting tin with water to come half way up sides of dish and cook, uncovered, in centre of oven for 20–30 minutes, or until just set and top is golden brown.

CUCUMBER WITH TOMATOES
Serves 4–6

1lb (½ kilo) tomatoes, peeled and sliced
½ cucumber, peeled and sliced
salt and pepper
pinch of nutmeg
pinch of sugar
½oz (12gm) butter

1. Preheat oven to moderate to moderately hot, 375 deg F or gas 5 (190 deg C).
2. Arrange layers of tomato and cucumber in a shallow casserole and season well with salt, pepper and a little nutmeg and sugar. Dot with butter.
3. Cover closely with lid or foil and cook just below centre of oven for about 30–40 minutes, or until cucumber is tender.

BUTTERED CUCUMBER
Serves 4

An unusual vegetable to serve with fish, pork or chicken.

1 cucumber
½ teaspoon salt
½ level teaspoon sugar
3 dessertspoons white wine vinegar
2oz (50gm) butter, melted
1 dessertspoon finely chopped parsley
2 tablespoons chopped chives or green salad onion tops
freshly ground black pepper

1. Peel cucumber and cut in half lengthways.
2. If seeds are rather large, scoop them out with a teaspoon and discard.
3. Cut cucumber into chunky pieces, then place in a bowl and sprinkle with salt, sugar and vinegar. Leave to stand for 1–2 hours, then drain well and dry on kitchen paper.
4. Preheat oven to moderate to moderately hot, 375 deg F or gas 5 (190 deg C).
5. Transfer prepared cucumber to a shallow casserole. Add butter, parsley and chives or green salad onion tops and season well with pepper.
6. Toss well together, then cook, uncovered, in centre of oven for about 25 minutes, or until cucumber is tender but still firm.

MARROW WITH MARJORAM
Serves 4–6

1 medium vegetable marrow
1oz (25gm) butter
salt and pepper
½ level teaspoon dried marjoram

1. Preheat oven to moderate to moderately hot, 375 deg F or gas 5 (190 deg C).
2. Peel marrow, cut in half, discard seeds and cut into 1-inch cubes.
3. Grease a casserole with ½oz (12gm) butter.
4. Transfer prepared marrow to casserole and sprinkle with salt, pepper and marjoram. Dot with remaining butter.
5. Cover closely with lid or foil and cook just below centre of oven for about 40 minutes, or until marrow is tender.

TOMATO AND ONION CASSEROLE
Serves 4–6

1lb (½ kilo) onions, peeled and sliced
salt and pepper
½ teaspoon marjoram or basil
½oz (12gm) butter
1lb (½ kilo) tomatoes, peeled and sliced
2oz (50gm) fresh breadcrumbs
2oz (50gm) cheese, grated
1oz (25gm) butter or bacon fat, melted

1. Boil the onions in salted water for 20 minutes. Drain well and season with salt, pepper and herbs.
2. Preheat oven to hot, 425 deg F or gas 7 (220 deg C).
3. Grease a casserole with butter.
4. Put half the onions in the base of casserole and arrange half the tomatoes on top.
5. Add a layer of mixed breadcrumbs and cheese.
6. Repeat these layers and pour melted butter or bacon fat over the top.
7. Cook, uncovered, in centre of oven for about 15–20 minutes, or until heated through.

TOMATO CZARDA
Serves 4

Serve this with pork, chicken or fish.

1 carton soured cream
2 tablespoons milk
½oz (12gm) butter
1lb (½ kilo) potatoes, peeled and thinly sliced
8oz (200gm) tomatoes, peeled and thinly sliced
1 garlic clove, peeled and crushed
salt
freshly ground black pepper
pinch of dried marjoram
chopped parsley

1. Preheat oven to very moderate, 325 deg F or gas 3 (170 deg C).
2. Mix soured cream with milk.
3. Grease a casserole with butter.
4. Arrange a layer of potatoes in the casserole, then a layer of tomatoes. Dot with garlic.
5. Pour a little soured cream mixture over and season with

salt, pepper and marjoram.
6. Continue these layers, finishing with a layer of potatoes and soured cream.
7. Cover closely with lid or foil and cook in centre of oven for about 1 hour, or until potatoes are tender.
8. Sprinkle with parsley before serving.

SAUCY ONIONS
Serves 4

Try this dish with fried sausages or grilled gammon.

4oz (100gm) streaky bacon rashers, trimmed and finely chopped
8 medium onions, peeled
½ pint (250ml) chicken stock
1oz (25gm) butter
1 packet (½ pint or 250ml) savoury white sauce mix
1 hard-boiled egg, roughly chopped
paprika pepper

1. Preheat oven to moderate, 350 deg F or gas 4 (180 deg C).
2. Fry bacon until lightly browned, then transfer with a draining spoon to a casserole.
3. Place onions in casserole, pour boiling stock over and dot with butter.
4. Cook, uncovered, in centre of oven for 1–1¼ hours, or until onions are tender.
5. Strain off liquor and make up to ½ pint (250ml) with water if necessary.
6. Use this liquor instead of milk to make up white sauce according to packet directions.
7. Add hard-boiled egg to sauce, pour over onions and sprinkle with paprika pepper before serving.

CHEESY ONION CUSTARD
Serves 3–4

A more substantial vegetable dish which can be served on its own or with ham or sausages.

3 large onions, peeled and sliced
1oz (25gm) butter
2 eggs
½ pint (250ml) milk
3oz (75gm) Cheddar cheese, finely grated
salt and pepper

1. Preheat oven to moderate, 350 deg F or gas 4 (180 deg C).
2. Boil onions in a little slightly salted water until just tender. Drain well.
3. Grease a casserole with ½oz (12gm) butter and arrange onions in the base.
4. Separate the eggs and beat the yolks with the milk. Stir in the cheese and season well to taste with salt and pepper.
5. Whisk the egg whites stiffly and stir into the milk mixture.
6. Pour prepared mixture over onions, dot with remaining butter and cook, uncovered, in centre of oven for about 35 minutes, or until just set.

BAKED ONIONS
Serves 4

4 large onions, peeled
1oz (25gm) butter
salt
freshly ground black pepper
¼ pint (250ml) chicken stock

1. Preheat oven to moderate, 350 deg F or gas 4 (180 deg C).
2. Arrange onions in a casserole, dot each with butter and sprinkle with salt and pepper.
3. Pour stock around onions.
4. Cover closely with lid or foil and cook in centre of oven for about 1 hour.
5. Remove lid and continue cooking for a further 15–30 minutes, or until onions are tender and golden brown.

SWEET AND SOUR BAKED ONIONS
Serves 4

Cook onions this way and try them served with pork or sausage dishes.

1lb (½ kilo) onions, peeled and thickly sliced
1oz (25gm) butter
3 level teaspoons sugar
3 tablespoons wine vinegar
3 tablespoons water
salt
freshly ground black pepper

1. Preheat oven to moderate, 350 deg F or gas 4 (180 deg C).
2. Arrange onions in a shallow casserole and dot with butter.
3. Sprinkle with sugar, pour vinegar and water over and season with salt and pepper.
4. Cover closely with lid or foil and cook in centre of oven for about 45 minutes.
5. Remove cover and continue cooking for a further 15 minutes, or until onions are tender and lightly browned.
6. Drain well before serving.

BRAISED LEEKS
Serves 4

Ideal to serve with fish or chicken.

1lb (½ kilo) leeks
1oz (25gm) butter
2–3 tablespoons stock
salt
freshly ground black pepper

1. Preheat oven to moderate, 350 deg F or gas 4 (180 deg C).
2. Remove coarse outer leaves of leeks, cut off and discard tops and roots, then cut into 1-inch pieces. Wash very thoroughly.
3. Melt butter in a flameproof casserole, add leeks and toss over gentle heat for 2–3 minutes.
4. Add stock and season well with salt and pepper.
5. Cover closely with lid or foil and cook in centre of oven for about 35–40 minutes, or until leeks are tender.
6. Drain before serving.

TIPSY LEEKS
Serves 4

1lb (½ kilo) leeks
1oz (25gm) streaky bacon, trimmed and diced
freshly ground black pepper
2–3 tablespoons white wine

1. Preheat oven to very moderate, 325 deg F or gas 3 (170 deg C).
2. Remove coarse outer leaves of leeks, cut off and discard tops and roots, then cut into 1-inch pieces. Wash very thoroughly.
3. Place leeks in a casserole together with bacon and season well with pepper. Pour wine over.
4. Cover closely with a lid or foil and cook in centre of oven for 45–50 minutes, or until leeks are tender. Serve with the juices from the dish.

ASPARAGUS CHARLOTTE
Serves 3–4

Serve with grilled gammon or as a light supper dish on its own.

½oz (12gm) butter
4–6 large slices bread and butter, crusts removed
1 can (15oz or 425gm) asparagus spears
4oz (100gm) Cheddar cheese, finely grated
3 eggs
1 pint (approximately ½ litre) milk
2 level teaspoons dry mustard
salt and pepper
Worcestershire sauce

1. Grease a 2½–3 pint (approximately 1¼–1½ litre) ovenproof casserole with butter.
2. Arrange half the slices of bread and butter in the casserole, top with drained asparagus and sprinkle with half the cheese.
3. Cover with remaining slices of bread and butter and sprinkle with remaining cheese.
4. Preheat oven to moderate to moderately hot, 375 deg F or gas 5 (190 deg C).
5. Whisk eggs with milk and add dry mustard, salt and pepper and Worcestershire sauce to taste.
6. Pour egg mixture into dish or casserole and leave to stand for 15 minutes.
7. Cook, uncovered, in centre of oven for about 45 minutes, or until cooked through and golden brown on top.

GARDENERS' CASSEROLE
(Illustrated on page 71)
Serves 4–6

Green beans with a cheese sauce
to serve with most meats.

1½lb (¾ kilo) fresh French beans
1 bayleaf
pinch of nutmeg
1oz (25gm) butter
½oz (12gm) flour
½ pint (250ml) milk
½ level teaspoon mustard
4oz (100gm) Cheddar cheese,
grated
salt and pepper
1 tablespoon of cream or top of
the milk

1. Preheat oven to hot, 425 deg F
or gas 7 (220 deg C).
2. Trim tops and tails from beans
and string if necessary. Leave
whole and cook in boiling, salted
water with bayleaf for 5–10
minutes, or until almost tender.
3. Drain well and discard bayleaf,
then toss in nutmeg and ½oz
(12gm) butter.
4. Arrange beans in casserole and
keep warm.
5. Melt remaining butter in a
saucepan, sprinkle in flour and
stir over gentle heat for 2 minutes.
6. Remove pan from heat and
gradually blend in milk.
7. Return to heat, bring to the
boil and simmer for 2 minutes,
stirring continuously.
8. Remove pan from heat and beat
in mustard and 3oz (75gm) cheese
until well blended. Season.
9. Stir cream or top of the milk
into hot cheese sauce and pour
over top of beans. Sprinkle top
with remaining cheese.
10. Cook, uncovered, towards top
of oven for about 15 minutes, or
until heated through and golden
brown.

NIAGARA BAKED SWEETCORN
Serves 3–4

½oz (12gm) butter
6 tablespoons tomato ketchup
½ level teaspoon dry mustard
pinch of salt
½oz (12gm) brown sugar
½ onion, peeled and chopped
1 can (11½oz or 326gm)
sweetcorn
2 streaky bacon rashers,
trimmed and diced

1. Preheat oven to moderate,
350 deg F or gas 4 (180 deg C).
2. Grease an ovenproof dish with
butter.
3. Mix together ketchup,
mustard, salt and sugar in a basin.
4. Add onion and sweetcorn,
toss well in mixture and pour
into ovenproof dish. Top with
bacon.
5. Cover closely with lid or foil
and cook in centre of oven for
40 minutes, or until bacon is
cooked.

MIXED VEGETABLE HOTPOT
Serves 4

2oz (50gm) butter
2 carrots, peeled and sliced
1 large turnip, peeled and diced
1 small head celery, washed,
trimmed and sliced
2 leeks, washed, trimmed and
sliced
2 medium onions, peeled and
sliced
1 pint (approximately ½ litre)
chicken stock
1 level teaspoon vegetable or
meat extract
8oz (200gm) potatoes

1. Preheat oven to moderately
hot, 400 deg F or gas 6 (200 deg C).
2. Melt 1oz (25gm) butter in a
flameproof casserole.
3. Add carrots, turnip, celery,
leeks and onions and turn with
a metal spoon until well coated
with butter.
4. Mix hot stock with vegetable

or meat extract and pour over
vegetables.
5. Peel and thinly slice potatoes
and arrange in a neat layer over
top.
6. Dot with remaining butter and
cover closely with lid or foil.
7. Cook in centre of oven for
about 45 minutes.
8. Remove cover and continue
cooking for a further 15–20
minutes, or until vegetables are
tender and top is golden brown.

VEGETABLE BAKE
Serves 6

1oz (25gm) butter
1 medium onion, peeled and
chopped
1 garlic clove, peeled and
crushed
2 streaky bacon rashers,
trimmed and cut into small
pieces
1lb (½ kilo) green beans,
cooked and drained
8oz (200gm) tomatoes, peeled
and sliced
1lb (½ kilo) cooked potatoes,
sliced
salt and pepper
1 packet (½ pint or 250ml)
parsley sauce mix
½ pint (250ml) milk
2oz (50gm) Cheddar cheese,
finely grated

1. Preheat oven to moderate,
350 deg F or gas 4 (180 deg C).
2. Melt butter in a pan and fry
onion and garlic gently together
for 2–3 minutes.
3. Add bacon and continue
cooking for 2–3 minutes.
4. Place a layer of green beans
in the base of a pie dish or
casserole, then add a little of the
fried onion and bacon mixture.
5. Arrange a layer of sliced
tomatoes and potatoes on top,
seasoning well with salt and
pepper. Continue in these layers,
finishing with a layer of potatoes.
6. Make up parsley sauce
according to packet directions
using milk, then pour over
vegetables and sprinkle with
cheese.
7. Cook, uncovered, in centre of
oven for about 30 minutes, or
until heated through and top is
golden brown.

Fruit

For those who believe the pudding to be the best part of the meal, here are a few simply prepared but rather special dishes which can be gently cooking while you are eating the main course.

PEARS IN RED WINE
Serves 8

This is a traditional method of preparing whole dessert pears and is ideal for a dinner party served hot or cold.

5oz (125gm) lump sugar
¼ pint (125ml) red wine
¼ pint (125ml) water
small piece stick cinnamon
8 firm dessert pears
little lemon juice

1. Preheat oven to very moderate, 325 deg F or gas 3 (170 deg C).
2. Place the sugar, wine, water and cinnamon in a pan and stir over gentle heat until sugar has dissolved. Bring to the boil and simmer for 2 minutes without stirring.
3. Peel the pears, leaving stalks on and brush the fruit with lemon juice to avoid discoloration.
4. Place the pears in a deep casserole and pour the prepared syrup over.
5. Cover with lid or foil and cook in centre of oven for about 2 hours, or until pears are tender. Serve hot or well chilled with cream.

COTSWOLD PEARS
Serves 4

Pears cooked in spiced ginger ale and redcurrant jelly.

1 can (1lb 14oz or 850gm) pear halves
1 bottle ginger ale
1 dessertspoon lemon juice
1oz (25gm) butter, melted
good pinch of cinnamon
2 cloves
2 tablespoons redcurrant jelly

1. Preheat oven to moderate, 350 deg F or gas 4 (180 deg C).
2. Drain pears (syrup could be used for a jelly) and arrange in a shallow casserole.
3. Pour ginger ale and lemon juice over, then add butter, cinnamon, cloves and redcurrant jelly.
4. Cover with lid or foil and cook in centre of oven for about 30 minutes, or until pears are heated through.
5. Serve with cream.

CASTLE PEARS
Serves 4–6

An old English recipe for pears baked in soured cream.

3 large pears, halved and cored
1 carton soured cream
3–4 level tablespoons demerara sugar
2 level tablespoons cake or biscuit crumbs
1 level teaspoon ground cinnamon

1. Preheat oven to moderate, 350 deg F or gas 4 (180 deg C).
2. Arrange pears in a shallow casserole.
3. Pour soured cream over top and sprinkle with sugar, cake or biscuit crumbs and cinnamon.
4. Cook, uncovered, just below centre of oven for about 30 minutes, or until pears are tender and top is golden brown.

COMPOTE OF PEARS
Serves 4

1½lb (¾ kilo) stewing pears, peeled, halved and cored
4oz (100gm) granulated sugar
¼ pint (125ml) water
juice of half a lemon
2 cloves
1-inch stick of cinnamon
2 tablespoons white wine (optional)

1. Preheat oven to moderate, 350 deg F or gas 4 (180 deg C).
2. Place pears in a casserole.
3. Place remaining ingredients in a strong pan. Heat gently until sugar has dissolved, then bring to the boil and boil for 2 minutes, or until syrupy.
4. Pour syrup over pears in casserole.
5. Cover closely with lid or foil and cook in centre of oven for about 30 minutes, or until pears are tender.
6. Serve hot or cold with cream or custard.

SPICED FRUITS
Serves 4–6

1 can (1lb or ½ kilo) pear halves
1 can (1lb or ½ kilo) peach halves
1 tablespoon honey
2 tablespoons mango chutney, chopped

1. Preheat oven to moderate, 350 deg F or gas 4 (180 deg C).
2. Drain fruits (syrup can be used in a jelly) and arrange in layers in a casserole.
3. Mix honey and chutney together and pour over the fruit.
4. Cover closely with lid or foil and cook below centre of oven for 45 minutes–1 hour, or until fruit is heated through.
5. Serve hot with vanilla ice cream.

STUFFED PEACHES
(Illustrated on page 72)
Serves 6

A short-cut sweet with a party finish.

1 can (1lb 14oz or 850gm) peach halves
2 tablespoons brandy
2oz (50gm) ratafias, finely crushed, plus 4 whole ratafias for decoration
2oz (50gm) ground almonds
1 level tablespoon caster sugar
¼ pint (125ml) double cream
strip of angelica

1. Preheat oven to moderate to moderately hot, 375 deg F or gas 5 (190 deg C).
2. Drain peaches, reserving the syrup, and arrange in a shallow, ovenproof dish.
3. Mix ¼ pint (125ml) reserved peach syrup with brandy and use a little of this to bind together the crushed ratafias and ground almonds.
4. Place a spoonful of the mixture in the hollow of each peach and sprinkle with a little sugar.
5. Pour remaining brandy syrup into the dish.
6. Cook, uncovered, above centre of oven for about 25 minutes.
7. Serve peaches hot with cream or chill and serve surrounded with piped whirls of whipped cream decorated with ratafias and chopped angelica.

ROSY APPLES
Serves 6

6 Granny Smith or small Bramley apples, peeled and cored
4oz (100gm) sultanas
finely grated rind and juice of 1 lemon
2oz (50gm) soft brown sugar
4 tablespoons seedless raspberry jam
¼ pint (125ml) apple juice
6 teaspoons redcurrant jelly

1. Preheat oven to moderate, 350 deg F or gas 4 (180 deg C).
2. Arrange apples in a shallow casserole.
3. Mix sultanas, lemon rind and sugar together and press in centres of apples.
4. Sprinkle apples with lemon juice and place a spoonful of

raspberry jam on top of each. Pour apple juice into casserole.
5. Cook, uncovered, in centre of oven until apples are tender, about 40 minutes according to variety and size of fruit.
6. Baste apples with liquid from the dish, decorate top of each with a teaspoonful of redcurrant jelly and return to oven for a further 5–6 minutes.

SPIKED APPLES
(Illustrated on page 72)
Serves 4

Apples baked in cider and spiked, hedgehog fashion, with almonds.

4 cooking apples, peeled, halved and cored
3oz (75gm) demerara sugar
2oz (50gm) chopped candied peel
1 pint (approximately ½ litre) cider or unsweetened apple juice
2oz (50gm) almonds, blanched and cut into spikes

1. Preheat oven to moderate, 350 deg F or gas 4 (180 deg C).
2. Arrange apples in a shallow casserole. Sprinkle with sugar, scatter with peel and pour cider or apple juice over.
3. Cover with lid or foil and cook towards base of oven for about 1 hour, or until apples are tender but still retain their shape.
4. Transfer apples carefully to a serving dish and spike with almonds.
5. Pour liquid from the dish into a pan, boil until well reduced, then pour over the apples.
6. Serve hot or cold with cream or custard.

BAKED APPLES MAMBA
Serves 6

2 bananas
1 tablespoon lemon juice
pinch of cinnamon
1 tablespoon honey
6 medium cooking apples,
cored
¼ pint (125ml) orange juice

1. Preheat oven to moderate to
moderately hot, 375 deg F or gas 5
(190 deg C).
2. Peel bananas, then mash
them with lemon juice, cinnamon
and honey.
3. Cut through skin of each
apple with a sharp knife around
centre.
4. Place apples in a casserole,
fill centres with banana mixture
and pour orange juice around the
apples.
5. Cover closely with lid or foil
and cook in centre of oven for
about 45 minutes, or until apples
are tender, basting from time to
time with the orange juice.
6. Serve hot or cold with custard
or cream.

YORKSHIRE SAVOURIES
Serves 4

4 ¼-inch slices buttered bread
2oz (50gm) Cheddar cheese,
grated
2 apples, peeled and thinly
sliced
1 egg
¼ pint (125ml) milk
finely grated rind of half a
lemon
½oz (12gm) sugar

1. Preheat oven to moderate,
350 deg F or gas 4 (180 deg C).
2. Cut bread into small cubes and
put a layer in the base of four
individual fireproof dishes.
3. Sprinkle cheese over.
4. Place a layer of apple on top.
5. Use remaining bread to form
another layer, and finish with a
layer of apple.
6. Lightly beat egg. Heat milk to
blood heat, pour over egg and add
lemon rind.
7. Pour this into dishes and
sprinkle with sugar.
8. Cook in centre of oven for
30 minutes, or until heated
through and golden on top.

WEST COUNTRY PRUNES
(Illustrated on page 72)
Serves 4

Prunes plumped up in a spicy
cider.

8oz (200gm) prunes
½ pint (250ml) sweet cider
4 tablespoons caster sugar
small strip of lemon rind
small piece of cinnamon stick

1. Soak prunes overnight in
cider to cover.
2. Preheat oven to very moderate,
325 deg F or gas 3 (170 deg C).
3. Transfer prunes and cider to a
small casserole and add sugar,
lemon rind and cinnamon stick.
4. Cover closely with lid or foil
and cook below centre of oven
for about 40 minutes, or until
prunes are tender.
5. Serve hot or cold with lightly
whipped cream.

SUNNY SALAD
Serves 6

4oz (200gm) stoned prunes
4oz (200gm) dried apricots
cold tea
1½oz (37gm) butter
3 bananas
1oz (25gm) sultanas
3 tablespoons clear honey
½ pint (250ml) orange juice
finely grated rind of 1 orange
¼ level teaspoon cinnamon
1oz (25gm) flaked almonds,
lightly toasted

1. Soak prunes and apricots
overnight in cold tea to cover.
Drain well.
2. Preheat oven to moderate,
350 deg F or gas 4 (180 deg C).
3. Grease a shallow casserole
with ½oz (12gm) butter.
4. Peel bananas, cut into slices
and arrange in casserole.
5. Cover with prunes and
apricots and scatter sultanas
over top.
6. Blend honey with orange juice
and rind and cinnamon, then
pour over fruit.
7. Dot with remaining butter
and cook, uncovered, in centre
of oven for about 30 minutes, or
until fruit is tender.
8. Sprinkle top with almonds and
serve hot with whipped cream.

CHERRIES IN WINE
Serves 6

4oz (100gm) granulated sugar
¼ pint (125ml) water
2lb (1 kilo) red cherries
½ bottle white wine
½ small stick cinnamon

1. Preheat oven to very moderate,
325 deg F or gas 3 (170 deg C).
2. Place sugar and water in a
heavy saucepan and stir over
gentle heat until sugar has
dissolved. Bring to the boil, then
simmer for 2–3 minutes, or until
syrupy.
3. Place cherries in a casserole
and pour prepared syrup over
together with white wine. Stir
well together, then add
cinnamon stick.
4. Cover closely with lid or foil
and cook towards base of oven for
20–30 minutes, or until cherries
are tender.
5. Thicken, if liked, before
serving with a little arrowroot
blended with water.
6. Chill before serving.

CALYPSO BANANAS
Serves 6

6 medium bananas
¼ pint (125ml) fresh orange
juice
1 tablespoon rum (optional)
2oz (50gm) demerara sugar
2oz (50gm) butter
2oz (50gm) desiccated coconut

1. Preheat oven to moderate,
350 deg F or gas 4 (180 deg C).
2. Peel bananas, cut into quarters
and arrange in a shallow
casserole.
3. Mix orange juice, rum (if used)
and demerara sugar together
and sprinkle over the bananas.
4. Dot with butter and sprinkle
with coconut.
5. Cook, uncovered, above centre
of oven for 15–20 minutes, or
until bananas are tender and
top is golden brown.
6. Serve hot with cream.

SPICE ISLAND BANANAS
Serves 4

4 firm bananas
½oz (12gm) butter
4oz (100gm) cream cheese
1oz (25gm) soft brown sugar
¼ level teaspoon cinnamon
pinch of ground mace
4 tablespoons double cream
nutmeg

1. Preheat oven to moderate, 350 deg F or gas 4 (180 deg C).
2. Peel bananas and cut in half lengthways, then across into quarters.
3. Melt butter in a pan and lightly fry banana pieces until golden brown.
4. Arrange half the prepared bananas in a shallow casserole.
5. Beat cream cheese with sugar, cinnamon, mace and 1 tablespoon double cream, then spread this mixture over the bananas in casserole.
6. Top with remaining bananas and spoon remaining cream over them.
7. Cook, uncovered, in centre of oven for 15–20 minutes, or until bananas are tender.
8. Finely grate a little nutmeg over the top before serving.

CARIBBEAN SALAD
Serves 4

4 oranges
2 small pieces preserved ginger, finely chopped
2 tablespoons syrup from preserved ginger
1–2 tablespoons Cointreau or Grand Marnier liqueur
2 tablespoons desiccated coconut, lightly toasted

1. Preheat oven to very moderate, 325 deg F or gas 3 (170 deg C).
2. Peel oranges, removing all white pith. Cut across into slices and remove any pips.
3. Arrange orange slices in a shallow casserole and scatter chopped ginger over.
4. Pour ginger syrup and liqueur over top.
5. Cover closely with lid or foil and cook below centre of oven for about 30 minutes, or until oranges are cooked through.
6. Scatter toasted coconut over top before serving.

BUTTERED FRUITS
(Illustrated on page 72)
Serves 8

A quickly prepared sweet with a difference, and one which can be cooked at the same time as the main meal.

1 can (1lb or ½ kilo) pineapple chunks
1 can (1lb 14oz or 850gm) peach halves
1 can (1lb or ½ kilo) apricot halves
2oz (50gm) butter
6oz (150gm) soft brown sugar
1 level teaspoon mixed spice
juice of half an orange
6 glacé cherries, halved

1. Preheat oven to moderate, 350 deg F or gas 4 (180 deg C).
2. Drain fruits well. (The syrup can be used to make a jelly.)
3. Arrange the fruits in a casserole.
4. Melt butter in a pan and add sugar, spice and orange juice. Mix well together.
5. Sprinkle mixture over top of fruit.
6. Cook below centre of oven for 45 minutes–1 hour, or until fruit is heated through.
7. Decorate the top with glacé cherries and serve hot with cream or ice cream.

PINEAPPLE POLL
Serves 4–6

1 fresh pineapple
½ pint (250ml) medium sweet white wine
small piece cinnamon stick
1 level tablespoon honey
glacé cherries
1–2 tablespoons flaked almonds, lightly toasted

1. Preheat oven to moderate, 350 deg F or gas 4 (180 deg C).
2. Peel pineapple, cut into slices, remove hard core and arrange in a shallow casserole.
3. Boil together wine, cinnamon and honey for 5 minutes, then pour over pineapple in casserole.
4. Cover closely with lid or foil and cook below centre of oven for about 30 minutes, or until pineapple is heated through.
5. Place a cherry in centre of each pineapple slice and scatter almonds over before serving.

PLUMS IN WINE
Serves 4–6

1½lb (¾ kilo) plums
caster sugar
¼ pint (125ml) sweet white wine
2 tablespoons water
good pinch of cinnamon

1. Preheat oven to cool, 275 deg F or gas 1 (140 deg C).
2. Stone plums and arrange in a shallow casserole.
3. Sprinkle with sugar to taste.
4. Mix together wine, water and cinnamon and pour over prepared fruit.
5. Cover closely with lid or foil and cook in centre of oven for about 45 minutes, or until fruit is tender but still whole.
6. Serve chilled with whipped cream.

Index

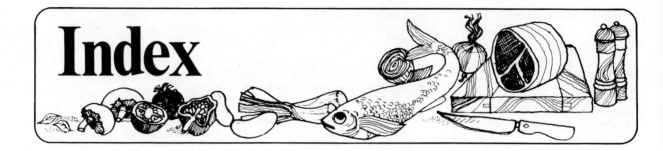

Apples:
Baked apples mamba 100
Rosy apples 99
Spiked apples 99
Yorkshire savouries 100
Arabian lamb 37
Asparagus Charlotte 96
Aubergines:
Aubergines à la provençale 93
Lombardy casserole 93
Stuffed aubergines 93
Aztec chicken 68

Bacon:
Bacon chop pot 45
Bacon pot au feu 46
Californian platter 45
Chiltern casserole 45
Danish casserole 46
Riviera casserole 46
Bacon, ham and sausages,
pages 45–50
Baked apples mamba 100
Baked fish Martinique 86
Baked onions 96
Bananas:
Banana Singapore 94
Banana togo 94
Baked apples mamba 100
Calypso bananas 100
Spice island bananas 101
Bavarian red cabbage 91
Beef, pages 6–15
Beef and barley 10
Beef bordelaise 15
Beef and peach paprika 12
Beef Riviera 13
Belgian chops 32
Bell Inn smokies 88
Bistro casserole 13
Blenheim casserole 61
Boeuf bourguignonne 15
Boeuf en daube 15
Boeuf provençal 15
Boeuf Roussy 12
Braised beef 11
Braised celery 92
Braised chicken 60
Braised chicory 92
Braised leeks 96

Braised pork chops 41
Braised sweetbreads 58
Braised veal 16
Buckingham braise 74
Budget beano 50
Buttered cucumber 95
Buttered fruits 101

Cabbage gratin 91
Caernarvon casserole 51
Californian platter 45
Calypso bananas 100
Calypso curry 70
Carbonnade of beef 12
Carelian hotpot 42
Caribbean salad 101
Carmen casserole 67
Casserole caprice 65
Casserole of kidneys 52
Casserole of pheasant 77
Castle pears 98
Chalet veal 21
Cheesy onion custard 96
Chelsea supper 50
Cherries in wine 100
Chicken, pages 60–70
Chicken Amalfi 63
Chicken americano 67
Chicken Antigua 70
Chicken bonne femme 66
Chicken cacciatore 67
Chicken Cicero 68
Chicken goulash 61
Chicken Josephine 64
Chicken montemare 68
Chicken with pineapple 63
Chicken Samantha 69
Chicken Valencia 68
Chicken vermouth 65
Chicken with walnuts 62
Chiddingly hotpot 7
Chilli con carne 11
Chiltern casserole 45
Chops with rosemary 20
Clementine chicken 65
Cod:
Baked fish Martinique 86
Cod crème gratin 85
Cod Panama 86
Cod portuguese 86
Cod provençal 85

Fish Antonio 86
Junior hotpot 85
Pedro's fancy 89
Scottish supper 85
Sunset bake 87
Sweet fish curry 87
Viking casserole 87
Colonial pork casserole 42
Compote of pears 99
Cook's favourite 40
Coonawarra casserole 31
Coq au vin 66
Corn and sausage casserole 48
Cotswold pears 98
Cottage casserole 80
Country dumpling casserole 79
Country hotpot 29
Country sausage bake 49
County lamb 28
Courgettes:
Courgettes with herbs 94
Gratin aux courgettes 94
Tomato and courgette rice 94
Creamed lamb curry 37
Cucumber with tomatoes 94
Cupboard love 50
Curried chicken 70
Curried rabbit 81
Curried veal 23

Daleside pheasant 76
Danish casserole 46
Dawlish chicken 60
Devilled halibut 89
Devilled tongue 57
Devil's rolls 52
Dijon beef 13
Duckling, pages 73–75
Duckling with grapes 73
Duckling Monte Cristo 75
Duckling with peaches 73
Duckling with sweet and sour
cherries 74
Dutch casserole 41

Empire stew 8

Family casserole 57
Family filler 9
Ferry boat liver 55
Festive casserole 8
Fish, pages 83–90
Fish Antonio 86
Flemish casserole 82
Fricassee of veal 23
Fruit, pages 98–101

Game, pages 76–82
Gammon and peaches 47
Gammon rarebit 47
Gardeners' casserole 97
Gingered carrots 92
Gingered lamb chops 34
Gipsy beef 9
Golden casserole 19
Grange casserole 19
Gratin aux courgettes 94
Gratin du Jabron 91
Greek gratiné 33
Grendon casserole 39
Grove casserole 55

Haddock:
  Baked fish Martinique 86
  Bell Inn smokies 88
  Fish Antonio 86
  Haddock in cheese sauce 88
  Innsbruck casserole 87
  Louisiana bake 88
  Norwegian casserole 88
  Pedro's fancy 89
  Summer fish casserole 88
  Sunset bake 87
  Sweet fish curry 87
  Viking casserole 87
Hadrian's casserole 10
Halibut with tarragon cream
  sauce 89
Ham and gammon:
  Gammon and peaches 47
  Gammon rarebit 47
  Ham and banana rolls 47
  Ham and pineapple crunch 47
  Ham Taormina 46
Hampton casserole 40
Handy casserole 40
Hare:
  Flemish casserole 82
  Jugged hare 82
  Minster casserole 82
Herby hotpot 25
Herrings:
  Herring hotpot 83
  Herring and tomato casserole 84
  Herrings Margareta 84
  Soused herrings 83
  Sozzled herrings 84
  Westside herrings 83
High days hotpot 26
Highland pheasant 76
Holiday chicken 62
Homestead casserole 39
Hot bangers and beans 48
Hungarian goulash 13
Hunters' rabbit 80
Hunters' stew 11

Innkeepers' casserole 8
Innsbruck casserole 87
Irish stew 25
Italian casserole of lamb 31

Jugged beef 11
Jugged hare 82
Junior hotpot 85

Kensington casserole 19
Kentish casserole 61
Kentucky casserole 63
Kidney and onion stew 52

Laird's casserole 78
Lamb, pages 25–37
Lamb bretonne 31
Lamb and butter beans 25
Lamb chop pot 27
Lamb creole 32
Lamb Djuvec 34
Lamb Genevieve 32
Lamb goulash 37
Lamb with lentils 30
Lamb with marjoram 29
Lamb Orlando 27
Lamb Pompey 32
Lamb Rochelle 31
Lamb with savoury dumplings 28
Lamb Shanghai 33
Lamb Woodstock 28
Lamb Versailles 30
Lancashire casserole 59
Lancashire hotpot 27
Lincolnshire duckling 74
Liver:
  Devil's rolls 52
  Family casserole 57
  Ferry boat liver 55
  Grove casserole 55
  Liver with savoury dumplings 57
  Liver in sherry sauce 56
  Neapolitan liver 55
  Porkers 56
  Stuffed liver 56
Lodge duckling 73
Lombardy casserole 93
London veal rolls 20
Louisiana bake 88

Mackerel in barbecue sauce 84
Mackerel in cider 84
Manor house chicken 60
Marinaded lamb 33
Marrow with marjoram 95
Marynka 22
Mexicana pork 42
Minster casserole 82
Mixed vegetable hotpot 97
Monday favourite 29
Monday potatoes 92
Mutton curry 37

Navarin of lamb 32
Neapolitan liver 55
Niagara baked sweetcorn 97
Norfolk rabbit 80
Normandy duckling 75
Norwegian casserole 88

Offal, pages 51–59
Old English casserole 52
Onions:
  Baked onions 96
  Cheesy onion custard 96
  Saucy onions 95
  Sweet and sour baked
    onions 96
Osso buco 24
Oxtail:
  Caernarvon casserole 51
  Old English casserole 52
  Oxtail casserole with onion
    dumplings 51

Paprika lamb 34
Paprika veal 22
Partridge with cabbage 77
Partridges Algarve 78
Patio casserole 49
Pears:
  Castle pears 98
  Compote of pears 99
  Cotswold pears 98
  Pears in red wine 98
  Spiced fruits 99
Pedro's fancy 89
Pembroke braise 6
Pennsylvania casserole 64
Peppery chicken 69
Pheasant:
  Casserole of pheasant 77
  Daleside pheasant 76
  Highland pheasant 76
  Pheasant with chestnuts 76
Pigeon in a pot 78
Pigeons with cherries 79
Pigeons in red wine 79
Pineapple poll 101
Plaice flamingo 90
Plaice Lancelot 90
Plums in wine 101
Pork, pages 38–44
Pork 'n apple 40
Pork and apple hotpot 38
Pork with barbecue sauce 44
Pork and celery casserole 39
Pork Charlotte 38
Pork chops Macon 42
Pork chops in mushroom sauce 41
Pork chops with orange 40
Pork chops Savannah 41
Pork Madras 44
Pork Peking 43
Pork surprise 39
Pork vindaloo 44
Porkers 56
Pot of veal 16

Potatoes:
Gratin du Jabron 91
Monday potatoes 92
Potatoes Gruyère 92
Scalloped potatoes Mathilda 92
Tomato czarda 95
Vegetable bake 97
Poulet basque 64
Poulet en cocotte 66

Quicky tuna 90

Rabbit:
Cottage casserole 80
Country dumpling casserole 79
Curried rabbit 81
Hunters' rabbit 80
Norfolk rabbit 80
Rabbit in tarragon mustard
sauce 81
Tucker bag casserole 81
Ragout of beef with prunes 14
Riviera casserole 46
Roadhouse casserole 7
Rosy apples 99
Rustic casserole 7

Saucy onions 95
Sausages:
Budget beano 50
Chelsea supper 50
Corn and sausage casserole 48
Country sausage bake 49
Cupboard love 50
Hot bangers and beans 48
Patio casserole 49
Sausage capers 48
Sausage fandango 50
Sausage Flavius 49

Sausage hotpot 50
Savoury sausage pot 49
Smothered sausages 48
Sweet curried sausages 48
Savoury hearts 58
Savoury meatballs 10
Savoury sausage pot 49
Savoury veal casserole 19
Scalloped potatoes Mathilda 92
Scalloped tripe 59
Scandinavian meatballs 12
Scottish supper 85
Sesame veal 21
Sicilian casserole 75
Smothered sausages 48
Soused herrings 83
Sozzled herrings 84
Spanish chicken 67
Speedy supper 57
Spice island bananas 101
Spiced chicken and apricots 69
Spiced fruits 99
Spiced steak 10
Spiked apples 99
Steak and mushrooms 6
Steak and onions 6
Stratford casserole 26
Stuffed aubergines 93
Stuffed liver 56
Stuffed peaches 99
Summer fish casserole 88
Sunny salad 100
Sunset bake 87
Sutton casserole 62
Sweet and sour baked onions 96
Sweetbreads country style 58
Sweet curried sausages 48
Sweet fish curry 87
Sweet pork casserole 43
Sweet September casserole 30
Swiss steak 14

Taipan pork 43
Tangy beef casserole 7
Tarragon chicken with orange 62
Thatchers' casserole 9
Thursday casserole 38
Tipsy leeks 96
Tivoli hotpot 14
Tomatoes:
Cucumber with tomatoes 94
Tomato and courgette rice 94
Tomato czarda 95
Tomato and onion casserole 95
Transatlantic casserole 30
Trout with mint 90
Tripe lyonnaise 59
Tucker bag casserole 81
Tyrolean casserole 77

Valencia beef casserole 14
Veal, pages 16–24
Veal Angostura 20
Veal balalaika 24
Veal chasseur 22
Veal goulash 21
Veal with parsley 16
Veal polonaise 20
Veal sombrero 22
Veal Sorrento 24
Vegetables, pages 91–97
Vegetable bake 97
Vienna casserole 23
Viking casserole 87
Village casserole 26

Wealden casserole 29
Welsh casserole 27
West country prunes 100
Westside herrings 83
Winter casserole 26

Yankee chicken 64
Yorkshire savouries 100